CRITICAL MASSES AND CRITICAL CHOICES

CRITICAL MASSES AND CRITICAL CHOICES

EVOLVING PUBLIC OPINION ON NUCLEAR WEAPONS, TERRORISM, AND SECURITY

KERRY G. HERRON

HANK C. JENKINS-SMITH

UNIVERSITY OF PITTSBURGH PRESS

Published by the University of Pittsburgh Press, Pittsburgh, Pa., 15260

Manufactured in the United States of America
Printed on acid-free paper
10 9 8 7 6 5 4 3 2 1

Library of Congress Cataloging-in-Publication Data

Herron, Kerry G.
 Critical masses and critical choices : evolving public opinion on nuclear weapons, terrorism, and security / Kerry G. Herron, Hank C. Jenkins-Smith.
     p.   cm.
 Includes bibliographical references and index.
 ISBN 0-8229-5934-8 (pbk. : alk. paper)
 1. Nuclear weapons—United States—Public opinion. 2. National security—United States—
Public opinion. 3. United States—Military policy—Public opinion. 4. Political culture—United
States. 5. Public opinion—United States. 6. Social surveys—United States. I. Jenkins-Smith,
Hank C. II. Title.
 UA23.H464 2006
 355'.033073—dc22   2006015727

For Carol Silva, the love of my life and the center of my universe.
—Hank C. Jenkins-Smith

With love and appreciation to Marilyn, Kristina, and Kimber, the women in my life.
—Kerry G. Herron

CONTENTS

PREFACE

When we set out to write this book in early 2001, our chief interest was to understand how members of the American public were adjusting their perspectives on international nuclear threats and security policies in the context of monumental changes wrought by the collapse of the Soviet Union and the end of the Cold War. The terrorist strikes on September 11, 2001, changed the world again, leading us to extend our investigations for another two and a half years to assess how these new shocks would affect public opinion on security issues. The result is an assessment of the expressed opinions of Americans about security issues spanning a full decade—a decade that saw the unfolding of some of the most remarkable and wrenching changes in American history. Throughout that period, however, our focus remained consistent: how are Americans' beliefs and preferences regarding the appropriate means to manage security threats abroad and at home evolving in a rapidly changing world?

Our approaches to the multidimensional issue of security, and to our study of the ways in which ordinary citizens apprehend and respond to security concerns, were shaped by the positions from which we conducted our research. For the bulk of the period in which we engaged in this analysis, we worked in an academic institution that focused on the conduct of policy-oriented survey research. Our academic colleagues, at our home institutions and across the country, provided the kind of feisty and intellectually demanding critiques that prevented us from becoming too complaisant or comfortable with our developing analyses. (We include the anonymous reviewers of our papers, who were often kind and supportive but almost as often pointedly critical in their evaluations.) This experience was greatly enriched by extensive opportunities to engage and argue with an array of extraordinary experts and officials who work in various positions in the field of security, ranging from the national laboratories to executive agencies, and from local emergency responders to senior policy officials. The effect of this contact was, in part, to keep us aware of the very difficult strategic and operational issues that face policymakers in this complex issue domain. We trust that these interactions served as effective antidotes to facile assumptions and too-easy conclusions about the characterizations, trade-offs, and implications of the security dilemmas that face the United States. But it was a third aspect of our research environment—a deep and long-term engagement with a diverse cross section of the American public—that most fundamentally affected our work. This engagement grew in part from our personal involvement in conceptualizing and implementing opinion survey research. Both of us designed and alternately led twenty-one focus groups in which we sought to stimulate discussions about security among Americans from ten cities and suburbs ranging from San Diego to Boston, and from New Orleans to Chicago. This proved to be an amazingly easy task. In most instances, the discussions would be moving at full throttle when the allotted time was up. In the design of our initial surveys, we personally interviewed citizens on the telephone. And—most importantly—we analyzed the responses to over 13,500 interviews with members of the general public on nuclear postures, international threats, domestic considerations of security policies, terrorism, and political beliefs conducted in the years spanning 1993 to 2003. (Although not reported in this book, we also interviewed more than 4,200 technical and policy elites during the same ten-year period, asking many of the identical questions posed to participants from the general public.) The substance and structure of those interviews are described in the chapters that follow, but all this engagement fundamentally influenced our understanding of public opinion. Traditional elite characterizations of extremely limited public capacities and tendencies toward volatility do not explain the kinds of stable patterns and common sense we measured. The longer we investigate public opinion, the more we respect and value it. We appreciate the generosity of our respondents who took time from their busy lives to answer our lengthy surveys. We deeply value their considerable efforts freely given, their contributions of rich personal experience and analogy, and the deliberate management of uncertainty that shaped and informed their answers to our questions. We also directly observed occasions in which respondents appeared to be ill informed, glib, or thoughtless in their answers, but these were the exceptions and may be among the irreducible ingredients of public opinion. Overall, we are deeply impressed with ordinary citizens' capacities and willingness to engage in relatively complex and extended discussions about pressing national issues. Their lives are touched by the policy concerns in question; they *have* thought about them, and they are willing (and sometimes eager) to provide their views. From all this we conclude that it is well worth listening carefully to what these people have to say about public policy—especially on complex and urgent issues such as security.

Our extended evaluation of public opinion on security has not led us to advocate particular security policy positions. We have our own policy preferences, of course, though we differ from each other almost as often as we agree. But that is not the point of this book. What we do advocate is that policymakers, opinion leaders, and scholars take a hard and informed look at expressed public values concerning terrorism, security, and US strategies involving nuclear weapons. Public opinion needs to be understood, not because it is right or wrong—indeed, that is the "wrong" question—but because policy must be informed by how it is understood and evaluated by the public. Deep and resilient policy beliefs and preferences among the American people provide the parameters within which stable security policies can be constructed. They warn when policy is on unsure ground, subject to sustained and broad dissent of the sort that may undermine or delegitimize security efforts. Without such input, security policies, whether focused outside or inside the United States, are much less likely to provide and protect the very security that is their objective. Responsible decision makers in a representative republic like the United States are obliged to attend to the nature of public support for security policies. That does not mean policy should be based primarily on polling or developed by referenda. It only means that public opinion, even about the most complex security issues, should be a valued input to policy processes.

In taking on a project of this magnitude, we have enjoyed the generosity and support of many people and institutions. (Because of the span of time over which we have worked on this project, some individuals who supported this research changed institutional affiliations or retired during the course of the project. In this section we acknowledge contributions based on the primary institution with which the named individuals were affiliated at the time of their involvement.) Primary funding and institutional support was generously provided by Sandia National Laboratories, the George Bush School of Government and Public Service at Texas A&M University, and the Institute for Public Policy at the University of New Mexico. As we note below, other organizations also were involved in important ways.

At Sandia National Laboratories we are indebted to senior leaders who made the necessary financial and institutional support possible. They include the current president and director, Dr. Thomas O. Hunter; former president and director, Dr. C. Paul Robinson; Dr. Joan B. Woodard, executive vice president and deputy laboratories director for nuclear weapons; and Dr. Alton D. Romig Jr., senior vice president and deputy laboratories director for integrated technologies and systems. We especially want to acknowledge the sustained contributions of Dr. Roger L. Hagengruber, senior vice president, emeritus, whose institutional support, professional expertise, and personal interest, advice, and encouragement were essential to all of the research efforts and findings reported in this volume. This project would not have been possible without his personal participation. Richard Schwoebel and David McVey helped conceive and initiate the project. Stan Fraley, Laura Gilliom, Clyde Layne, and John Taylor were key partners and administrators of associated contracts. Others who made important contributions include Arlin Cooper, David Cunnington, Aida Garcia, Victor Johnson, Jerry Langheim, Dennis Miyoshi, William Nickell, David Nokes, Arian Pregenzer, Dick Smith, and Stan Spray. Among the many compliments that we could pay the people at the Sandia National Laboratories, we most appreciate that they took the risk of giving us the latitude to design and implement this project without once seeking to interfere with the nature of the questions asked or the content of the analyses conducted.

We have received the kind of intellectual and financial support from Texas A&M University of which most researchers can only dream. The faculty at the George Bush School of Government and Public Service has been an unstinting source of constructive criticism and encouragement. Professor Carol Silva is a research partner who has participated in all of the surveys reported in this book. She contributed importantly to theoretical development, survey design, and data collection efforts. Her intellectual and methodological contributions have been of immense value and are matched only by her charm, wit, and ability to win any argument about the deteriorating effects of age on senior male academics. Professor Guy Whitten (from the Texas A&M Department of Political Science) is another research partner who contributed importantly. We especially value his international expertise and his participation in surveys conducted in Europe. Professors Larry Lynn, Warren Eller, Mike Desch, Kishore "The Enforcer" Gawande, Jeffrey Engels, James Lewis, and the infamous GBS Brown Bag group have all provided important critiques, suggestions, and support. Others who provided valuable support include Matthew Henderson, Laura Templeton and Joe Dillard. Crucial financial support was provided by the endowment of Joe R. and Teresa Lozano Long, who are heroes to us because of their unstinting support of education and research. And we wish to warmly acknowledge the unflinching support (even when we behaved like pesky academics) of the dean of the George Bush School of Government and Public Service, Lieutenant General (Retired) Richard A. (Dick) Chilcoat.

From the University of New Mexico we continued to receive the crucial support of Dr. Roger Hagengruber, who after retiring from senior leadership positions at Sandia National Laboratories assumed directorship of the UNM Institute for Public Policy and established the Office for Policy, Security and Technology. His support and participation through his roles at UNM remain vital to our research. We also want to especially acknowledge the contributions of Amy Goodin and Amelia Rouse, who contributed importantly to survey designs and directed data collections. Professor Neil Mitchell (who left New Mexico in 2005 for the University of Aberdeen in Scotland) made significant conceptual inputs to research design and analysis of results from surveys in Europe. Gilbert St. Clair participated in the design and implementation of our first survey in this series. Scott Hughes contributed importantly to interviewing and analysis. Others at UNM who provided valuable administrative support include Carol Brown, Rudy Gallegos, Adam Pool, and Eric Whitmore. We also want to acknowledge the hard work and energetic support we received from the many graduate and undergraduate students who served as survey interviewers at the UNM Institute for Public Policy Survey Research Center.

We also wish to thank Robert O'Connor, Director of the Decision, Risk and Management Sciences Division of the National Science Foundation (NSF). NSF grant number 0234119 provided the resources needed to collect the panel data analyzed in chapter 5 of this book.

We deeply appreciate the participation and continuing friendship of Professor Richard Barke at the Georgia Institute of Technology, who helped develop the first survey in this series. We acknowledge the support of Karl Braithwaite, Scott Duncan, and Janet Langone, all at Los Alamos National Laboratory. We appreciate the support of John Hirsh at Pacific Northwest Laboratory. Klaus Berkner, at Lawrence Berkeley Laboratory, provided assistance. We are indebted to Stan Neeley, at the Battelle Seattle Research Center. Bob Bland, at the Union of Concerned Scientists, was very helpful. Among many others at various institutions in the United States and abroad, we gratefully acknowledge the contributions of Ayaz Akhtar, Kathleen Bailey, Dinah Bisdee, Alessia Damato, Simon Glanville, Dennis Gormley, Marilyn Herron, Thomas Mahnken, Antoline Monteils, Uwe Gerd Oberlack, Cyrille Pinson, and Laura Turino.

While all these people, and many others, contributed importantly to the work reported in this book, they bear no responsibility for any errors, misinterpretations, or omissions. We have only ourselves to acknowledge for any such failures.

CRITICAL MASSES AND CRITICAL CHOICES

OBJECTIVES, CONCEPTS, AND THEORIES

1

THE CENTRAL ORGANIZING principle of international security in the twentieth century was a struggle among the competing ideologies of fascism, democracy, and communism. The massive destruction of two world wars was succeeded by a cold war between the open markets and societies of the West and the closed societies and centralized economies of the Soviet bloc. Today that conflict has been replaced by an emerging struggle between the forces of modernity and societies seeking to preserve religious and cultural traditions threatened by globalizing social, political, economic, and technological trends. The proliferation of weapons of mass destruction and their potential uses by some states and transnational terrorist groups trying to stem the tide of modernity has become the contemporary dynamic around which international security is reorganizing.

The huge nuclear arsenals that evolved during the Cold War are being reconsidered in the absence of superpower confrontation and in light of the difficulties of deterring amorphous terrorist groups. At the same time, maintaining and safeguarding existing nuclear weapons and materials continue to require substantial resources. The number of states possessing nuclear weapons increased by one-third when India and Pakistan fielded operational nuclear weapons systems.[1] In February 2005, North Korea officially declared that it possesses nuclear weapons, and Iran is thought to be vigorously pursuing nuclear capabilities. Growing threats of mass-casualty terrorism are demanding large investments in defensive preparedness against nuclear, chemical, and biological weapons. The prospects of further horizontal nuclear proliferation to other states and to terrorist organizations, combined with vertical proliferation in nuclear capacities and sophistication among those who possess or acquire nuclear weapons, constitute persistent threats to US interests. Coupled with these developments, the reemergence of previously subdued ethnic conflicts is producing civil wars that demand international intervention, the Israeli-Palestinian conflict persists, a global war on terrorism is underway, and the long-range outcome of the war in Iraq may be problematic. In this volatile security environment, the United States is reducing its nuclear arsenal, fielding an embryonic system of national ballistic missile defenses, restructuring its military, and reorganizing its government to fight terrorism. The implications of these trends for future nuclear deterrence, security investments, and military postures are continuously evolving, and they raise critical questions about associated policy processes and outcomes.

One of the most important considerations relates to the role of the public. American citizens are key stakeholders in the future of US security, and because of the requirement for public support, security issues have critical implications for domestic politics, elections, and the boundaries within which sustainable security policy can evolve. To what degree can policymakers expect or desire the US public to participate directly or indirectly in dynamic foreign and strategic policy processes? Do the rapid changes and associated complexities of the security situation exceed the capacities of most Americans to understand and contribute to the shaping of new security designs? How are American views of nuclear security evolving in such a dynamic environment? How does the general public perceive the efficacy of nuclear deterrence in the face of new and different post–Cold War threats? Do Americans support the elimination of nuclear weapons? If not, do they support further development and testing of new and more tailored nuclear weapons capabilities? How is the growing threat of mass-casualty terrorism affecting public views of security? How are initial US efforts in the ongoing war on terrorism being assessed by the American public? What are public views of trade-offs in personal security and personal freedoms? What are acceptable conditions for the use of US military force in the struggle against terrorism? These are but a few questions illustrating the kinds of twenty-first-century security issues facing the American people and the international community. What should we expect of the abilities of ordinary citizens to usefully grapple with these issues?

Rationale and Objectives

We have two modest objectives in this book. One is to examine empirically the views of the US general public about post–Cold War security, with special emphasis on the nuclear dimensions of security and the growing challenges to security posed by terrorism. Another objective is to contribute to the continuing debate about the capacities of publics to help guide policies in complex domains. Nuclear security and terrorism are particularly well suited for both objectives, for they constitute the central elements of strategic planning in the post–Cold War era and provide challenging tests of competing theories of public capacities. We pursue our objectives by analyzing extensive data about nuclear security and terrorism obtained in a series of six national surveys measuring the views of almost 10,000 members of the American public conducted biennially between 1993 and 2003. We analyze responses from core questions asked in each of the six surveys that provide a unique view of the changing nature of security from a period beginning eighteen months after the collapse of the Soviet Union and extending through the next decade of the post–Cold War era, encompassing the terrorist attacks in the United States on September 11, 2001 (9/11), the conflicts in Afghanistan and Iraq, and ongoing global efforts in the war on terrorism.

Our examination of public views on nuclear security includes a wide spectrum of measures ranging from broad impressions of the changing security environment to quite specific beliefs and policy preferences. Included are conceptual questions about the viability of nuclear deterrence, beliefs about the risks and benefits associated with nuclear weapons, and assessments of specific nuclear security issues such as the appropriate size of the US nuclear arsenal. We track more specific preferences concerning investments in nuclear weapons capabilities and views about strategic arms control. Our analyses include data collected before the attacks of 9/11, immediately following 9/11, and two years later. These data permit us to investigate public assessments of terrorist threats, preferences for response options, and views of progress in the continuing struggle against terrorism.

Strong Test Cases

Nuclear security is a challenging policy area for public participation for several reasons. First, the design, testing, maintenance, transportation, safeguarding, and employment of nuclear weapons all have highly technical aspects that require specialized expertise. For example, whether US nuclear weapons can be reliably maintained for the foreseeable future without operational nuclear testing is a debatable technical issue. How the stewards of nuclear weapons will safeguard them and their associated nuclear materials for thousands of years is a continuing technical question with implications that exceed human experience. Certainly nuclear security poses very difficult technical hurdles for many ordinary citizens, and the factual knowledge gap between elites and members of the mass public is especially high in this policy area.

Second, nuclear security has a long-standing tradition of limited public access. US development of the world's first nuclear weapons was conducted without public knowledge under strict secrecy. After World War II, nuclear espionage was a real and threatening attribute of the Cold War, and nuclear advantage remains a competitive objective of some states in the post–Cold War era. The potential for transnational networks of terrorists to acquire and use nuclear devices as the ultimate terror weapons adds even greater requirements for secrecy and protection. Nuclear security policy options often are debated by officials and technical experts in arenas not accessible to the media and the vast majority of American citizens. In relative terms, public access and participation is highest in domestic policy processes, more restricted in general foreign and security policy processes, and even more restricted in matters of nuclear security.

Third, most citizens have no personal experience with nuclear technologies and related policy choices. This stands in contrast to public experience with many other complex policy domains. For example, health care, education, and social security all are complex policy areas, and each has technical dimensions requiring specialized expertise, but the vast majority of adult citizens have some degree of personal or family experience in dealing with associated issues. That level of personal experience is not present in the case of nuclear security. All these aspects of nuclear weapons policy make it more difficult for citizens to be informed of alternative choices and significantly restrict public participation in nuclear security policy processes. The challenges in the way of coherent—let alone rational—public beliefs and preferences on nuclear security issues would thus seem to be nearly insurmountable.

Because of the threat of nuclear and other forms of mass-casualty attacks, transnational terrorism also provides a tough case for policy participation. Terrorism is different conceptually, because it is highly resistant to deterrence. To be effective, deterrence (nuclear or otherwise) has two prerequisites: accountability and retribution. The source of attacks must be identifiable to a high degree of certainty, and retribution must be unavoidable and unacceptable to the attacker. Because of the nature of transnational terrorism, both requirements are problematic. Terrorist networks are amorphous, ill defined, borderless, and make attribution much more difficult than state-level threats. The facts that transnational terrorist groups may have members from multiple countries, may receive support from multiple sources, and may train and prepare in multiple locations also make retribution more complex and less certain. Together, the problematic nature of attribution and retribution make deterring terrorism particularly challenging.

Terrorism provides the nexus for the dangerous confluence of the proliferation of weapons of mass destruction, ideological and cultural conflict, and the challenges of securing an increasingly globalized economy and transportation network. This means that no one state, or even an alliance of several states, is likely to successfully combat transnational terrorism. The requirement for international cooperation in the struggle against terrorism exceeds that required in most state-level conflicts and makes public participation in policy processes for combating terrorism much more complex.

Early Post–Cold War Optimism

The liberation of Eastern Europe, capped by the fall of the Berlin Wall in 1990 and the dissolution of the Soviet Union in December 1991, set the stage for optimistic expectations about a post–Cold War world. Nuclear policy trends during the last decade of the twentieth century included the following promising developments: reductions in the numbers of US and allied nuclear weapons as well as prospects for a smaller Russian nuclear arsenal; safe removal of Soviet-era nuclear weapons from the newly independent states of Ukraine, Kazakhstan, and Belarus to the possession and operational control of Russia; a moratorium on US nuclear weapons testing and debate about a comprehensive nuclear test ban; efforts to develop a treaty limiting the production of fissile materials; the indefinite extension of the Nuclear Non-proliferation Treaty; destruction of previously undeclared nuclear weapons by South Africa; and optimistic domestic debate about a "peace dividend." Even the Persian Gulf War of 1990–1991 did not long dampen the strategic outlook for a more peaceful future following the half-century of nuclear brinksmanship between the United States and the Soviet Union and their respective allies.

We began research early in this period of optimism partly to measure what we anticipated would be a devaluation of US nuclear weapons capabilities after the Cold War. We expected to document public assessments of the diminishing relevance of nuclear weapons and to track the rates at which nuclear devaluation occurred over time. We began designing the first survey little more than a year after the dissolution of the Soviet Union, and though we could not reference a baseline survey employing the same core set of questions during the Cold War, we sought to establish reference points early in the new security environment against which subsequent measures could be compared as we progressed further into the post–Cold War era.

Analytical Framework

Before writing the first survey question, we developed the analytical framework in figure 1.1, within which we hypothesize key relationships expected to influence opinions and preferences about nuclear issues. From this framework, we constructed baseline questions designed to meet our twin objectives of measuring and documenting public views on nuclear weapons as well as

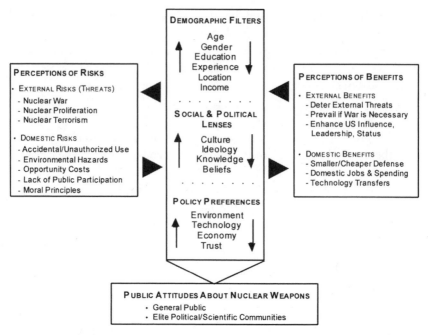

Figure 1.1. Analytical framework

gaining insights into the larger theoretical questions about public capacities to hold and express coherent views on complex policy issues.

Our framework suggests that public attitudes about nuclear security partially are functions of interactive beliefs about risks and benefits associated with nuclear weapons. These beliefs are held within the context of a number of factors specific to each individual. Among them are three key sets of variables: (1) demographic factors such as age, gender, education, income, training, experience, and place of residence; (2) social and political lenses shaped by political culture and ideology, subject knowledge, and belief systems; and (3) preferences about related public policy issues such as the environment, the role of science and technology in society, economic considerations, and trust in public institutions and policy processes. This framework is central to our analysis of trends in public views, because it suggests issues and relationships for which questions can be designed, and it provides a map for testing hypotheses about the capacities of publics to employ policy-relevant structured beliefs. During the design stages of our various surveys between 1993 and 2003, we explored issues and relationships suggested by our model in discussions among twenty-one focus groups in ten different cities. Results helped us hone and refine survey questions.[2]

After designing the initial survey instrument, our objectives for subsequent surveys included retaining and improving the core set of questions intended to elaborate our analytical framework as well as incorporating additional related topical issues. For example, in addition to the nuclear security and terrorism issues discussed in this book, we also surveyed opinions about a range of other topics including nuclear energy, philosophical approaches to science and research, relationships among American technical communities, US national science policies, cooperation among American and Russian nuclear scientists, and personal security issues. Though the issue content varies among our surveys, the set of comparative questions about nuclear security forms the leading core of most surveys, followed by other issues and lines of investigation. In subsequent chapters, we summarize policy-relevant findings about mass views on nuclear security and terrorism, but before examining those data, it is necessary to establish the larger theoretical questions about public capacities that we address.

Theoretical Questions

The nature and role of public opinion in democratic theory has long been debated. Though separate concepts of "public" and "opinion" can be traced to ancient times, Jean-Jacques Rousseau is credited with using the combined term "*l'opinion publique*" (public opinion) around 1744 (Noelle-Neumann 1984).[3] How to differentiate "public opinion" from among the mass of conflicting views present in the body politic was a central dilemma of liberal philosophy (Price 1992). The concept and role of public opinion was discussed by the US Founding Fathers, debated in the Federalist Papers (Hamilton, Madison, and Jay [1788] 1961), and critiqued by de Tocqueville ([1835, 1840] 1945) in his essays on American democracy. One of the central issues in the philosophic struggles between republicanism and federalism was the argument between James Madison and Alexander Hamilton about the role of public opinion. As Sheehan (2004) notes:

For Madison, republicanism meant the recognition of the sovereignty of public opinion and the commitment to participatory politics. Hamilton advocated a more submissive role for the citizenry and a more independent status for the political elite. While Madison did not deny to political leaders and enlightened men a critical place in the formation of public opinion, he fought against Hamilton's thin version of public opinion as "confidence" in government. . . . Hamilton recognized that Madison's opposition to him and the Federalists was propelled by a fundamental philosophic disagreement over the nature and role of public opinion in a republic. (405–6)

Throughout the eighteenth century, the concept of public opinion most often referred to general social behavior, but by the nineteenth century, theorists such as Bentham ([1838–1843] 1962) and Mill ([1863] 1992) evolved a more utilitarian political role for public opinion in government (Price 1992). Ultimately, the Bentham/Mill utilitarian perspective provided the foundation for the most broadly accepted construct of public opinion in the twentieth century and the rationale for the evolution of systematic attempts to measure it through opinion polling (Minar 1960). In this evolution, concepts from the Enlightenment period in which public opinion was conceived as an expression of the general will gave way to utilitarian notions of contemporary public opinion comprising the most commonly held ideas (Price 1992).

Traditional Expectations of Public Capacities

Modern concepts of public opinion and its proper role in US policy processes evolved to an elitist perspective characterized by three interacting components: (1) a philosophy of minimal capacities of mass publics to understand and contribute to complex policy domains—especially foreign and security policies; (2) empirical evidence suggesting that the belief systems of ordinary citizens are insufficiently structured to inform and constrain policy choices in areas where individuals lack specialized knowledge or experience; and (3) criticism of means for systematically measuring and understanding public views. This perspective gained wide acceptance among political sophisticates, theorists, and academics, and became the "traditional" view that informed much of the common wisdom about what elites should expect from the general public in terms of policy participation and influence.

Modern philosophical underpinnings of this traditional perspective are featured most prominently in the writings of Walter Lippmann (1922, 1925, 1955). Lippmann's deep reservations about the capacities of publics to usefully contribute to policy processes is apparent throughout much of his work, but three of Lippmann's books most directly address the limitations of publics and their opinions. In the aptly titled *Public Opinion* (1922), Lippmann expresses his doubts about the abilities of common citizens to understand the complexities of public policy while emphasizing the role of elites:

I argue that representative government, either in what is ordinarily called politics, or in industry, cannot be worked successfully, no matter what the basis of election, unless there is an independent, expert organization for making the unseen facts intelligible to those who have to make the decisions. (31)

In the absence of institutions and education by which the environment is so successfully reported that the realities of public life stand out sharply against self-centered opinion, the common interests very largely elude public opinion entirely, and can be managed only by a specialized class whose personal interests reach beyond the locality. (310)

In the sequel *The Phantom Public* (1925), Lippmann builds on the construct of limited public capacities by specifying an appropriately limited role for public activism. He cautions about the dangers of a polity whose members largely are in continuing pursuit of individual interest and subject to manipulation by special interests. For Lippmann, the role of the masses must be circumscribed.

The environment is complex. Man's political capacity is simple. (78)

The true public, in my definition of that term, has to purge itself of the self-interested groups who become confused with it.... [T]he true public will not stay mobilized very long for anything. (112)

A false sense of democracy can lead only to disillusionment and to meddlesome tyranny.... The public must be put in its place, so that it may exercise its own powers, but no less and perhaps even more, so that each of us may live free of the trampling and the roar of a bewildered herd. (155)

[I]n this theory the public intervenes only when there is a crisis of maladjustment, and then not to deal with the substance of the problem but to neutralize the arbitrary force which prevents adjustment. It is a theory which economizes the attention of men as members of the public, and asks them to do as little as possible in matters where they can do nothing very well.... It is by the private labors of individuals that life is enhanced. I set no great store on what can be done by public opinion and the action of masses. (199)

A quarter of a century later, Lippmann had become even more pessimistic about the influence of public opinion and its role in shaping policy—especially foreign and security policies. The following quotation from *The Public Philosophy* (1955) illustrates Lippmann's dire assessment in mid-twentieth century. "When mass opinion dominates the government, there is a morbid derangement of the true functions of power. The derangement brings about the enfeeblement, verging on paralysis, of the capacity to govern. This breakdown in the constitutional order is the cause of the precipitate and catastrophic decline of Western society. It may, if it cannot be arrested and reversed, bring about the fall of the West" (15).

In addition to Lippmann, others such as Almond (1950, 1956), Bailey (1948), Berelson, Lazarsfeld, and McPhee (1954), Campbell et al. (1960, 1966), Kennan (1951), Markel (1949), and Morgenthau (1948) added to and enriched the philosophical concept of minimal public capacities. Though each expressed reservations and expectations about public opinion somewhat differently (and often less stridently than Lippmann), together, they helped shape what became an elite consensus that the US general public is ill informed about foreign and security policy issues and unsuited for active participation in many important policy decisions. Mass views are criticized for being emotionally volatile, lacking coherence, being insufficiently responsive to the policy situation, and, once aroused, being susceptible to overreaction. The one saving grace seems to be that mass opinions are not very influential in shaping policies having great consequences for the safety and security of the United States. As Holsti (1992, 1996) puts it, traditionalists consider mass opinions about foreign policy to be volatile, unstructured, and largely irrelevant.

In 1964, Philip Converse wrote a seminal piece on the role of belief systems in shaping policy preferences among mass and elite publics that provides supporting evidence about the lack of systematic opinion structures among ordinary citizens. In "The Nature of Belief Systems in Mass Publics," Converse concludes that belief structures that constrain and limit policy preferences among elites having higher levels of education and specialized issue knowledge are not present among mass publics. According to Converse, such predispositions are lacking to such an extent that members of the general public are not equipped even to use the liberal-conservative continuum to help guide their choices (235). From his own polling, he reports that only about 17 percent of the American public has an accurate understanding of liberal-conservative distinctions. Another 46 percent have some understanding of the terms, but only within narrow applications for some issues, and those applications do not hold across different policy domains. Converse finds that more than a third of the public (37 percent) hold extremely vague, if any, understandings of the terms "liberal" and "conservative," and cannot employ ideology as a heuristic for simplifying issue choices. He considers the concept of ideology and its practical application using a liberal-conservative continuum to be "a rather elegant high-order abstraction, and such abstractions are not typical conceptual tools for the man in the street" (215), therefore "it is not surprising that there is little active use of the continuum as an organizing dimension" (223).

Converse also concludes that unless an issue directly concerns individual members of the general public or important groups in obviously rewarding or punishing ways, the general public lacks the contextual grasp of the political system and its policy processes necessary to recognize how members should respond to an issue without being told by elites and political parties who hold their confidence (216). Converse argues that "the unfamiliarity of broader and more abstract ideological frames of reference among the less sophisticated is more than a problem in mere articulation. Parallel to ignorance and confusion of these ideological dimensions among the less informed is a general decline in constraint among specific belief elements that such dimensions help to organize. It cannot therefore be claimed that the mass public shares ideological patterns of belief with relevant elites at a specific level any more than it shares the abstract conceptual frames of reference" (231).

Where loosely organized political beliefs are present among mass publics, Converse finds that "these beliefs are extremely labile over time" (241), and thus not systematically related to policy preferences in predictable ways. Converse concludes that hypotheses about comprehensive and highly integrated belief systems and their behavioral consequences partially can be substantiated among elite publics, but largely are disconfirmed among the masses below them (255). He ends his often-cited piece as follows:

> The broad contours of elite decisions over time can depend in a vital way upon currents in what is loosely called "the history of ideas." These decisions in turn have effects upon the mass of more common citizens. But, of any direct participation in this history of ideas and the behavior it shapes, the mass is remarkably innocent. We do not disclaim the existence of entities that might best be called "folk ideologies," nor do we deny for a moment that strong differentiations in a variety of narrower values may be found within subcultures of less educated people. Yet for the familiar belief systems that, in view of their historical importance, tend most to attract the sophisticated observer, it is likely that an adequate mapping of a society (or, for that matter, the world) would provide a jumbled cluster of pyramids or a mountain range, with sharp delineation and differentiation in beliefs from elite apex to elite apex but with the mass bases of the pyramids overlapping in such profusion that it would be impossible to decide where one pyramid ended and another began. (256–57)

Converse's findings reinforce the philosophical framework espoused by Lippmann and others in which mass publics are led by elite opinion makers through opaque processes to enlightened policies that most members can neither understand nor appreciate. Converse suggests that, unlike their elite elements, general publics lack sufficiently structured belief systems to participate in complex policy processes, such as foreign and security policymaking. Mass publics have little to contribute beyond their role in general elections to select legislative and executive elites who can guide policy processes and outcomes. Together, the elitist philosophical framework and Converse's findings about belief structures solidify a traditionalist perspective that has proven enduring.[4]

In the second half of the twentieth century, major gains were made in survey research methods that promised to afford more systematic sampling and measurement of public views on policy issues.[5] These advances support increased scholarly investigation of public capacities, and we summarize key aspects of some of those findings below, but the rise of polling and its implications for how public capacities are understood is not without criticism. John

Zaller (1992) is critical both of average public capacities and the methodologies for measuring public opinion. To Zaller, the key to public capacities lies in political awareness. He draws strong distinctions among differing levels of political attentiveness.

There is a small but important minority of the public that pays great attention to politics and is well informed about it. . . . At the other end of the attentiveness spectrum is a larger group of people who possess almost no current information about politics. . . . People at this level of inattentiveness can have only the haziest idea of the policy alternatives about which pollsters regularly ask them to state opinions, and such ideas as they do have must often be relatively innocent of the effects of exposure to elite discourse. Most citizens, of course, fall between these extremes. . . . But even so, it is easy to underestimate how little typical Americans know about what for a time they do understand. (16)

The two main points about political awareness, then, are (1) that people vary greatly in their general attentiveness to politics, regardless of particular issues, and (2) that average overall levels of information are quite low. More succinctly, there is high variance in political awareness around a generally low mean. (18)

Zaller also is doubtful of the stability of public opinions because of tenuous ties between higher level beliefs and policy preferences. He argues that responses to opinion surveys are more a function of salience and cues than of underlying dispositions.

I abandon the conventional but implausible view that citizens typically posses "true attitudes" on every issue about which a pollster may happen to inquire, and instead propose a model of how individuals construct opinion reports in response to the particular stimuli that confront them. (35)

Which of a person's attitudes is expressed at different times depends on which has been made most immediately salient by chance and the details of questionnaire construction, especially the order and framing of questions. The notion that citizens have "just one" attitude on typical issues is made to look foolish every time multiple polling agencies become involved in trying to measure opinion on some issue. What they find is not evidence of the public's "true attitude," but of its many different attitudes. (93)

Critics of survey methods and the rapid growth of polling continue to caution about the difficulties of measuring public opinion and the uses to which such efforts are directed. In a critique of the shortcomings of survey methodologies and the pernicious effects of widespread polling on policy processes, Weissberg (2001) concludes that contemporary polls are not offering respondents the kinds of hard choices faced by legislatures or policy analysts. By measuring only wishes for a world of benefits without related costs and risks, polls do not provide worthwhile advice about policy choices. To Weissberg, the innate capacity to understand the issues when members of the public are well informed and engaged is less the problem than is the fact that modern polling can provide only what respondents know the moment the question is asked. As a result, current survey methodology is incapable of extracting sound policy counsel. Weissberg also is concerned about how the ascendancy of public opinion in today's world of instant polling sets boundaries on legitimate policy debates, can be manipulated to influence public agendas, and shifts the burden of proof to those who oppose "majority preferences." As a result, polling crosses the line between reporting what may or may not be actual public sentiments to becoming a political tool with counterproductive implications for policymaking.

From these and other contributions to the core of traditional theory about the potential of mass publics in participative systems, we trace a stream of reasoning that considers common citizens to have minimal capacities to understand complex policy choices, to be unlikely to rise above self-interest in pursuit of the larger societal good, to lack sufficiently coherent beliefs and values that provide a political ideology and worldview, to be so politically unaware as to comprehend neither trade-offs in policy choices nor the processes within which they are made, and to be sufficiently befuddled as to frustrate most attempts at measuring and understanding their views with methodologies inadequate to the task. From this perspective, it follows that the public must be kept well within the limited expectations of participating in elections to select elites qualified to operate the levers of power and conduct the business of government.

Revisionist Expectations of Public Capacities

These traditional assumptions and characterizations of public capacities certainly have not stood without challenge. As methods for opinion survey research evolve and are refined, criticisms of earlier survey methods and conclusions are offered, and a growing body of academic quality opinion research yields new empirical evidence challenging the traditionalist consensus.

Responding to traditional criticisms of volatility and "moods" among mass views, Caspary (1970) finds that public opinion about foreign policies is more stable and more permissive of international involvements than previously represented. Achen (1975) also finds that evidence of instability cited by traditionalists is more methodologically driven than actual reflections of variation in public opinion. In a meta-analysis of dozens of surveys and responses to hundreds of questions, Page and Shapiro (1992) and Shapiro and Page (1988, 1994) illustrate stability over time in public views about foreign policy and highly rational reactions and evolution of views that are driven by events.

Traditional assumptions about the lack of structure and constraints within mass opinion also are challenged by a number of studies reporting evidence of structured belief systems and sophisticated heuristics shaping and constraining public opinions about not only domestic policies but also international issues and foreign policies (Chittick, Billingsley, and Travis 1995; Hinckley 1991; Holsti 1996; Hurwitz and Peffley 1987, 1990; Peffley and Hurwitz 1985; Sniderman, Brody, and Tetlock 1991; Sniderman and Tetlock 1986; and Wittkopf 1981, 1983, 1986, 1990, 1994). The evidence these and other revisionists cite contrasts sharply with the unstructured and unconstrained "nonattitudes" lacking ideological consistency described by Converse (1970). While acknowledging lower levels of factual information among mass publics, methodologically rigorous research by revisionists finds that mass public views about domestic, foreign, and security relationships appear to be coherently organized around complex belief systems. These beliefs are filtered by social cognition processes and contextual influences and guided by heuristics that partially offset the effects of shortfalls in factual information.

Even though the public is generally less well informed about complex issues than are elites, Lupia and McCubbins (1998) argue that the reasoned choice necessary for contributing to policy processes does not require complete information. The most important requirement is the ability to predict the consequences of actions. Rather than trying to master complete information about a given issue, people are cognitive misers, *choosing* to disregard most of the information they could acquire and selectively retaining those kinds of information that help them avoid costly mistakes and secure their welfare. It is both rational and efficient for people to rely on the expertise and advice of others whom they consider to be more informed about specific issues. Citizens use issue debates and political institutions to help them choose which advice to follow and which to ignore.[6] As to the instability in public opinion cited by traditionalists to illustrate the absence of structured beliefs, Sniderman, Tetlock and Elms (1999) note that some of the variation in public views reflects responses to wording variations in surveys and actually might demonstrate sophisticated abilities to include nuance in formulating policy positions.

In his fascinating analysis of collective judgments, James Surowiecki (2004) identifies four conditions that characterize "wise" publics: *diversity of information* (including technical and impressionistic knowledge); *independence* (lack of pressure to conform to group consensus); *decentralization* (individuals are able to include local knowledge and are not constrained by institutional dictates); and *aggregation* (means exist for turning individual judgments into collective decisions or policies). He cites numerous historical examples to show that if these conditions are met, public judgments are likely to be correct. Like Page and Shapiro (1992), Surowiecki notes the tendency of errors and extremes to cancel themselves out. "If you ask a large enough group of diverse, independent people to make a prediction or estimate a probability, and then average those estimates, the errors each of them makes in coming up with an answer will cancel themselves out. Each person's guess, you might say, has two components: information and error. Subtract the error, and you're left with the information" (10). While acknowledging that public decisions are not infallible and that they are susceptible to what John Stuart Mill described as "tyranny of the majority,"[7] Surowiecki concludes:

[T]he idea that the right answer to complex problems is simply "ask the experts" assumes that experts agree on the answers. But they don't, and if they did, it's hard to believe that the public would simply ignore their advice. Elites are just as partisan and no more devoted to the public interest than the average voter. More important, as you shrink the size of a decision-making body, you also shrink the likelihood that the final answer is right. Finally, most political decisions are not simply decisions about how to do something. They are decisions about what to do, decisions that involve values, trade-offs, and choices about what kind of society people should live in. There is no reason to think that experts are better at making those decisions than the average voter. (267)

These and other challenges to traditional orthodoxy are not limited to public views of domestic issues. Revisionists also dispute conventional wisdom about the reliability of mass views on foreign and security policies as compared to views of more informed elites. Oldendick and Bardes (1982) and Wittkopf (1987) report different patterns of beliefs and preferences about foreign policies between mass publics and elite groups, but those differences do not necessarily mean that elite views are more (or less) valid than the aggregate views of ordinary citizens. After studying differences in views of leaders and citizens on a wide range of foreign and domestic policy issues surveyed over time by the Chicago Council on Foreign Relations (CCFR), Page and Barabas (2000) conclude the following:

Taken as a whole, the gaps that CCFR surveys have revealed between the foreign policy preferences of citizens and those of leaders do not generally appear to us to result from a contrast between leaders' wisdom and expertise and the public's ignorance, misunderstanding, selfishness, or short-sightedness. In many cases public opinion may be reasonably well informed and deliberative, and the gaps may reflect differences between leaders and citizens with respect to values, goals, and interests. In such cases, democratic theory would seem to recommend responsiveness to what the citizens favor. (362)

As to traditional characterizations of the unsuitability of mass opinions for guiding foreign and security policies, Page and Shapiro (1983) find that government actions are more likely to respond in the direction of evolving public opinions about foreign policy than vice versa. That view was supported when Monroe (1998) analyzed policy outcomes for more than five hundred issues between 1980 and 1993 and reported that foreign policy decisions tend to be among the most consistent (67 percent) with public opinion. Addressing traditional criticisms about the public being slow to respond and then overreacting to events, Knopf (1998) studied mass opinions about military spending from 1965 to 1991 and concluded that public reactions to foreign policy events generally are moderate, and that the public responds to relevant information about changing circumstances with varying support for military spending. Russett (1990) concludes that rather than a source of perturbations for long-term strategic planning, public opinion actually operates as a stabilizing force on military spending. Jentleson (1992) and Jentleson and Britton (1998) find public support for the use of military force abroad to be differentiated by cause and to be responsive to political decisions about committing US forces. After analyzing a number of different foreign and security policy issues of the 1980s, Hinckley (1991) writes: "The overall conclusion is that public opinion is a significant element in the decision making process and that it behooves those in national security policymaking positions to be attentive to what the public thinks and understand why the public thinks that way" (129).

Comparing views among samples of elite scientists, state legislators, and the US general public, our own research (Herron and Jenkins-Smith 2002) indicates that at the aggregate level ordinary citizens relate beliefs about nuclear weapons to preferences about nuclear security policies in much the same ways as the two elite groups. When we compare patterns of beliefs among samples of the American and British publics (Jenkins-Smith, Mitchell, and Herron 2004) we find evidence of similar hierarchical belief structures among both publics across three different policy domains ranging from foreign affairs to domestic energy policy. In short, reasonably structured systems of beliefs are not merely the province of elites, and they extend across mass publics in different countries.

These and other challenges to the tradition of minimal public capacities have loosened the dominance of traditional views about the role of the public in shaping security policies, but debate continues about the degree to which the general public should participate in foreign and security policy processes, and assumptions about the greater validity and importance of expert opinion are widespread. From revisionist perspectives emerges a countervailing theory about public capacities that we summarize and contrast with traditional views in table 1.1.

Table 1.1. Contrasting traditional and revisionist theories of public capacities

Axioms of traditional theory	Axioms of revisionist theory
1. Ordinary citizens lack the cognitive capacities to understand politically sophisticated and technically complicated issues and are insufficiently knowledgeable about complex policy domains to develop reasoned preferences.	1. Complete information is not required for reasoned policy choice. Citizens are cognitive misers, disregarding most of the information they could acquire while selectively retaining information most important to their individual and collective welfare. Selective information processing is more a sign of rationality and sophistication than of limited capacities.
2. Underlying dispositions among the general public are insufficient to provide systematic structure and coherence of views about complex policy issues.	2. Well-defined belief systems and complex heuristics support and constrain mass opinions in both domestic and foreign policy domains in much the same ways they provide structure and coherence to views of elite publics.
3. Public opinion at the individual level is unstable, subject to rapid swings, and susceptible to overreaction. Public opinion at the mass level tends to be dominated by organized special interests or to be characterized by a wide range of incompatible views.	3. Fluctuations in issue salience should not be equated with changes in preferences. Longitudinal analyses show long-term stability in collective opinions related to underlying beliefs or key events. Though organized interest groups help define debate parameters, they do not fully control mass opinions.
4. Ordinary citizens depend on elites to determine policy priorities, set agendas, and evaluate alternative policy options. Mass views are subject to manipulation by policy elites.	4. Though ordinary citizens use debates among elites and opinion leaders whose beliefs are most closely aligned with their own to provide heuristic shortcuts, mass preferences shape government policies over the long term.
5. The less apparent and immediate the connection of policy issues to individual prerogatives, the less willing and able are members of the public to actively participate in policy processes.	5. While mass public activism in policy processes may vary directly with self-interest and near-term implications, history is replete with examples of individual sacrifices for society's sake—especially in terms of security policies.

Implications of Theory for Public Views on Nuclear Security and Terrorism

Traditional theory predicts that nuclear security policy is too complex in strategic scope and too technical in detail for ordinary citizens to hold rational and stable opinions about such issues as the new and evolving strategic security environment, trade-offs among risks and benefits deriving from nuclear weapons, the efficacy of nuclear deterrence, the advisability of arms control, and how spending should change for nuclear weapons capabilities. Traditionalists argue that the public lacks the requisite belief structures to consistently and reasonably connect broad integrating beliefs, such as political ideology, with specific beliefs and preferences about security policy. This view of public capacities warns of the dangers of public overreaction to traumatic events like 9/11 and cautions against undue influence by special interests. And traditionalist concepts suggest that while terrorism may focus the public on immediate threats to security, the more distant threat of state-level nuclear conflict is of little interest in the absence of a clear and present nuclear danger.

Unsurprisingly, revisionist theory predicts very different public capabilities. Revisionists expect to find at the aggregate level reasoned preferences deriving from stable and persistent belief structures in which logical connections exist between broad ideological dispositions and more specific policy beliefs. While expecting some perturbations in public views of specific issues relating to security, revisionists expect public opinions about nuclear security to be relatively stable over time. They predict that public assessments of the threat and support of forceful responses to terrorist attacks like 9/11 will be marked, but they also predict that such responses will be constrained by considerations derived from the broader structure of beliefs that operates in more ordinary times. Revisionist theory suggests that citizens follow public and political debates about the changing nature of security, but they rely on familiar heuristics such as ideology and partisanship to help guide preferences for strategic directions. Similarly, revisionists expect the general public initially to support measured calls for sacrifice to enhance security when the associated policies are adequately articulated by national leaders and pursued with consistency.

Our data provide a unique opportunity to contribute to democratic theory by testing these contrasting expectations. Having begun measuring public views of nuclear security early in the post–Cold War era, and having continued comparative measurements for a decade thereafter that included the rise of terrorism and the further proliferation of weapons of mass destruction, we can test empirically the kinds of expectations about mass public opinion in the United States present in these two very different theories of public capacities.

In addition to designing our research to help compare and test different concepts of public capabilities, we also seek to measure how policy-relevant views of security are changing in the post–Cold War environment. As we designed and planned this research, we predicted that public valuation of US nuclear weapons would decline significantly following the demise of the only other nuclear superpower, and our questions were intended to help track that trend. As we will show, the trends we have measured thus far reflect very different findings. We will show that rather than declining, assessments of the benefits afforded by US nuclear weapons have *increased* significantly in the post–Cold War era. Instead of quickly fading in relevance, the efficacy of nuclear deterrence remains strong in the views of most Americans. Rather than dissipating, US public support for investing in nuclear security actually strengthened. In chapter 2, we begin illustrating these counterintuitive findings by analyzing public views about the security environment, strategic threats, and beliefs about the risks and benefits of nuclear weapons.

2

TRENDS IN NUCLEAR
SECURITY ASSESSMENTS

THE LAST DECADE of the twentieth century was one of enormous change in the security of the United States and the world. The torrent of changes in Eastern Europe, culminating in the previously unimaginable collapse of the barriers between the two Germanys, shook long-held beliefs about the very foundations for stability and security. The ensuing disintegration of the Soviet Union forced a complete reassessment of national and international security policies amid the most sweeping strategic changes since World War II. The euphoria over the end of the Cold War was tempered, however, as new challenges and uncertainties loomed concerning nuclear proliferation and terrorism. These developments present opportunities and risks that are difficult for scholars, experts, and policymakers to assess, and they are no less challenging for publics the world over. In this chapter, we assess how the American people are adjusting to the momentous security developments of the early post–Cold War era. We analyze trends in public views of how the international security environment is evolving to include assessments of strategic threats posed by Russian and Chinese nuclear weapons capabilities. We illustrate how public views of broader external nuclear risks such as the likelihood of nuclear conflict, nuclear proliferation, and nuclear terrorism evolved between 1993 and 2003. Also we examine trends in beliefs about the risks associated with our own nuclear arsenal. We chart similar comparisons over time of public beliefs about the external and domestic benefits associated with US nuclear weapons.[1]

Trends in Perceptions of the Security Environment

Beginning in 1997, we employed the following questions to ask survey participants to rate how international security and US security have changed since the end of the Cold War.

(Lead-in) I want to ask you some questions about how you think the world may have changed since the end of the Cold War. We are interested in your perceptions. There are no right or wrong answers.

(Q4) Considering the international environment as a whole, and using a scale from one to seven where one means the world is much less secure, and seven means the world is much more secure, how do you think international security has changed since the end of the Cold War?

(Q5) Focusing more specifically on the US, and using the same scale from one to seven where one means much less secure, and seven means much more secure, how has US security changed since the end of the Cold War?

We compare grouped responses to each question for each of the four measurement periods in figures 2.1 and 2.2.[2]

When we began this series of questions in 1997, a majority of respondents considered international and US security to have improved since the end of the Cold War. This was consistent with much of the considered opinion of the time in which discussion of a "peace dividend" occupied considerable space in the pages of scholarly and policy opinion as well as popular media.[3] The proportion of respondents perceiving security to have improved declined by about 10 percent between 1997 and 2003, while the proportion of those who consider international and US security to have worsened increased by about the same amount. Changes in means for each question from 1997 to 2003 are statistically significant. While it seems likely the terrorist attacks of 9/11

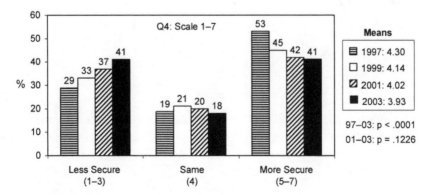

Figure 2.1. How international security has changed since the Cold War

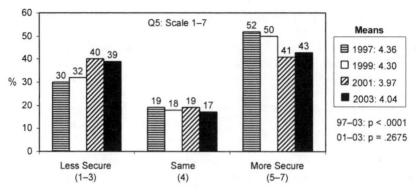

Figure 2.2. How US security has changed since the Cold War

influenced subsequent assessments, our measurements in 1999 suggest that the downward trend has earlier beginnings. In 2003 most respondents do not consider national or international security to have substantially improved over that which existed during the Cold War.

To focus on public understanding of more specific components of strategic security, we also asked the following four questions about current and prospective threats to the United States posed by Russian and Chinese nuclear forces.

(Lead-in) Now we want your overall assessment of current and future threats to the US from two sources.

(Q51) First, on a scale from zero to ten where zero means no threat, and ten means extreme threat, how would you rate the current threat to the US posed by Russia's nuclear weapons?

(Q52) Next, using the same scale from zero to ten where zero means no threat, and ten means extreme threat, how would you rate the current threat to the US from China's nuclear weapons?

(Q53) Turning now to your outlook for the future, and using the same scale from zero to ten, how would you rate the threat to the US in the next ten years from Russia's nuclear weapons?

(Q54) On the same scale from zero to ten, how would you rate the threat to the US in the next ten years from China's nuclear weapons?

We compare trends in grouped assessments of current threats from Russian and Chinese nuclear forces in figures 2.3 and 2.4, and we compare trends in ratings of future strategic nuclear threats in figures 2.5 and 2.6.

Several points are apparent. First, the mean public rating of the current nuclear threat from Russia is significantly lower in 2001 and 2003 than in earlier surveys in 1997 and 1999, while the corresponding mean rating of the cur-

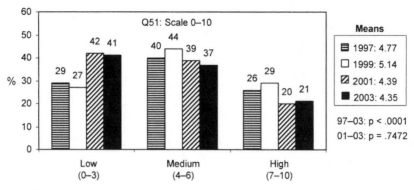

Figure 2.3. Trends in public assessments of the current Russian nuclear threat

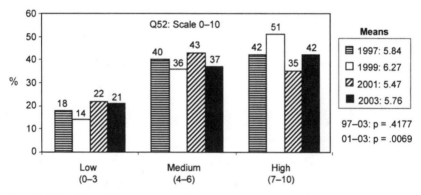

Figure 2.4. Trends in public assessments of the current Chinese nuclear threat

rent threat posed by China's nuclear weapons increases significantly between 2001 and 2003 to a value that statistically is unchanged from 1997. Second, the proportion of respondents in 2003 (42 percent) who rate the Chinese nuclear threat in the high range (7–10) is twice the proportion of respondents (21 percent) who rate the nuclear threat from Russia in the same range. Also note that in each measurement period, the mean nuclear threat rating for China is significantly higher than the corresponding rating for Russia ($p < .0001$ for each of the four years). Thus while our respondents consider general levels of security to be deteriorating, they also judge the more specific and traditional threats posed by Russian nuclear forces to be decreasing. This speaks to public abilities to absorb major strategic changes in nuclear relationships within the larger context of the evolving post–Cold War security environment.

Figures 2.5 and 2.6 show comparable public assessments of future Russian and Chinese nuclear threats projected over the next ten years.

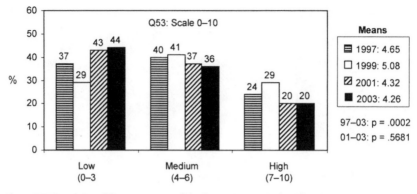

Figure 2.5. Trends in public assessments of the future Russian nuclear threat

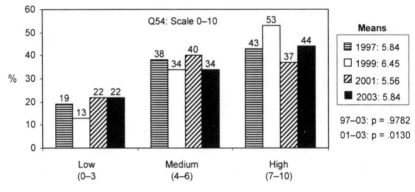

Figure 2.6. Trends in public assessments of the future Chinese nuclear threat

Note that the mean future nuclear threat rating for Russia in 2003 changes little from the previous measurement in 2001, but the mean future threat rating for China rises significantly above that measured two years earlier. Again, the mean ratings of future threats are significantly higher for China than for Russia in each of our four surveys ($p < .0001$ each year). While the public expects the threat posed by Russia's nuclear capabilities to remain at about the same level over the next decade, they predict that the Chinese nuclear threat will grow slightly over the same period.[4]

These findings suggest that China has replaced Russia in terms of public expectations of relative current and predicted nuclear threats to US security, and that publicly perceived nuclear threats from each are trending differently. Both current and projected mean nuclear threats from Russia decline significantly over the course of our measurements from 1997 to 2003. Mean current and projected nuclear threats from China vary across the different measurement periods, but by 2003 they are at levels that are statistically unchanged from our first measurements in 1997.

Trends in External Nuclear Risks

In each survey since beginning this project eighteen months after the breakup of the Soviet Union, we asked a series of six questions designed to measure three dimensions of evolving beliefs about external nuclear risks (risks from others' nuclear weapons). They consist of the following two questions about the risks of nuclear conflict, two questions about the risks of nuclear proliferation, and two questions about the risks of nuclear terrorism.

(**Q6**) How has the breakup of the Soviet Union affected the chances that the US will be involved in a war with any country in which nuclear weapons are used?

(**Q7**) How has the breakup of the Soviet Union affected the possibility that nuclear weapons will be used by any country against any other country?

(**Q15**) How do you think the breakup of the Soviet Union has affected the likelihood that nuclear weapons will spread to other countries?

(**Q16**) How would you rate the risk to the US if more countries have nuclear weapons?

(**Q17**) How would you rate today's threat of nuclear terrorism occurring anywhere in the world?

(**Q18**) How would you rate the threat of nuclear weapons being used by terrorists anywhere in the world during the next ten years?

Table 2.1 compares trends in mean response values for each of the six questions between 1993 and 2003.

Public assessments of the implications of the Soviet breakup remain remarkably steady over the decade. Respondents are divided about the effects on the likelihood of nuclear conflict, with judgments of the chances the United States will become involved in a nuclear conflict increasing modestly (but statistically significantly) over the period, and assessments of the likelihood that nuclear weapons will be used in nuclear conflict between any two countries holding steady at just above midscale. Opinion is equally steady, and less divided, about the effects of the Soviet demise on further nuclear proliferation, with most participants in each survey judging the risks to be higher. Similarly, most respondents consider the risks to the United States, specifically, of further nuclear proliferation to be higher after the Soviet breakup, and that perspective holds steady throughout the measurement period. As to the current and future threat of nuclear terrorism, participants consider the contemporary threat to be increasing, and forecast no reduction when asked

Table 2.1. Trends in mean public assessments of external nuclear risks

Mean external nuclear risks	1993	1995	1997	1999	2001	2003	'93 v '03 p-value
Effect of Soviet breakup on chances US will be involved in nuclear war (Q6: 1 = decreased greatly↔7 = increased greatly)	3.85	4.08	4.04	4.35	4.28	4.14	< .0001
Effect of Soviet breakup on chances nuclear weapons will be used by any country against any other country (Q7: 1 = decreased greatly↔7 = increased greatly)	4.54	4.67	4.41	4.66	4.61	4.50	.5951
Effect of Soviet breakup on further nuclear proliferation (Q15: 0 = greatly reduced↔10 = greatly increased)	6.49	6.02	6.04	6.62	6.10	6.34	.1560
Risk to the US if more countries have nuclear weapons (Q16: 0 = no risk↔10 = extreme risk)	7.65	7.81	7.45	7.65	7.59	7.67	.7413
Threat of nuclear terrorism occurring anywhere in the world today (Q17: 0 = no threat↔10 = extreme threat)	6.89	7.16	7.04	7.14	7.01	7.10	.0237
Threat of nuclear terrorism occurring anywhere in the world in the next 10 years (Q18: 0 = no threat↔10 = extreme threat)	7.00	7.23	6.83	7.09	7.06	7.11	.2432

to consider the next ten years. Clearly, our respondents do not consider the risks of nuclear conflict, nuclear proliferation, or nuclear terrorism to have abated after the Cold War, and judgments about those risks do not show large variations over time.

We combine responses to these six questions to form a composite index of external nuclear risks that provides a robust indication, comparable over time, illustrating trends in evolving beliefs about external nuclear weapons risks.[5] In figure 2.7 we show the distribution of responses in 2003, and in figure 2.8 we chart trends in mean external nuclear risk indices between 1993 and 2003.[6] In 2003, about 8 percent of respondents judge external nuclear risks to be low (0–3), 49 percent rate them moderate (4–6), and 42 percent place them in the high range (7–10). The modal value is 6.0, and the mean is 6.52.

Mean composite external nuclear risks remain notably steady over the course of the decade, even after the events of 9/11. Thus it appears that the general public differentiates between the nonnuclear risks deriving from the terrorist attacks of 9/11 versus the risks posed by others' nuclear weapons—including nuclear terrorism—and do not conclude that overall external *nuclear* risks have changed appreciably. As our findings show, from the perspectives of the US general public, average composite external nuclear risks vary only

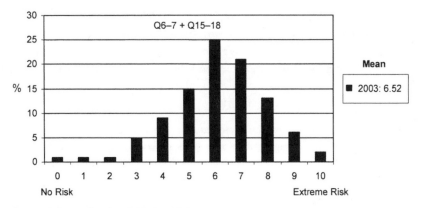

Figure 2.7. External nuclear risk index, 2003

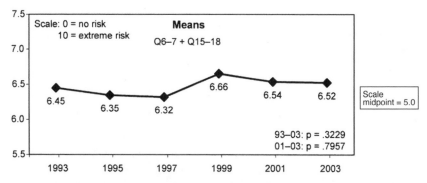

Figure 2.8. Trends in the mean external nuclear risk index, 1993–2003 (Note that here and in subsequent trend graphs, we truncate the vertical scale to better illustrate the data. We identify the scale midpoint to help orientation.)

0.34 on a scale from zero to ten over the decade from 1993 to 2003. But we note also that mean assessments are well above the scale midpoint of 5.0 in each measurement period, and that a substantial decrease in overall nuclear risks following the end of Cold War hostilities between the United States and the Soviet Union has yet to occur in the judgments of our respondents.

Trends in Domestic Nuclear Risks

In addition to measuring public assessments of risks deriving from others' nuclear weapons, we also measure domestic risks believed to derive from our own nuclear weapons. In each measurement period since 1993, we asked respondents from the general public to rate the domestic risks associated with manufacturing, transporting, storing, disassembling, and storing materials from disassembled US nuclear weapons. Additionally, we asked them to rate the likelihood that a US nuclear weapon might be employed without proper national authorization, and the likelihood that an accidental nuclear explosion might occur. The following questions allow us to compare trends in public beliefs about domestic nuclear risks.

(Lead-in) The next several questions ask for your perceptions about risks to American society associated with managing US nuclear weapons. Using a scale from zero to ten where zero means no risk, and ten means extreme risk, how would you rate the risk of each of the following items?

(Q8) Manufacturing nuclear weapons in the US

(Q9) Transporting nuclear weapons in the US

(Q10) Storing existing nuclear weapons in the US

(Q11) Disassembling nuclear weapons in the US

(Q12) Storing radioactive materials in the US from disassembled weapons

(Q13) On a scale from zero to ten, where zero means not at all likely, and ten means highly likely, how would you rate the likelihood of a US nuclear weapon being used within the next twenty-five years without presidential authorization?

(Q14) On the same scale from zero to ten, how would you rate the likelihood of an accident involving a US nuclear weapon causing an unintended nuclear explosion?

In table 2.2, we show mean responses to each question across the six surveys.

Note that in contrast to the previously charted steady or increasing public assessments of external nuclear risks, views of domestic nuclear risks deriving from US nuclear weapons capabilities show significant decreases in each category measured over the past decade. The reductions in mean perceived risks from the US nuclear arsenal range from a 14 percent decline in the likelihood of unauthorized use of a US nuclear weapon to a decrease of 23 percent in risks associated with manufacturing components for US nuclear weapons. These observations are recorded during a decade in which the United States is not developing, manufacturing, or testing nuclear weapons, though, presumably, some critical components are remanufactured. Of course, storage and transportation activities are ongoing, and nuclear weapons are being disassembled.

By combining responses to these questions we create a robust index of public beliefs about domestic risks associated with US nuclear weapons, as shown in figure 2.9.[7] By comparing composite mean assessments of the domestic nuclear risk index over time, we illustrate trends in figure 2.10. Grouped responses in 2003 indicate that 34 percent consider domestic nuclear risks to

Table 2.2. Trends in mean public assessments of domestic nuclear risks

Domestic risk measures	1993	1995	1997	1999	2001	2003	'93 v '03 p-value
Manufacturing nuclear weapons in the US (Q8: 0 = no risk↔10 = extreme risk)	6.54	5.74	5.10	5.42	5.07	5.06	< .0001
Transporting nuclear weapons in the US (Q9: 0 = no risk↔10 = extreme risk)	6.84	5.96	5.42	5.68	5.44	5.49	< .0001
Storing existing nuclear weapons in the US (Q10: 0 = no risk↔10 = extreme risk)	6.57	6.07	5.71	5.94	5.46	5.60	< .0001
Disassembling nuclear weapons in the US (Q11: 0 = no risk↔10 = extreme risk)	6.02	5.51	5.06	5.34	4.95	4.94	< .0001
Storing radioactive materials in the US from disassembled weapons (Q12: 0 = no risk↔10 = extreme risk)	7.64	6.25	6.12	6.39	5.86	5.92	< .0001
Likelihood of unauthorized use of US nuclear weapon in next 25 years (Q13: 0 = not at all likely↔10 = extremely likely)	4.06	4.34	3.91	4.24	3.08	3.50	< .0001
Likelihood of an unintended US nuclear weapon explosion (Q14: 0 = not at all likely↔10 = extremely likely)	4.79	4.98	4.57	4.70	3.78	4.09	< .0001

be low (0–3), 47 percent rate them moderate (4–6), and 18 percent judge them to be relatively high (7–10). The modal response is 5.0, and the mean is 4.93.

The downward trend in composite means from 6.06 in 1993 to 4.93 in 2003 clearly is statistically significant. The mean value for combined domestic nuclear risks fell below midscale both in 2001 and 2003, suggesting declining levels of public concern about safeguarding and controlling nuclear weapons. As will be shown in chapter 3, responses to direct questions about trust in

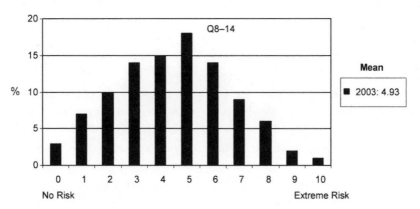

Figure 2.9. Domestic nuclear risk index, 2003

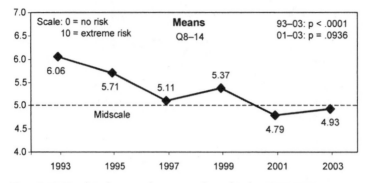

Figure 2.10. Trends in the mean domestic nuclear risk index, 1993–2003

the Departments of Energy and Defense, as well as US national laboratories, reflect substantial levels of public confidence in the US nuclear weapons establishment.

Trends in External Nuclear Benefits

To measure public assessments of external benefits believed to derive from the US nuclear arsenal, we posed questions about the importance of nuclear weapons for US influence and status, remaining a military superpower, preserving the American way of life, and providing nuclear deterrence. The questions are shown below in summary fashion.

(Q19) How important are US nuclear weapons for US influence over international events?

(Q20) How important are US nuclear weapons for maintaining US status as a world leader?

(Q21) How important is it for the US to remain a military superpower?

(Q22) How important have nuclear weapons been to preserving America's way of life?

(Lead-in) The next three questions ask about your perceptions of nuclear deterrence, which means preventing someone from using nuclear weapons against us, because they expect that we would retaliate by using nuclear weapons against them.[8]

(Q23) First, how important was nuclear deterrence in preventing nuclear conflict during the Cold War?

(Q24) How important are US nuclear weapons for preventing other countries from using nuclear weapons against us today?

(Q25) If more countries acquire nuclear weapons in the future, how effective will nuclear deterrence be in preventing nuclear wars from occurring anywhere in the world?

We compare mean responses to each question over time in table 2.3.

Mean assessments of the importance of US nuclear weapons for international influence and US status as a world leader, and the importance of remaining a military superpower increase significantly between our first survey in 1993 and our survey in 2003. Mean judgments of the importance of nuclear deterrence for preventing nuclear conflict during the Cold War and today are all high, and they remain steady throughout the measurement period. Finally, even when asked to assume that additional countries successfully acquire nuclear weapons, the future effectiveness of nuclear deterrence in a more proliferated world is rated above midscale and varies little over the six surveys. This continued strength of valuations of US nuclear weapons ca-

Table 2.3. Trends in mean public assessments of external nuclear benefits

Mean external nuclear benefits	1993	1995	1997	1999	2001	2003	p-value
Importance of nuclear weapons for US international influence (Q19: 0 = not at all important↔10 = extremely important)	6.10	6.39	6.32	6.70	6.84	6.74	'93 v '03 < .0001
Importance of nuclear weapons for US status as a world leader (Q20: 0 = not at all important↔10 = extremely important)	6.25	6.67	6.59	7.06	7.16	7.12	'93 v '03 < .0001
Importance of US remaining a military superpower (Q21: 0 = not at all important↔10 = extremely important)	7.62	8.00	8.18	8.46	8.76	8.32	'93 v '03 < .0001
Importance of nuclear weapons for preserving US way of life (Q22: 0 = not at all important↔10 = extremely important)	6.07	6.30	6.28	6.47	6.57	6.22	'93 v '03 .1904
Importance of nuclear deterrence during Cold War (Q23: 0 = not at all important↔10 = extremely important)	NA	7.79	7.63	7.66	7.88	8.02	'95 v '03 .0023
Importance of nuclear deterrence today (Q24: 0 = not at all important↔10 = extremely important)	NA	7.60	7.41	7.66	7.62	7.47	'95 v '03 .1458
Future effectiveness of nuclear deterrence if more countries acquire nuclear weapons (Q25: 0 = not at all effective↔10 = extremely effective)	NA	5.99	6.00	5.92	6.99	5.85	'95 v '03 .1741

pabilities more than a decade after the end of the Cold War is surprising. We anticipated a decline in public views of the importance of US nuclear weapons in the post–Cold War era.

We combine responses to these questions to form an external nuclear benefit index for which the distribution of responses in 2003 is shown in figure 2.11, and the means are charted over time in figure 2.12.[9] This distribution pattern clearly shows that respondents in 2003 attribute substantial external security benefits to the US nuclear arsenal. About 58 percent of respondents rate the combined external benefits of nuclear weapons in the high range (7–10), while only about 7 percent of respondents place them in the low range (0–3). About 35 percent rate external nuclear benefits in the middle range (4–6). The modal response is 7.0, and even the mean is in the high range at 7.11.

The trend in our composite index of mean external nuclear benefits since 1995 generally is upward, with a turn downward in 2003. Note, however, that mean assessments are well above midscale in each period. A dozen years af-

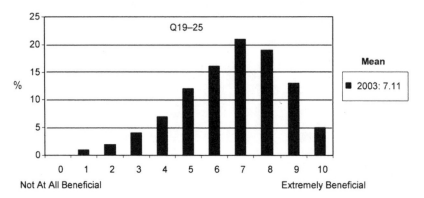

Figure 2.11. External nuclear benefit index, 2003

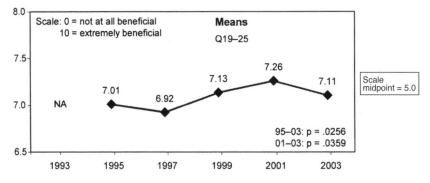

Figure 2.12. Trends in the mean external nuclear benefit index, 1995–2003

ter the end of the Cold War, mean public views of the benefits of US nuclear weapons for achieving national objectives have not declined from those values recorded shortly after the collapse of the Soviet Union, and have actually increased somewhat. Clearly, the devaluation of US nuclear weapons we expected in the post–Cold War period has not yet occurred.

Trends in Domestic Nuclear Benefits

Public assessments of domestic benefits related to US nuclear weapons are more difficult to gauge than the other three dimensions of nuclear risks and benefits. Measuring domestic benefits requires differentiating nuclear investments from those that are nonnuclear, and that is problematic. For example, some US weapon systems are designed to employ both nuclear and nonnuclear munitions. In some cases, weapon systems such as aircraft or naval vessels are designed for and employed primarily in conventional, nonnuclear roles, but also have the capacity to be used for employing nuclear weapons. Other systems, such as the B-1 bomber, may originally be designed primarily for nuclear roles but later are adapted to conventional missions. Also, expenditures for personnel and support equipment and facilities are not easily separated into nuclear and conventional components, because many of the same skills and equipment are applicable to both nuclear and nonnuclear combat environments.

The same is true for investments in research and development that can encompass both conventional and nuclear systems as well as dual-role systems. Other types of investments, such as those for strategic intelligence and command and control are even harder to differentiate, because they are not publicly reported with sufficient clarity to definitively categorize them as to their nuclear vs. conventional applicability. Some of the investment categories that may be applicable to nuclear systems and capabilities are made outside the defense budget, and tracking all nuclear-related investment categories across the entire federal budget is extremely complex. These and other factors make the separation of nuclear and nonnuclear expenditures and investments very difficult, and thus measuring the domestic benefits of the nuclear categories is a daunting task for technical experts, and is even more problematic for most citizens.[10]

For these and other reasons, we limit our questions to three broad inquiries into public beliefs about potential domestic benefits associated with nuclear weapons. As shown below, the three questions address cost trade-offs in nuclear and nonnuclear military capabilities, the economic value of jobs related to defense industries, and the potential benefit of technology transfers from the defense sector to other sectors of the US economy.

(Q37) Using a scale from one to seven where one means you strongly disagree, and seven means you strongly agree, please respond to the following statement. "Having a nuclear arsenal means the US can spend less for national defense than would be necessary without nuclear weapons."

(Lead-in) The next two questions deal with the economic value of defense industry jobs and defense-related technologies. Both use a scale from one to seven where one means little economic value, and seven means great economic value.

(Q38) First, how do you rate the economic value of defense industry jobs in America?

(Q39) Next, how do you rate the economic value of technological advances in defense industries for other areas of the US economy?[11]

We compare trends in mean responses to each question in table 2.4.

Even in an environment in which the numbers of US nuclear weapons are being reduced, perceived domestic benefits of US nuclear capabilities are not declining; in fact, mean responses to each question have increased significantly since we first asked them. For comparative purposes, we combine responses to each question to form a domestic nuclear benefit index, and we chart the distribution of the index for 2003 in figure 2.13.[12]

Responses are grouped mostly toward the middle and upper portions of the scale, with 40 percent of respondents placing domestic nuclear benefits in the high range (7–10) and 46 percent rating them in the midrange (4–6). About 14 percent of respondents judge them to be low (0–3). The pattern shows a modal response value of 6.0 and a mean of 6.55, which, as shown in figure 2.14, has remained remarkably stable since 1995.

This pattern of means shows a sustained level of valuation from 1995 (the first year in which all three questions were asked) to 2003 that is well above midscale. The previously discussed difficulties in judging domestic nuclear benefits do not prevent consistent evaluations, and the fact that they are not grouped around midscale suggests that most respondents are able to form

Table 2.4. Trends in mean public assessments of domestic nuclear benefits

Mean domestic nuclear benefits	1993	1995	1997	1999	2001	2003	p-value
US nuclear arsenal means we can spend less than would be necessary without nuclear weapons (Q37: 1 = strongly disagree↔7 = strongly agree)	3.43	3.94	4.15	4.02	3.69	3.87	'93 v '03 < .0001
Economic value of defense industry jobs (Q38: 1 = little value↔7 = great value)	4.55	4.88	5.13	5.22	5.50	5.26	'93 v '03 < .0001
Economic value of technological advances in defense industries for other areas of US economy (Q39: 1 = little value↔7 = great value)	NA	5.29	5.60	5.69	5.82	5.67	'95 v '03 < .0001

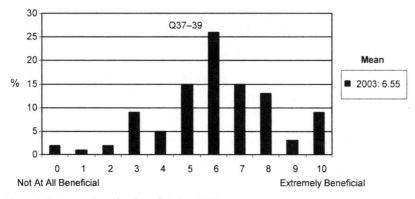

Figure 2.13. Domestic nuclear benefit index, 2003

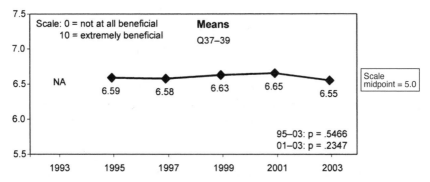

Figure 2.14. Trends in the mean domestic nuclear benefit index, 1995–2003

opinions about the benefits of defense investments for the US domestic economy.

We employ these four indices of public beliefs about external and domestic nuclear risks and benefits as important measures of domain beliefs when we analyze mass belief structures in chapter 6. But next we examine trends in public views about specific nuclear security issues, such as the contemporary relevance of nuclear weapons, the efficacy of nuclear deterrence, nuclear security policy and spending preferences, and trust in key elements of the US nuclear weapons establishment.

TRENDS IN POLICY AND SPENDING PREFERENCES

THE PREVIOUS CHAPTER focused on trends in public perceptions of broad issues of security and general perceptions of the utility of the US nuclear arsenal. Overall, we find that—contrary to expectations—during the early post–Cold War era, Americans perceived an eroding security environment and ascribed a continuing and even elevated value to the US nuclear arsenal. This chapter evaluates specific policy beliefs that might be expected to flow from the more general security frame of reference. We are asking whether the broad-brush public perceptions recounted in chapter 2 carry over into specific beliefs about important but more detailed policy correlates. Our approach is to analyze public views of selected nuclear security policies and investments by addressing the following kinds of questions.

In the midst of an unconventional war against terrorism, do nuclear weapons continue to be relevant to national and international security?

Does nuclear deterrence remain important to the public's sense of security?

Do Americans support reducing the size of the US nuclear arsenal, and if so, to what minimum levels?

Can nuclear weapons be eliminated?

How does the public assess the importance of underground nuclear testing and the prospects for a comprehensive test ban treaty?

How do Americans think spending for nuclear security capabilities and infrastructure should change?

Do Americans support developing new small-yield nuclear weapons capable of penetrating deep underground?

Do they support national missile defenses?

Do members of the general public systematically relate their assessments of the risks and benefits of nuclear weapons to their preferences for associated policies?

Trends in responses to these kinds of questions provide insights about public assessments of the future viability and efficacy of nuclear security. Moreover, responses to questions about these more specific and nuanced policy beliefs and preferences can be judged for consistency with respondents' broader aggregate assessments of the security environment. The challenge is whether, in the aggregate, public beliefs are integrated and coherent within this cognitively demanding policy domain.

Relevance of Nuclear Weapons

To investigate views about the relevance of nuclear weapons, we posed a series of questions about the potential for their elimination and about public beliefs regarding the utility and importance of US nuclear weapons. In each of our security studies, beginning in 1993, we asked participants to respond to the following statements about the feasibility of eliminating all nuclear weapons using a scale from one (strongly disagree) to seven (strongly agree).[1] We show trends in mean responses to both in figure 3.1.[2]

(Q34) It is feasible to eliminate all nuclear weapons worldwide within the next twenty-five years.

(Q35) Even if all the nuclear weapons could somehow be eliminated worldwide, it would be extremely difficult to keep other countries from building them again.

Several points are noteworthy. First, as shown by the bottom trend line, in each survey, the mean response to the statement that "it is feasible to eliminate all nuclear weapons worldwide within the next twenty-five years" is *below* midscale, indicating a mean position of disagreement. Note that variation is

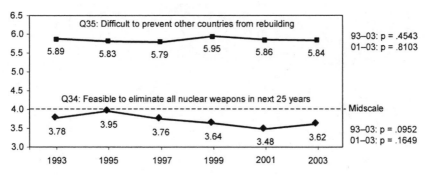

Figure 3.1. Trends in mean prospects for eliminating all nuclear weapons

modest, with change over the decade not statistically significant. Moving to the top trend line, note that in each of our surveys, mean responses to the statement that "even if all nuclear weapons could somehow be eliminated, it would be extremely difficult to prevent other countries from building them again" all are *above* midscale, indicating aggregate agreement. Also note that mean responses to this statement do not change appreciably across the decade of measurements.[3]

In further probing public views of the prospects for nuclear abolition, we also began asking a question in 1995 that places the issue within the context of arms control agreements and mutual arms reductions. We asked respondents how they feel about the United States agreeing to an arms control provision that requires eventually eliminating all of our nuclear weapons. No reference is made to treaty commitments such as Article VI of the Treaty on the Non-proliferation of Nuclear Weapons (NPT).[4] Responses are provided on a scale of one (strongly oppose) to seven (strongly support). We chart the trend in mean responses since 1995 in figure 3.2.

Public support of a treaty calling for the elimination of US nuclear weapons in the context of mutual elimination of all nuclear arsenals worldwide declined significantly between 1995 and 2001. Note, however, that the mean value in 2003 returned to above midscale, apparently reversing the prior trend.

Further insight into public views about the continued relevance of nuclear weapons after the Cold War is apparent in the patterns of responses to questions asking participants to rate the importance of the US nuclear arsenal for various security functions. Some of these questions are described briefly in chapter 2 as components of our external nuclear benefits index, but here we chart mean responses over time to graphically illustrate trends. We reiterate that, at the outset of this project and in the aftermath of the Cold War, we an-

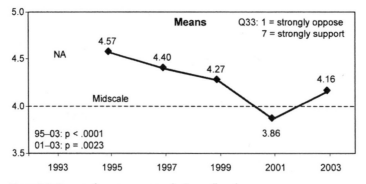

Figure 3.2. Support for agreement to eliminate all nuclear weapons

ticipated a sustained decline in the perceived importance of the nuclear arsenal for this array of purposes. Figures 3.3–3.6 thus illustrate what was (for us) an unexpected growth in public valuation of US nuclear weapons by charting mean responses to the following five questions, each of which is answered on a scale from zero (not at all important) to ten (extremely important). Note that vertical scales vary.

(Q19) How important are US nuclear weapons for US influence over international events?

(Q20) How important are US nuclear weapons for maintaining US status as a world leader?

(Q21) How important is it for the US to remain a military superpower?

(Q36) How important is it for the US to retain nuclear weapons today?

These response patterns show generally upward trends in public valuations of US nuclear weapons since the end of the Cold War, but each also

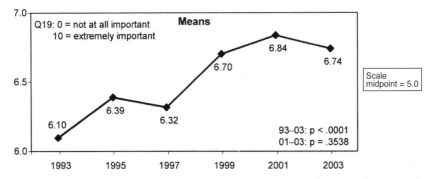

Figure 3.3. Trends in mean importance of nuclear weapons for US influence

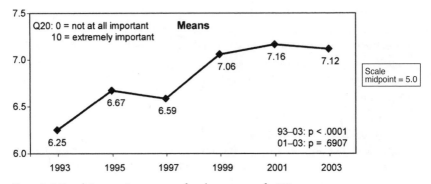

Figure 3.4. Trends in mean importance of nuclear weapons for US status

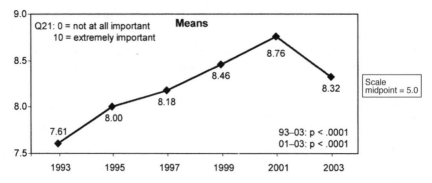

Figure 3.5. Trends in mean importance of the United States remaining a military superpower

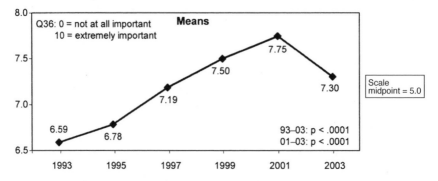

Figure 3.6. Trends in mean importance of retaining US nuclear weapons

shows a downturn in 2003. Note that mean values for each question in each measurement period all are well above the midscale value of 5.0. And starting from above midscale in 1993, the mean valuation of the importance of US nuclear weapons for international influence (figure 3.3) increases 10.5 percent by 2003, while the mean rating of the importance of nuclear weapons for US status as a world leader (figure 3.4) grows 13.9 percent. During the same period, the mean importance of the United States remaining a military superpower (figure 3.5) increases 9.3 percent. Finally, in this series, mean assessments of the importance of retaining US nuclear weapons (figure 3.6) increase 10.8 percent over the ten-year measurement period. For each question, these differences in means from 1993 to 2003 would have occurred by chance fewer than one in 10,000 times ($p < .0001$).

It is clear that post–Cold War devaluation of nuclear weapons for achieving national objectives and for providing national security not only has yet to materialize, but public valuations of US nuclear weapons have *increased* significantly across the board since our first measurements. Note, however, that these questions do not address numbers or types of nuclear weapons, nuclear research investments, delivery vehicles, alert postures, or support force structures. Thus, the responses detailed so far should not be interpreted to imply public support for a larger nuclear arsenal, new nuclear weapons, or broader force postures—issues to which we return later. Rather, they reflect only mean levels of public assessments of the broad importance of US nuclear weapons for achieving national objectives. The key finding is that such valuations have not declined, but rather have significantly increased during the first twelve years of the post–Cold War era. We note, however, that the downturns in 2003 reverse the direction of trends in earlier measurements.

Efficacy of Nuclear Deterrence

How have the dissolution of the Soviet Union, greater cooperation with Russia, and an economically growing China influenced public views of nuclear deterrence? As noted in the preceding chapter, we began in 1995 a series of questions designed to measure different dimensions of the deterrence issue. The first question asks participants to assess retroactively the importance of nuclear deterrence in preventing nuclear conflict during the Cold War; the second asks the importance of deterrence for preventing nuclear conflict in the present period. Both are answered on a scale from zero (not at all important) to ten (extremely important). We compare response trends in figure 3.7.

As shown by the solid line, mean assessments of the importance of nuclear deterrence during the Cold War trend upward from 1997 and are statistically significantly higher in 2003 compared to our first measurements in 1995 ($p = .0023$). Note that *all* mean assessments are above 7.6 on a scale from zero to ten. As shown by the dashed line, mean assessments of the current impor-

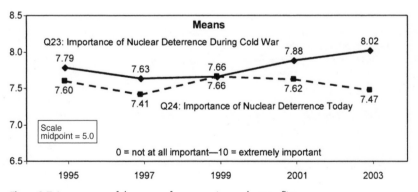

Figure 3.7. Importance of deterrence for preventing nuclear conflict

tance of nuclear deterrence for preventing other countries from using nuclear weapons against the United States vary only from a low of 7.41 to a high of 7.66, and differences from 1995 to 2003 are not statistically significant (p = .1458). Note that all means are above 7.4 on a zero-to-ten scale, but that the trend since 1999 is declining.

Another interesting aspect involves the relative trends in these two measures. In aggregate and across the entire survey period, the perceived difference in importance is modest. Roughly 30 percent believe nuclear deterrence has become less important, 45 percent see no change, and 25 percent think deterrence has actually increased in importance since the Cold War. Over the period of our surveys, however, public opinion shifts noticeably. In 1995, respondents are roughly evenly divided on the question of whether deterrence has declined or increased in importance compared to the Cold War period (28 percent to 23 percent). By 2003, the balance shifts to 36 percent believing deterrence is less important now compared to only 21 percent who think deterrence is more important now. This shift is statistically significant (chi-square p < .001). Thus, public views of the relative value of nuclear deterrence are evolving, with perceptions of its importance for preventing nuclear conflict during the Cold War increasing retrospectively, while perceptions of its contemporary importance are relatively lower and trending in the opposite direction.

Our third question in this series shifts focus and response options to ask participants to estimate the future *effectiveness* of nuclear deterrence if other countries gain nuclear weapons. Responses are on a scale from zero (not at all effective) to ten (extremely effective). We graph trends in responses in figure 3.8.

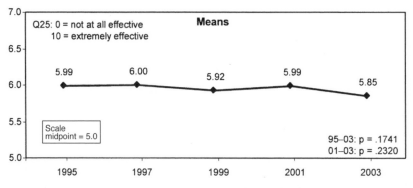

Figure 3.8. Effectiveness of deterrence in preventing nuclear conflict if more countries acquire nuclear weapons in the future

As expected, changing the frame of reference to the future and adding the assumption of further nuclear proliferation results in lower mean assessments of the future effectiveness of nuclear deterrence relative to the two previous questions. Nevertheless, mean public ratings vary little across the five measurement periods, and the mean in 2003 is statistically unchanged from our first measurement in 1995. Note that all means are above midscale.

Of course, the value of deterrence can be seen to extend beyond prevention of nuclear conflict. Beginning in 1999, we added the following deterrence question asking respondents to rate the importance of US nuclear weapons for preventing other countries from using chemical or biological weapons.

(Q26) Now we want you to think about preventing the use of chemical and biological weapons against the US today. Using a scale from zero to ten where zero means not at all important, and ten means extremely important, how important are US nuclear weapons for preventing other countries from using chemical or biological weapons against us today?

We compare distributions and mean responses in figure 3.9.

Though distributional patterns are similar in each measurement period, mean assessments of the importance of US nuclear weapons for preventing other countries from using chemical or biological weapons against the United States decrease significantly from 1999 to 2003. Thus, as with deterrence against nuclear conflict, public perceptions of the importance of nuclear weapons for deterring the use of other types of weapons of mass destruction have diminished as the post–Cold War era evolves.

Another consideration underlying the value of deterrence relates to the implications of increasingly effective alternatives to nuclear weapons for de-

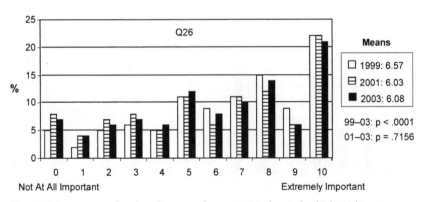

Figure 3.9. Importance of nuclear deterrence for preventing chemical or biological weapons being used against the United States today

terring aggression against the United States. Technological improvements in conventional armaments that allow munitions to be delivered with pinpoint accuracy led to a class of weapons known as precision guided munitions (PGMs) or "smart bombs." The increasing effectiveness of PGMs compared to air-delivered unguided munitions was demonstrated in 1991 during the Persian Gulf War, in the war in Yugoslavia over the province of Kosovo in 1999, and again in Afghanistan and Iraq in 2002 and 2003.[5] To gain insight about the degree to which members of the general public may relate US combat experiences with PGMs to their potential for deterring potential enemies, we provided the following lead-in and question about the degree to which smart bombs can replace nuclear weapons for purposes of deterrence.

(Lead-in) As shown in Afghanistan and Iraq, precision-guided munitions, often called smart bombs, can be delivered very accurately by airplanes and cruise missiles. Some people argue that smart bombs that do not have nuclear warheads can take the place of nuclear weapons for preventing attacks against the US. Others disagree, arguing that nothing except our own nuclear weapons can reliably prevent others from using nuclear weapons against us.

(Q60) On a scale from zero to ten where zero means not at all, and ten means completely, to what degree, if any, do you think smart bombs can replace US nuclear weapons for purposes of deterrence?

We previously asked this question in 1999, and in figure 3.10 we compare those responses with answers in 2003.[6]

Since first asking this question in 1999, the effectiveness of PGMs in conducting combat operations in Afghanistan and Iraq may have influenced public assessments of the utility of smart bombs for deterrence. Note that while

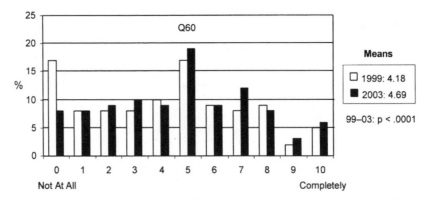

Figure 3.10. Degree to which smart bombs can replace US nuclear weapons for purposes of deterrence

the mean in 2003 still is below midscale, it is significantly greater than in 1999. Most notably, 17 percent of respondents in 1999 rate at zero the degree to which conventional PGMs can replace nuclear weapons for deterrence, but by 2003 only 8 percent of respondents choose that category.

Our findings about deterrence indicate that, on average, the public continues to value the efficacy of nuclear deterrence for preventing other countries from using nuclear weapons against the United States. Additionally, while less emphatic than similar judgments about deterring nuclear conflict, the public also believes nuclear weapons have value for deterring the use of other weapons of mass destruction. These judgments, however, do not speak to public beliefs in the efficacy of nuclear deterrence for preventing the use of weapons of mass destruction by transnational terrorist organizations. Coupled with our evidence suggesting that a growing minority of the public considers precision-guided conventional munitions to have potential for replacing nuclear weapons for purposes of deterrence, these findings suggest that public views of deterrence are evolving importantly within the context of the post–Cold War security environment.

Nuclear Security Policy and Spending Preferences

Given that public perspectives on the nature of the benefits and risks of the nuclear arsenal have changed, have more specific policy preferences changed as well? In this section, we address this question by characterizing the evolution of public views about sizing the US nuclear arsenal, arms control issues, and investment preferences relating to nuclear security.

Size of the US Nuclear Arsenal

Arms control agreements to reduce the size of the existing nuclear arsenal were augmented by unilateral (but coordinated) announcements late in 2001 by the presidents of the United States and Russia of intentions to deeply reduce existing nuclear stockpiles.[7] To explore and monitor changes in public views about minimum acceptable levels of US nuclear weapons, we began asking the following question in 1997.

(Q27) Under the terms of arms reductions agreements, the US and Russia are reducing their stockpiles of nuclear weapons. Recent published reports estimate that the US and Russia each have between 6,000 and 7,000 strategic warheads deployed today. For this question, assume that 7,000 is the maximum number and zero is the minimum. If mutual reductions in the number of US and Russian nuclear weapons can be verified, to approximately what level would you be willing to reduce the number of US nuclear weapons?

Response categories begin at 7,000–6,501 and decrease in increments of 500 to a value of zero. Figure 3.11 compares distributions and shows median values for each survey.

Though distributional patterns are similar across all response periods, a substantial increase in the proportion of 2003 responses in the range of 500–1 moves the median range lower. Note, however, the trend in declining proportions in the lowest response category (zero) across the four surveys. One of the key findings from these observations is that members of the general public support substantial reductions—exceeding 50 percent—from the current level of US nuclear weapons, but declining numbers of citizens support eliminating the nuclear arsenal, even in the context of mutual and verifiable reductions in Russia's nuclear weapons.

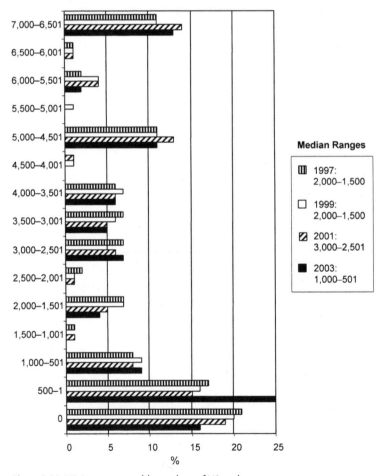

Figure 3.11. Minimum acceptable numbers of US nuclear weapons

A second indicator of public acceptance of reduced numbers of nuclear weapons relates to China's future. As reported in chapter 2, figures 2.3–2.6, comparative public assessments of the current and future threats posed by Russia and China indicate that most respondents consider China to have replaced Russia as the preeminent state-level nuclear threat. As the size of the US nuclear arsenal decreases, and as China assumes an increasingly competitive economic role in Asia, how are public views of US nuclear requirements likely to change? Beginning in 1997 we asked participants to respond to the two following statements about China's nuclear role in relation to efforts to reduce the US nuclear arsenal. Responses are given on a scale from one (strongly disagree) to seven (strongly agree). We compare results in figures 3.12 and 3.13.

(**Q28**) The number of China's nuclear weapons should not influence the number of US nuclear weapons.

(**Q29**) The US should not reduce below the number of nuclear weapons that China maintains.

As shown in figure 3.12, similar patterns since 1997 indicate that most participants disagree with the statement that the number of China's nuclear weapons should not influence the number of US nuclear weapons, but the mean in 2003 is significantly above that first reported in 1997, suggesting increasing agreement with the assertion. Note the bimodal pattern of responses in each year grouped near the ends of the scale. Responses to the second assertion (figure 3.13) show high levels of agreement across the four surveys, with the modal response in each being seven. Though no proposed policy change would bring US nuclear weapons levels near the currently much lower levels of Chinese nuclear weapons, this finding suggests that should China expand

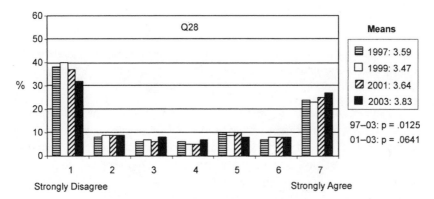

Figure 3.12. Number of Chinese nuclear weapons should not influence number of US nuclear weapons

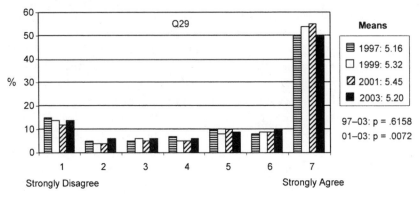

Figure 3.13. The United States should not reduce its nuclear weapons below number of Chinese nuclear weapons

its number of nuclear weapons as the United States reduces its nuclear arsenal, public support for future US reductions may be sensitive to the comparative sizes of the US and Chinese arsenals.

Arms Control

Underground Nuclear Testing

We posed two questions dealing with the issue of underground nuclear testing. In the first, we asked participants in 2001 and 2003 to rate the importance of underground nuclear testing for assuring the integrity of the US stockpile. The second question, which is included in each survey since 1995, inquires about support for a comprehensive nuclear test ban. We show both questions below and graph responses in figures 3.14 and 3.15.

(Q30) Using a scale from zero to ten where zero is not at all important and ten is extremely important, how do you rate the importance of underground nuclear testing for assuring the safety and reliability of US nuclear weapons?

(Q31) Using a one to seven scale where one means strongly oppose and seven means strongly support, how do you feel about the US participating in a treaty that bans all nuclear test explosions?

As shown in figure 3.14, opinion about the importance of underground nuclear testing for the safety and reliability of US nuclear weapons is widely distributed in 2003, but with a significant decrease in mean value compared to 2001. These responses suggest that participants in both surveys do not see a strong connection between underground nuclear testing and maintaining the safety and reliability of the US nuclear arsenal.

In figure 3.15, though mean support for a comprehensive nuclear test ban

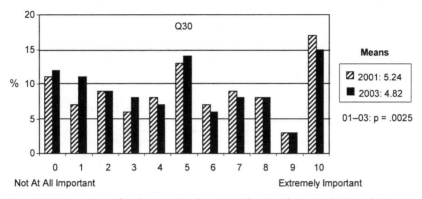

Figure 3.14. Importance of underground nuclear testing for the safety and reliability of US nuclear weapons

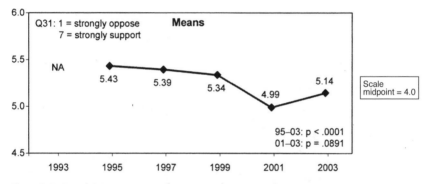

Figure 3.15. Trends in mean support for a comprehensive test ban treaty

treaty remains above midscale, the overall trend is downward, with mean support in 2003 significantly below that first measured in 1995.

Fissile Material Cutoff

Beginning in 1995, we also asked participants how they would feel about the United States participating in a treaty that bans production of nuclear materials that could be used to make nuclear weapons. Responses are provided on a scale from one (strongly oppose) to seven (strongly support). We compare mean responses in figure 3.16.

Mean responses in each survey are above midscale, indicating sustained levels of support, with some variation around the time of our survey in 2001 immediately following the events of 9/11.

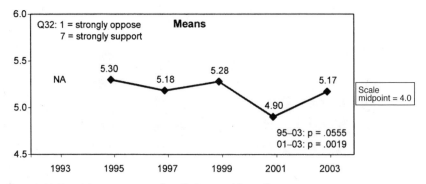

Figure 3.16. Trends in mean support for a fissile material cutoff treaty

National Missile Defenses

We made five inquiries relating to public views about the prospects for a national system of missile defenses. We began with the following knowledge question.

(**Q55**) There is an ongoing debate about defending the US from attacks by long-range nuclear-armed missiles. To the best of your knowledge, does the US currently have a defensive system for shooting down long-range ballistic missiles that have been launched against the US homeland?

Table 3.1 compares responses in 2003 to those in 2001 and in 1999.

Table 3.1. Does the US currently have a national missile defense system?

	%		
	No	Yes	Don't know
1999	26	63	10
2001	31	60	9
2003	31	61	8

While substantial majorities of respondents each year were unaware that the United States did not at the time of the surveys have defenses that could shoot down long-range ballistic missiles, the percentage of respondents correctly answering the question increases modestly from 1999 to 2001, and remains at that level in 2003.[8] Nevertheless, only about one in three members of the US public were aware that the United States did not have operational defenses against intercontinental-range ballistic missiles at the time of the surveys.

After participants responded to the above knowledge question, we provided the following information and contrasting arguments.

Actually, we do not currently have any defenses that can shoot down long-range ballistic missiles. People opposed to national missile defenses say that they are not needed, because the threat of US nuclear retaliation will deter all missile launches against us except for those that are accidental. They argue that missile defenses cost too much, will not work, and will lead to another arms race. People in favor of national missile defenses say that our government has a responsibility to protect us, and that such a system would defend against a few missiles launched accidentally or from an attack by a rogue state like North Korea.[9]

Then we asked participants to respond to the following three statements about missile defenses on a scale from one (strongly disagree) to seven (strongly agree).[10]

(Q56) The US government has a responsibility to build a national ballistic missile defense system to protect us from attacks by nuclear missiles.

(Q57) Money to build a national ballistic missile defense system for the US would be better spent on other programs.

(Q58) A US national ballistic missile defense system would lead to a new arms race with Russia and China.

In figures 3.17–3.19 we compare responses in 2003 to those provided in our surveys in 2001 and 1999.

As shown in Figure 3.17, most respondents agree with the statement that the US government has a responsibility to build a national ballistic missile defense system, and the modal response value is seven in each of the three surveys. The mean in 2003 remains above midscale at 4.97, but is significantly lower than either previous measurement. Responses to the statement that money to build a national ballistic missile defense system for the US would be better spent on other programs (Figure 3.18) are more widely distributed,

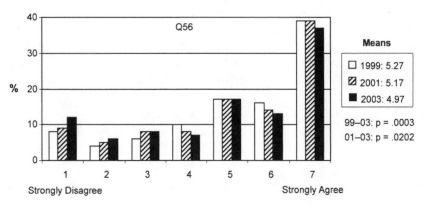

Figure 3.17. US government has responsibility to build national missile defenses (NMD)

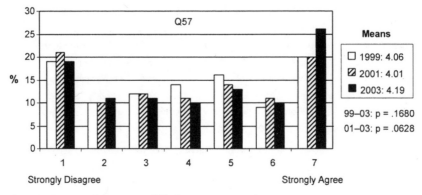

Figure 3.18. Money for NMD would be better spent on other programs

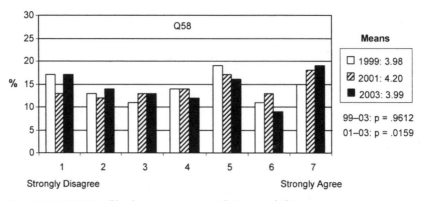

Figure 3.19. US NMD will lead to new arms race with Russia and China

with the mean in 2003 just above midscale at 4.19, which is little changed from the mean in 1999. Reactions to the third statement that US national missile defenses will lead to a new arms race with Russia and China (Figure 3.19) are almost evenly distributed across the full response scale, and the mean in 2003 is statistically unchanged from that in 1999. The distribution of public responses to all three of these questions about missile defenses remains quite stable over time.

To conclude this series, we asked participants to indicate their preference for building a national missile defense system by responding to the following question. Figure 3.20 compares responses in 2003 to those in 2001 and 1999.

(**Q59**) On a scale from one to seven where one means the US definitely should *not* build a national ballistic missile defense system, and seven means the US definitely

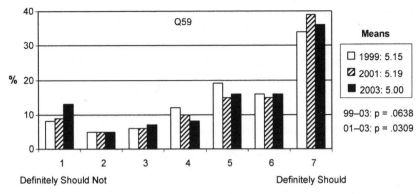

Figure 3.20. Should the United States build a national ballistic missile defense system?

should build such a system, what is your preference about building a system to defend the US against attacks by long-range nuclear-armed ballistic missiles?

Responses in 2003 are similar to those in earlier surveys, with most participants indicating a preference for building national missile defenses. The mean in each reporting period is well above midscale, and the modal response is a value of seven in each survey. However, there are subtle shifts in the distribution pattern in 2003 that suggest opinions may be firming somewhat. Note that the undecided respondents at a scale value of four are trending downward, while those opposed to building missile defenses at a scale value of one are trending upward. These slight trends notwithstanding, it appears that despite an array of countervailing considerations, public support for a system of national missile defenses is substantial and remains relatively stable between 1999 and 2003.

Nuclear Investment Preferences

Based on focus group discussions, we expected few members of the general public to be well informed about absolute levels of spending in various nuclear investment categories.[11] But gaining insight into impressions and preferences about nuclear investments can be useful when assessing trends over time in public valuation of nuclear security. To provide this kind of directional trend information, in each of our security surveys we asked respondents how they think spending should change for a set of functions directly related to US nuclear weapons capabilities. In the absence of alternative spending categories against which trade-offs are compared, and without more sophisticated metrics (such as contingent valuation measures), we are cautious about interpreting results in an absolute sense. Nevertheless, taken together, these indicators provide useful insights into trends over time in public preferences about investments in nuclear infrastructure.

The following five questions were asked in each biennial survey since 1993. Each was answered on a continuous scale from one (substantially decrease) to seven (substantially increase).

How should government spending change for each of the following?

(Q40) Developing and testing new nuclear weapons

(Q41) Maintaining existing nuclear weapons in reliable condition

(Q42) Research to increase the safety of existing nuclear weapons

(Q43) Training to ensure the competence of those who manage US nuclear weapons

(Q44) Maintaining the ability to develop and improve US nuclear weapons in the future

We compare trends in mean responses to each in figure 3.21.

For each spending category, public support for investments increases significantly over the 1993–2001 time period, with a notable turn downward in the 2003 survey. Note that of all the categories, only spending for developing and testing new nuclear weapons (Q40) remains below midscale, on average,

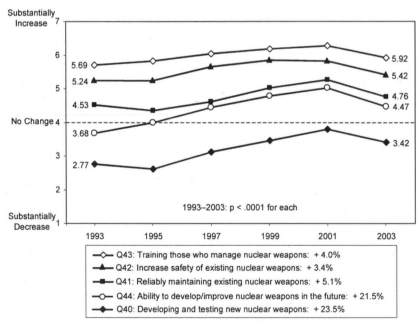

Figure 3.21. Trends in mean nuclear weapons spending preferences

in each of our surveys. Though each mean level of funding support for reliably maintaining existing nuclear weapons is above midscale, after an initial decline from 1993 to 1995, means increase steadily through 2001, then decline again in 2003. Similar patterns of increases followed by declines in 2003 are evident in each of the remaining spending categories. It is noteworthy that support for investments in maintaining the ability to develop and improve US nuclear weapons in the future (nuclear infrastructure) is the only nuclear weapons spending category to increase from below midscale in 1993 (indicating a mean preference for reducing spending) to midscale in 1995 and above midscale in subsequent years, with a cumulative gain in support of 21.5 percent by 2003.

Overall trends in public support for investing in these various nuclear weapons categories clearly are upward. The changes are not only statistically significant, but also seem to reflect policy-relevant growth in public support for nuclear security. These trends are consistent with trends in public assessments of the importance of US nuclear weapons shown in figures 3.3–3.6, and with trends in nuclear weapons risk and benefit indices reported in chapter 2. However, it appears that support for investments in nuclear weapons categories may have peaked during our survey in 2001 immediately following the terrorist attacks of 9/11.

Our final two investment categories deal with spending for preventing the further spread of nuclear weapons to other countries and spending to prevent nuclear terrorism. We summarize the questions below and compare trends in mean preferences in figure 3.22. Again, responses are on a scale from one (substantially decrease) to seven (substantially increase).

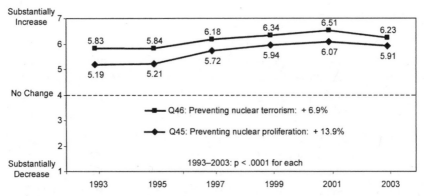

Figure 3.22. Trends in mean spending preferences for preventing nuclear proliferation and terrorism

(Q45) How should government spending change for preventing the spread of nuclear weapons?

(Q46) How should government spending change for preventing nuclear terrorism?

Unsurprisingly, mean public support for both of these spending categories is high in absolute terms in each measurement period, perhaps reflecting public awareness of threats posed by nuclear proliferation and the potential for nuclear terrorism. Overall trends are upward for both, followed by downturns in 2003.

Developing New Smaller-Yield Penetrating Warheads

Efforts by some countries, such as North Korea, to site key command and control centers, clandestine research and production facilities, and weapons of mass destruction and their components deep underground in caves and subterranean bunkers require US military planners to consider how best to destroy such facilities while producing minimum collateral damages. Even the largest conventional weapons (the equivalent of 15,000 pounds of high-energy explosives) will not always produce sufficient blast, heat, and shock deeply enough to yield high probabilities of destroying such subterranean facilities. In some defense policy communities, consideration is being given to the efficacy of employing new, smaller-yield nuclear weapons specifically designed to penetrate deeply into the earth before detonation. The large-yield warheads designed and produced during the Cold War for use in air or surface-level bursts are much larger than may be necessary for a specific high-value underground target, and their use likely would produce large amounts of collateral damage, including radioactive fallout. Because debate about these kinds of developments was in preliminary stages at the time of our survey in 2003, we provided respondents with background information and brief statements about the pro and con arguments that might be made about producing new, smaller-yield nuclear weapons capable of penetrating to destroy deeply buried targets. Then we asked several questions about initial public reactions to this issue. The informational lead-in and pro and con arguments are shown below. The order of the pro and con information was rotated so that half of the respondents heard supportive rationale first, followed by counterarguments, and the other half of respondents heard the information in reverse order.

(Lead-in) Currently there is a debate in the US about developing new lower energy nuclear weapons that can penetrate deep into the ground before exploding. Although these small-yield nuclear weapons would have much less destructive power than current large-yield weapons, the devices would be ten times or more as powerful as the largest *non*-nuclear weapons used in the war against Iraq. The primary purpose for these small-yield nuclear weapons is to destroy deeply buried weapons of mass

destruction and command bunkers that cannot be destroyed with non-nuclear weapons.[12]

Supporters of small-yield nuclear weapons argue that the US needs these weapons for two reasons. First, they believe such weapons will allow the US to destroy existing deeply buried targets while producing less radioactive fallout. Second, they believe these new weapons will strengthen deterrence, because such weapons will make it more difficult for other countries to protect weapons of mass destruction and their command bunkers located underground, which would limit their ability to retaliate against the US.

Opponents of small-yield nuclear weapons argue that the US should not develop these new weapons for two reasons. First, they believe such weapons will weaken deterrence, because developing these new nuclear weapons would encourage other countries to build new nuclear weapons. Second, if the US used such weapons to destroy deeply buried targets, other countries could then justify their use of nuclear weapons, which would increase the chances for widespread nuclear war.

With this in mind, please respond to the following statements using a scale from one to seven where one means strongly disagree, and seven means strongly agree.

(**Q61**) If the US had small-yield nuclear weapons, other countries and terrorists would be less likely to use their weapons of mass destruction against us.

(**Q62**) If the US had small-yield nuclear weapons, other countries and terrorists would be less likely to successfully protect their weapons of mass destruction by burying them deep underground.

We chart responses to the two statements in figures 3.23–3.24.

Responses suggest that participants are skeptical and divided (note the bimodal distribution) about the contributions new small-yield US nuclear weapons might make for deterring the use of weapons of mass destruction against the United States, but most agree that having such capabilities would

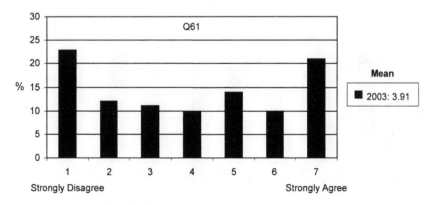

Figure 3.23. New small-yield US nuclear weapons would enhance deterrence

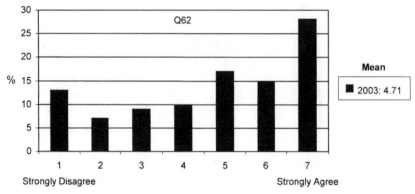

Figure 3.24. New small-yield US nuclear weapons would reduce attempts to protect high value targets by burying underground

reduce the likelihood of others successfully protecting weapons of mass destruction by burying them deep underground.

Because of previously cited evidence of sustained public support for a comprehensive ban on all nuclear test explosions (see figure 3.15), we wanted to know how the testing issue might affect support for developing new small-yield nuclear warheads. Accordingly, we ask the following two questions in the sequence shown. We chart responses in figures 3.25 and 3.26, respectively.

(**Q63**) On a scale from one to seven where one means the US definitely should *not* develop new small-yield nuclear weapons, and seven means the US definitely *should* develop such weapons, what is your view?

(**Q64**) Now consider that the US has not conducted a nuclear test explosion since 1992, but a limited number of underground nuclear tests might be required if we develop a new nuclear warhead. Using a scale from one to seven where one means the

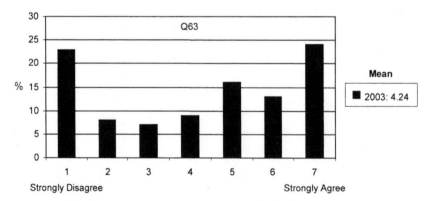

Figure 3.25. Should the United States develop new small-yield nuclear weapons?

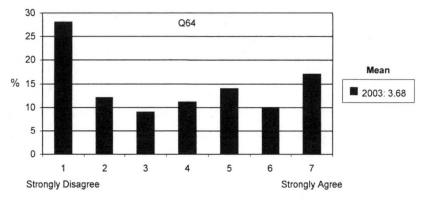

Figure 3.26. Should the United States develop new small-yield nuclear weapons even if some nuclear test explosions are required?

US definitely should not develop new small-yield nuclear weapons if doing so requires nuclear testing, and seven means the US definitely should develop such weapons, even if it does require some testing, what is your view?

As we hypothesized, when nuclear testing is not mentioned, mean support for developing new small-yield nuclear warheads is significantly higher than when the possibility of underground testing to help develop such warheads is specifically mentioned ($p < .0001$). This suggests that should the issue of new small-yield nuclear development be widely debated, the question of potential underground testing will be a factor in public support or opposition.

Trust in the US Nuclear Establishment

In nuclear security policy matters, the public has to rely on others. Technical complexities, security restrictions, and hierarchical government agencies all act as barriers to direct public access to information and decision making. In such a policy domain, levels of trust in those who make and manage policy are a prime ingredient in shaping related beliefs and preferences. For that reason, in 1995 we began using the following questions to ask respondents to our security surveys to rate the levels of trust they place in key players in the US nuclear establishment.

(Lead-in) On a scale from zero to ten where zero means no trust, and ten means complete trust, how much do you trust the following organizations to safely manage nuclear resources such as nuclear weapons or radioactive materials?[13]

(Q47) The Department of Defense

(Q48) Public utility companies

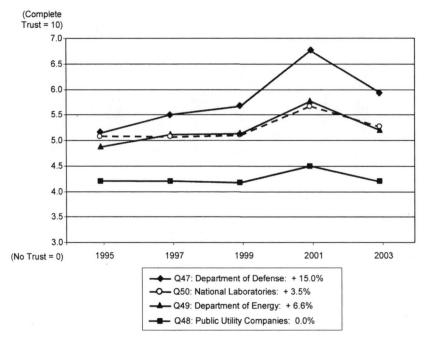

Figure 3.27. Trends in mean levels of trust in the nuclear establishment

(**Q49**) The Department of Energy

(**Q50**) National laboratories

In figure 3.27, we compare trends in mean levels of trust since 1995.

Though none of these key elements of the nuclear weapons establishment garners uniformly high levels of trust, the Department of Defense is consistently accorded the highest mean ratings. Substantial increases for each element in 2001, followed by moderation in 2003, suggest temporary changes associated with the timing of the survey in 2001 immediately following the terrorist attacks of 9/11. Upward trends for the Departments of Defense and Energy, however, are apparent prior to our 2001 survey, indicating that public trust in these departments has been growing since the mid-1990s.

Relating Nuclear Risks, Benefits, and Policy/Spending Preferences

Our analytical framework for nuclear security (figure 1.1) hypothesizes that public beliefs about nuclear weapons risks and benefits are related to policy preferences in predictable ways. In this section, we test that hypothesis by modeling the relationships among beliefs about the risks and benefits of nuclear weapons and public preferences for nuclear security policies. Our objective is to illustrate how respondents in our 2003 survey relate risks and benefits to policy choices and to determine if these patterns are persistent attributes of public opinion about nuclear security.

Before examining key relationships for multiple issues, we illustrate pairs of relationships among beliefs by showing the individual effects of each of our four risk and benefit indices on a single issue using bivariate regressions. One virtue of this approach is that the relationships can be easily presented graphically. We expect, however, that the effects of the risk and benefit indices will be both cumulative and overlapping. For that reason we also examine the combined effects of the risk and benefit indices on the same issue over time. Finally, we summarize relationships between the integrated risk-benefit beliefs and multiple nuclear security policy issues among our 2003 sample.

Bivariate Relationships

We begin by using each of our four risk and benefit indices as an independent variable in separate bivariate regressions to predict change in the importance of retaining US nuclear weapons among respondents in 2003.[14] The dependent variable for this illustration is question 36, which asks respondents to rate the importance of retaining US nuclear weapons today on a scale from zero (not at all important) to ten (extremely important). Table 3.2 summarizes results of the bivariate regressions, and figure 3.28 graphs the resulting estimated relationships between these variables. Note that all relationships are statistically significant and, logically, the domestic nuclear risk index is related negatively, while each of the other risk and benefit indices are related positively to preferences for retaining US nuclear weapons.

As shown graphically in figure 3.28, the importance of retaining US nuclear weapons in 2003 is most strongly related to beliefs about the external nuclear benefits of nuclear weapons. For each one-point increase in the external nuclear benefit index, the importance of retaining US nuclear weapons increases 0.862 on the zero-to-ten importance scale ($p < .0001$). The next strongest relationship is with beliefs about domestic benefits, where each one-point

Table 3.2. Relating nuclear risk and benefit indices to importance of retaining US nuclear weapons, 2003 (bivariate regressions)

Independent variables	Intercept	Coefficient (slope)	t-value	p-value	Adj. R²
External nuclear risk index	6.34	.146	3.54	.0004	.01
Domestic nuclear risk index	8.17	– .178	– 5.42	<.0001	.02
External nuclear benefit index	1.17	.862	28.66	<.0001	.39
Domestic nuclear benefit index	4.71	.397	12.42	<.0001	.11

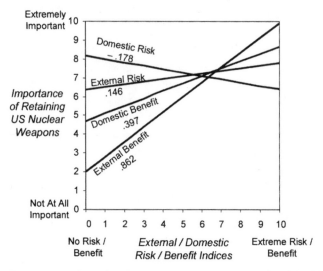

Figure 3.28. Nuclear risk and benefit indices vs. importance of retaining US nuclear weapons, 2003 (bivariate regressions)

increase in the domestic nuclear benefit index produces an increase of 0.397 in the importance of retaining nuclear weapons ($p < .0001$). As beliefs about external nuclear risks increase one point, the importance of retaining nuclear weapons increases 0.146 ($p = .0004$). Finally, as assessments of domestic nuclear risks increase one point, the importance of retaining US nuclear weapons decreases 0.178 ($p < .0001$).

Multivariate Relationships

Next we examine the integrated relationships of all four risk-benefit indices to a range of nuclear policy issues. To do that, we calculate multiple regressions in which our four risk and benefit indices are used together as independent variables to predict preferences for the following issues:

(Q27) Minimum acceptable number of nuclear weapons

(Q30) Importance of underground nuclear testing

(Q31) Support for a comprehensive nuclear test ban

(Q32) Support for a fissile material cutoff treaty

(Q36) Importance of retaining nuclear weapons today

(Q40) Funding for developing and testing new nuclear weapons

(Q44) Funding to sustain nuclear weapons infrastructure

(Q59) Support for building a national system of missile defenses

(Q63) Support for developing new smaller-yield penetrating warheads

Multiple regression results are in table 3.3; the coefficients reflect the relationship of each index when the other three indices are held constant.

Results illustrate the relative strength of beliefs about nuclear weapons benefits (as compared to beliefs about nuclear weapons risks) for predicting policy preferences. In determining the minimum acceptable number of US nuclear weapons (Q27), the most influential and statistically significant independent variable is the index of external nuclear benefits. Regarding the importance of underground nuclear testing for ensuring the safety and reliability of US nuclear weapons (Q30), only beliefs about benefits are related systematically to nuclear testing. Support for a nuclear test ban (Q31) and a treaty to prohibit production of fissile materials that could be used to make nuclear weapons (Q32) is related positively to the domestic risk index and related negatively to the external benefit index. Consistent with our findings in the bivariate regressions portrayed in Figure 3.28, the importance of retaining US nuclear weapons is related negatively to domestic nuclear risks and positively to assessments of external and domestic nuclear benefits. Beliefs about domestic risks are related negatively, while external and domestic benefits

Table 3.3. Relating risk and benefit indices to selected policy and spending issues, 2003 (multiple regressions: $^*p < .05$; $^\dagger p < .01$; $^\ddagger p < .001$)

Issue (dependent variable)	External risk index	Domestic risk index	External benefit index	Domestic benefit index	Adj. R^2
Minimum acceptable number of US nuclear weapons (Q27: scale reversed; increments of 500: 1 = zero↔15 = 6,500–7,000)	.003	−.157*	.805‡	.027	.10
Importance of underground nuclear testing (Q30: 0 = not at all important↔10 = extremely important)	−.057	.049	.597‡	.193‡	.15
Support for a comprehensive nuclear test ban (Q31: 1 = strongly oppose↔7 = strongly support)	.084*	.135‡	−.163‡	.004	.05
Support for a fissile material cutoff treaty (Q32: 1 = strongly oppose↔7 = strongly support)	.021	.182‡	−.158‡	.043	.05
Importance of retaining nuclear weapons today (Q36: 0 = not at all important↔10 = extremely important)	.047	−.167‡	.785‡	.122‡	.41
Funding for new nuclear weapons (Q40: 1 = substantially decrease↔7 = substantially increase)	.031	−.045	.300‡	.154‡	.19
Funding to sustain nuclear weapons infrastructure (Q44: 1 = substantially decrease↔7 = substantially increase)	.025	−.046	.415‡	.178‡	.26
Should US build national missile defenses? (Q59: 1 = definitely should not↔7 = definitely should)	.121‡	−.041	.374‡	.181‡	.22
Should US build new small-yield nuclear weapons? (Q63: 1 = definitely should not↔7 = definitely should)	.041	−.091†	.421‡	.188‡	.21

are related positively to support for funding for developing and testing new nuclear weapons (Q40). Funding for maintaining the ability to develop and improve nuclear weapons in the future (Q44) is related positively to beliefs about external and domestic nuclear benefits, and unrelated systematically to beliefs about external and domestic nuclear risks. Support for building a national missile defense system (Q59) is related positively to beliefs about external nuclear risks and both benefit indices. And finally, domestic nuclear risks are related negatively, while external and domestic benefits are related positively to building new small-yield nuclear warheads capable of penetrating deep underground (Q63).

These findings show how ordinary citizens relate, in sensible and predictable ways, policy preferences about a variety of nuclear security issues to their beliefs about risks and benefits associated with nuclear weapons. We will return to more detailed analyses of beliefs and their structures in chapter 6, but next we shift focus from beliefs about nuclear security to beliefs about terrorism.

4 ‖ TERRORISM

THUS FAR, THIS book has focused on nuclear security. In this chapter, we analyze public views on the related security issue of terrorism. Clearly this is the kind of issue that, in Lippmann's terms, should bring out some of the worst in public opinion. Extreme responses to the terror of events like the attacks of September 11, 2001, in New York and Washington DC, coupled with the cultural divides separating American experience and values from those of the attackers, could well be expected to generate public demands for policies that make it difficult for policymakers to act with deliberation or, when necessary, decisiveness. Clamor for injudicious retribution, or willingness to trade away domestic rights and liberties in the name of security, might well be expected of a public prone to act with the "trampling and the roar of a bewildered herd" (Lippmann 1925, 155). This chapter tackles the issue of how the public understands and responds to terrorism.

In order to develop a reasonably complete picture of public beliefs and policy preferences about terrorism, we approached the issue from several different directions and levels of generality. At the most abstract level, we asked our respondents about their perspectives on current and future threats of nuclear and other forms of terrorism. We then turned to the more specific matters of prospects for preventing terrorism, preferences for responding to terrorism, and trade-offs between security and individual prerogatives.

The duration of our project permits us to evaluate changes in public views on terrorism over time. We included inquiries about the threat of nuclear terrorism in each of our security surveys, and in 1995 we added a module of questions about public views of terrorism in more general terms. In 1997 and 2001, we asked participants to evaluate the vulnerabilities to terrorism of critical US infrastructures. By coincidence, our 2001 security survey began the day following the terrorist attacks of 9/11, affording the opportunity to gauge immediate public reactions to those traumatic events, and the terrorism questions previously asked in 1995 and 1997 provide pre-attack reference points against which to compare post-attack views. In 2003 we continued some of the questions used in earlier surveys while adding new questions relevant to the ongoing war on terrorism. Where possible, we employed the same questions to compare pre-9/11 assessments with those immediately following 9/11 and those two years later in the fall of 2003.

Assessing the Threat of Terrorism

We included both of the following questions about the current and future threat of nuclear terrorism in each of our surveys, and we chart trends in mean assessments in figures 4.1 and 4.2.[1]

(Q17) On a scale from zero to ten where zero means there is no threat of nuclear weapons being used by terrorists, and ten means there is extreme threat, how would you rate today's threat of nuclear terrorism occurring anywhere in the world?

(Q18) On the same scale from zero to ten where zero means no threat, and ten means extreme threat, how would you rate the threat of nuclear weapons being used by terrorists anywhere in the world during the next ten years?

Note that mean responses to both questions in each of the six national surveys are above 6.8 on a scale from zero to ten. Note also that mean responses from 1993 to 2003 vary only within a relatively narrow range, and they do

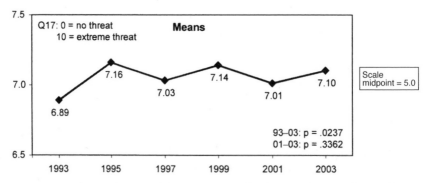

Figure 4.1. Trends in assessments of the current threat of nuclear terrorism occurring anywhere in the world

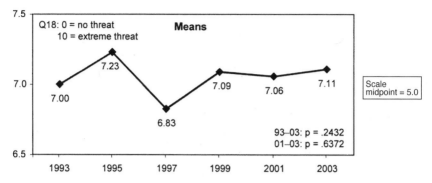

Figure 4.2. Trends in assessments of the threat of nuclear terrorism occurring anywhere in the world in the next ten years

not vary appreciably whether considering current or future threats. Public estimates of current and future threats of nuclear terrorism consistently are high in absolute terms and comparatively stable over time.

We posed the following broader question about public views of overall threats to the United States from all forms of terrorism in our 1997, 2001, and 2003 surveys, and thus it affords pre- and post-attack comparisons.

(Q65) Considering both foreign and domestic sources of terrorism, and considering both the likelihood of terrorism and its potential consequences, how would you rate *today's* threat of all kinds of terrorism in the US on a scale from zero to ten where zero means no threat, and ten means extreme threat?

In figure 4.3, we compare distributions and mean responses in 2003 with those in 1997 and 2001.

Mean assessments of the current threat from all forms of terrorism in-

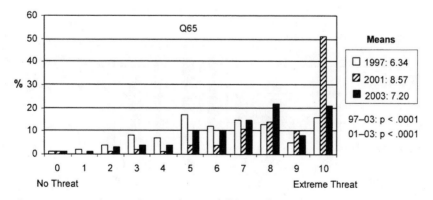

Figure 4.3. Current threat to the United States of all forms of terrorism

crease significantly in 2001 over the earlier measurements in 1997, and then decline significantly by 2003. Note that the modal response in 2001 is ten, the highest scale value, reflecting a predictable spike immediately following the events of 9/11. While initial reactions moderate significantly by the time of our survey in 2003, the mean remains significantly higher than the pre-9/11 measure in 1997.

We combine responses to these three questions to create a terrorism threat index, and in figure 4.4 we comparatively chart composite threat assessments in 1997, well before the attacks of 9/11, with those reported in 2001 immediately following 9/11, and those provided two years later in 2003.[2]

The pattern of public responses over this period can be taken to be consistent with either the traditionalist perspective of Lippmann and Converse or the revisionist views of Page and Shapiro. Traditionalists would point to the large swing upward from 1997 to 2001, and subsequent regression in 2003. Revisionists would point out that experts and leading policymakers—including the Bush administration itself—were caught by surprise by the attacks, leading some to call for a new "post 9/11 mind-set" to underpin appropriate policy responses (National Commission on Terrorist Attacks Upon the United States 2004). The subsidence of the perceived threat (by roughly half the magnitude of the 1997–2001 increase) can be taken as a reasonable recalibration after the absence of subsequent attacks and the implementation of a heightened US security posture. But these data cannot be taken as providing compelling support for either the traditionalist or revisionist arguments. Whether Americans are better characterized as a bewildered herd or a reasoning public requires delving into their more specific beliefs and preferences regarding the specter of terrorism.

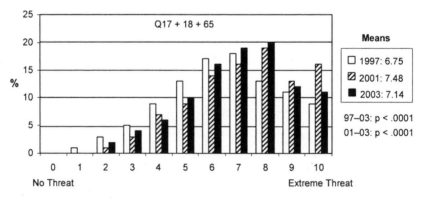

Figure 4.4. Terrorism threat index, 1997, 2001, 2003

Critical Infrastructure Vulnerabilities

Our first foray into public understanding of the complexities of antiterrorism takes aim at perceptions of specific US vulnerabilities to terrorism. In 1997 and 2001, we asked our respondents to rate US critical infrastructures in terms of their vulnerabilities to attacks by terrorists. We began by asking respondents to assess the overall threat to US critical infrastructures from terrorism sponsored by foreign and domestic groups or individuals. Then we inquired more specifically about individual infrastructure systems. The lead-in to this series and the first two general assessment questions follow:

(Lead-in) The next series of questions deals with critical infrastructures in the US such as telecommunications, electrical power systems, gas and oil supplies and services, banking and finance, transportation systems, water supply systems, emergency services, and continuity of government.

First, I want to know your perceptions about potential threats to these kinds of infrastructures as a group. On a scale from zero to ten where zero means no threat, and ten means extreme threat, please rate each of the following as potential threats to critical US infrastructures.

(Q84) Significant damage to critical US infrastructures resulting from terrorism sponsored by *foreign* groups or individuals

(Q85) Significant damage to critical US infrastructures resulting from terrorism sponsored by *US* groups or individuals

We compare responses in 2001, immediately following 9/11, with those provided in 1997 in figures 4.5 and 4.6.

Two observations about these response patterns seem relevant. First, whether the source is foreign or domestic, the overall terrorist threat to US critical infrastructures is judged significantly higher, on average, in 2001 than

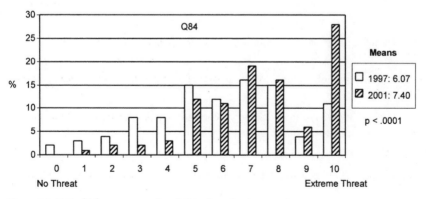

Figure 4.5. Critical infrastructure vulnerabilities from foreign terrorism

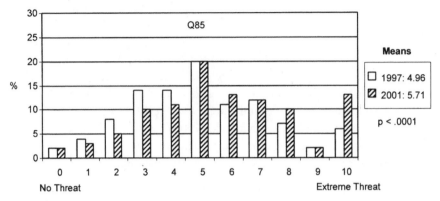

Figure 4.6. Critical infrastructure vulnerabilities from domestic terrorism

in 1997. Second, our respondents consider the foreign terrorist threat to be substantially higher than the domestic threat.

We followed the two introductory questions with the lead-in shown below, and specific questions about each of eight individual critical infrastructures.[3]

(Lead-in) Turning now to individual types of US infrastructures, some people have suggested that terrorists might pose physical threats to property and people and electronic threats to computer networks and other technologies. On a scale where zero means no threat, and ten means extreme threat, please rate the threat that you think terrorists pose to each of the following categories of essential services in the US. Please consider both the likelihood of such terrorist acts occurring and their potential consequences.

(Q86) Telecommunications such as telephones, television, radio, and the Internet

(Q87) Electrical power systems, including generating, transmitting, and distributing electrical power

(Q88) Gas and oil supplies and services, including producing, refining, transporting, and distributing petroleum products and natural gas

(Q89) Banking and finance, including checking services, credit cards, and stock markets

(Q90) Transportation systems, including capabilities for all forms of travel and freight shipments

(Q91) Water supply systems, including watersheds, aquifers, water treatment, and water distribution for all purposes

(Q92) Emergency services, such as medical, police, fire, and rescue

(Q93) Continuity of government, meaning preserving institutions and functions of government at all levels

We present responses by mean risk quartile among the eight categories of infrastructure, beginning in figures 4.7 and 4.8 with the two infrastructures judged to be most threatened by terrorism: gas and oil supplies and services, and transportation systems. Within this top quartile of infrastructure vulnerabilities, response patterns are similar, and differences in mean ratings between the two categories in 2001 are insignificant. Notice, however, that vulnerability in both categories is rated significantly higher, on average, in 2001 than in 1997, and the modal response in 2001 is ten for both questions.

The second quartile of infrastructure threats includes water supply systems and electrical power systems; the third quartile includes threats to telecommunications and banking/finance; and the fourth quartile includes the threat of terrorism to the continuity of government and to emergency services. In table 4.1 we summarize central tendencies and show the percentages of increases in means by infrastructure category between 1997 and 2001.

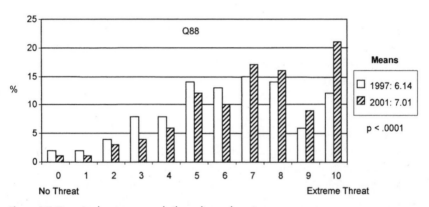

Figure 4.7. Terrorist threat to gas and oil supplies and services

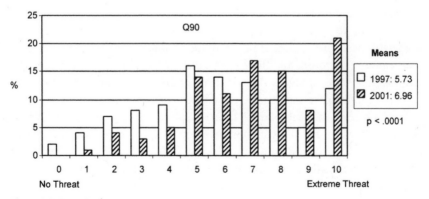

Figure 4.8. Terrorist threat to transportation systems

Table 4.1. Summarizing mean infrastructure vulnerabilities to terrorism

Risk quartile: 2001	US critical infrastructures	1997 (means)	2001 (means)	Change (%)
1	Gas and oil supplies and services	6.14	7.01	+14.2
	Transportation systems	5.73	6.96	+21.5
2	Water supply systems	5.83	6.86	+17.7
	Electrical power systems	5.83	6.56	+12.5
3	Telecommunications	6.12	6.42	+4.9
	Banking and finance	5.61	6.39	+13.9
4	Continuity of government	5.06	5.72	+13.0
	Emergency services	4.80	5.60	+16.7

Following the attacks of 9/11, mean terrorist threats to critical US infrastructures are rated higher across all eight categories than in 1997, with the largest increase in threat vulnerability being reported for transportation systems. In terms of relative order, gas and oil supplies and services are at the top in both measurement periods, but transportation moves from a mid-ranking in 1997 to the second position (and is statistically tied for first) in 2001. In the second quartile, water and electrical supply systems are judged next most vulnerable. Telecommunications and banking and finance systems and services comprise the third quartile, and continuity of government and emergency services are judged least at risk from terrorism in both 1997 and 2001.

Our last test of relative infrastructure vulnerabilities is to analyze differences in 2001 mean ratings across the eight infrastructure categories using two-tailed t-tests to identify statistically significant differences in means. In table 4.2 we show differences in means for each of the paired comparisons, and the p-value of the t-test (indicating statistical significance). These paired comparisons show that most differences in means among the categories are statistically significant, attesting to respondents' abilities to differentiate beliefs about vulnerabilities of critical US infrastructures to terrorist attacks.

What are we to make of the public's perceptions of relative infrastructure vulnerabilities? If the public is not at all discerning, we would expect essentially random responses and therefore no discernible differences in perceived vulnerability across categories or over time. If the public is prone to mindless panic, we might expect extreme perceived vulnerability across all categories of infrastructure on the heels of the 9/11 terrorist attacks. And if the public is unable to make meaningful distinctions, we might expect to see little difference in the *change* in perceived vulnerabilities across the disparate categories of infrastructure following those attacks. But by our measures the public is neither indiscriminate nor uniformly prone to extreme reactions. Our respondents meaningfully differentiate across the vulnerabilities of different types of in-

Table 4.2. Paired comparisons of critical infrastructures, 2001 (two-tailed *t*-tests)

p-value	*Gas & oil*	*Transpor-tation*	*Water*	*Electrical*	*Telecom*	*Banking & finance*	*Continuity of govern-ment*	*Emer-gency services*
Gas & oil	NA							
Transportation	.3482	NA						
Water	.0259	.1721	NA					
Electrical	<.0001	<.0001	<.0001	NA				
Telecom	<.0001	<.0001	<.0001	.0167	NA			
Banking & finance	<.0001	<.0001	<.0001	.0093	.7709	NA		
Continuity of government	<.0001	<.0001	<.0001	<.0001	<.0001	<.0001	NA	
Emergency services	<.0001	<.0001	<.0001	<.0001	<.0001	<.0001	.0912	NA

frastructures to terrorism. Roughly speaking, those infrastructures requiring large fixed and exposed components (such as long pipelines, large generating plants, and extensive power transmission lines) are rated as more vulnerable. More broadly distributed or decentralized systems (such as emergency services and government) are ranked less vulnerable. And the single largest jump in perceived vulnerability is attributed to transportation systems—likely in response to the terrorists' use of aircraft in the 9/11 attacks. While one might argue with the accuracy of any of these perceptions, they surely cannot be considered undifferentiated or baseless.

Preventing Terrorism

Next, we examine what our respondents think can be done to prevent terrorism, and how preventive efforts might affect trade-offs in individual prerogatives. Most of the questions in this section were asked in our 1995 and 2001 security surveys, and they provide comparisons of views from long before the attacks of 9/11 with views immediately following those events, and again two years later in 2003.

Our first measures in this series ask participants to respond to the following three statements that gauge expectations about government's ability to stop terrorism and the associated costs in individual rights and privacy of doing so.

(Lead-in) The terrorist bombing in Oklahoma City on April 19, 1995, and the terrorist attacks in New York and Washington DC on September 11, 2001, have raised questions about what can be done to stop terrorism. Using a scale from one to seven

where one means you strongly disagree, and seven means you strongly agree, please respond to the following statements.

(Q66) There is nothing the government can do to stop determined terrorists.

(Q67) The government could stop terrorists, but only with unacceptable intrusions on people's rights and privacy.

(Q68) The government must try to stop terrorists, even if it intrudes on some people's rights and privacy.

In figures 4.9–4.11, we compare responses to each statement in 1995, 2001, and 2003.

Between 1995 and 2001, mean assessments of the requirement for government to act preventively against terrorism increases significantly. By the time of our measurements in 2003, public demands for government action

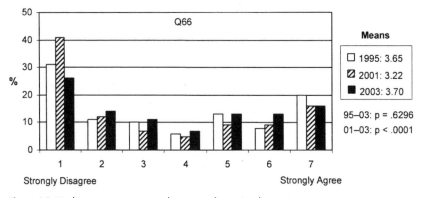

Figure 4.9. Nothing government can do to stop determined terrorists

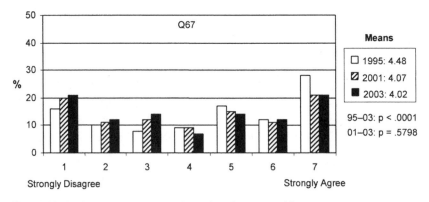

Figure 4.10. Government can stop terrorists only with unacceptable intrusions

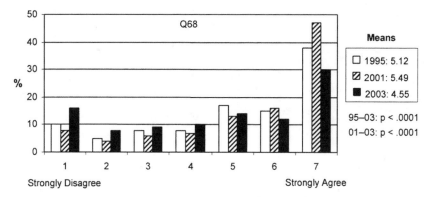

Figure 4.11. Government must try to stop terrorists even if intrusive

receded somewhat but still are above pre-9/11 levels. As shown in figure 4.9, respondents in 2001 more strongly disagree, on average, with the assertion that government can do nothing to stop determined terrorists than do our 1995 participants, but by 2003, respondents return to mean assessments in line with their pre-9/11 views. We note, however, that in each of the three surveys, mean assessments are below midscale, indicating enduring disagreement with the assertion. In figure 4.10, respondents in 2003 are significantly less in agreement than those in 1995 with the statement that in order to stop terrorists, government must make unacceptable intrusions into individual rights and privacy. And in figure 4.11, we show that respondents in 2003 agree less strongly, on average, than their counterparts in 2001 or 1995 that government must try to stop terrorists, even if those actions do intrude on some people's rights and privacy.

By reversing the scales to questions 66 and 67 and combining responses with those from question 68, we create a preventing terrorism index for which a value of one reflects minimum confidence that government can prevent terrorism, and a value of seven reflects maximum confidence that government can and must prevent terrorism, even at the cost of some individual prerogatives.[4] We compare index distributions and means for 1995, 2001, and 2003 in figure 4.12.

Mean confidence in government abilities to prevent terrorism, and support for preventive measures—even if they impinge on individual liberties—increases immediately following 9/11, then declines to pre-9/11 levels by 2003. These data suggest that following the attacks of 9/11, participants are much more inclined to expect and to tolerate intrusive government actions to prevent terrorism, but after implementing more intrusive measures (such as

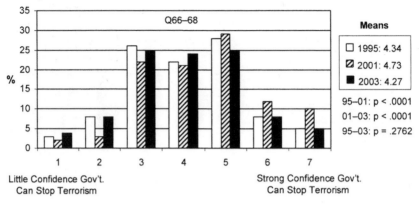

Figure 4.12. Preventing terrorism index, 1995, 2001, 2003

those in the Patriot Act) and two years of the war on terrorism, public support for such measures declines substantially.

To further explore this declining public support, we identified nine specific antiterrorist measures and asked respondents how they feel about the federal government exercising the powers necessary to implement each.[5] The lead-in to the questions and the response scales are as follows.

(Lead-in) Using a scale where one means strongly oppose, and seven means strongly support, how would you feel about giving the federal government the following powers to prevent terrorism?

The first two questions deal with privacy and search and seizure. We compare responses in 2003 with those from 1995 and 2001 in figures 4.13 and 4.14.

(Q70) The power to infiltrate and spy on organizations in this country that the government suspects of planning terrorist acts, even if the groups have not been convicted of any crime

(Q71) The power to search for and seize weapons from groups that are suspected of planning terrorist acts, even if the groups have not been convicted of any crime

Mean responses when we first posed these questions in 1995 are above midscale, and the means for both questions increase significantly by the time of our survey in 2001. By 2003, means recede from the peaks recorded in 2001, but each remains significantly above pre-9/11 means. Note that in each reporting period, the modal response to each question is ten—the maximum value on the scale. Between 1995 and 2003, mean support for the federal government infiltrating and spying on organizations suspected of planning terrorist attacks increases 4.2 percent, while support for federal powers to search

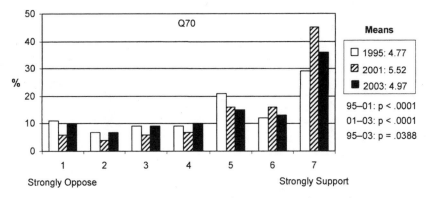

Figure 4.13. Power to infiltrate and spy on suspected organizations in the United States

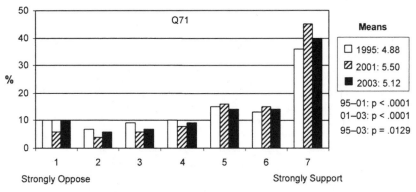

Figure 4.14. Power to search for and seize weapons from suspected groups in the United States

for and seize weapons from suspected terrorist groups increases similarly by 4.9 percent.

Next we examine responses to the two following questions about giving government the power to restrict speech and to ban certain types of information for the purposes of preventing civil violence.

(Q73) The power to ban people from speaking on radio or television if they advocate anti-government violence

(Q74) The power to ban information about bomb-making from computer networks

Figures 4.15 and 4.16 compare response distributions and means in 2003 with earlier measurements.

Response patterns for these two questions are revealing in two respects. They show that when compared to potential intrusions into privacy, such as those relating to surveillance and search and seizure of weapons (Figures

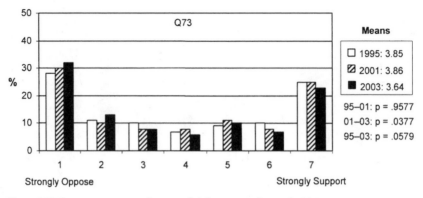

Figure 4.15. Power to suppress advocacy of violence on radio or television

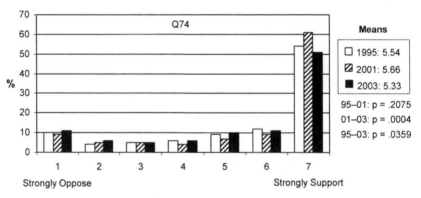

Figure 4.16. Power to ban bomb-making information from computer networks

4.13–4.14), freedom of public speech—even when used to advocate violence against the government—is much more guarded. Also, respondents differentiate between freedom of expression on radio and television and freedom of expression on computer networks such as the Internet (note the differences in vertical scales). In the former, the mean in each survey period is below midscale, and the modal response for each is a value of one (strongly oppose). In the latter, all means are well above midscale, and the modal response in each of the three surveys is a value of ten (strongly support). Also of note, mean responses to neither question after the 9/11 attacks differ significantly from those reported six years earlier, and by 2003, mean responses to both questions are *below* (indicating lower levels of agreement) those in 1995 or 2001.

The following question asks about government requirements for a national identification card. We chart responses in figure 4.17.

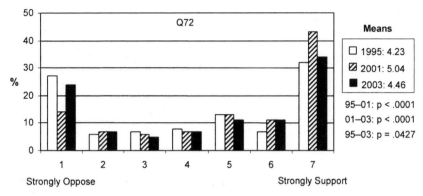

Figure 4.17. Power to require national identification cards

(Q72) The power to require national identification cards for all US citizens

Public support for a national identification card increases significantly between 1995 and 2001 and then moderates in 2003. Note that the marked bimodal distribution in 1995 and 2003 at the two extremes of "strongly oppose" and "strongly support" is not as evident in 2001, when 43 percent of participants choose the maximum support value of seven. This suggests that while a majority of respondents in each of our surveys support the concept of national identification cards, enduring opinion is deeply divided, with substantial fractions at each end of the scale. This division of opinion is muted only in the immediate aftermath of 9/11, and opinions are likely to remain divided unless future terrorist attacks again engender increased support.

Our next two questions in this series deal with restrictions on domestic and international travel and immigration into the United States. Neither was asked prior to 9/11. The questions are shown below and responses are graphed in figures 4.18 and 4.19.

(Q75) The power to restrict travel within the US

(Q76) The power to restrict travel to and from the US

Response patterns to these two options are almost mirror images, with modes at opposite ends of the scale and support averaging below midscale for domestic travel restrictions and above midscale for restricting travel to and from the United States. Also, mean support for restricting domestic travel to prevent terrorism declines significantly in 2003, while mean support for restrictions on travel to and from the United States declines slightly, but does not change significantly between survey periods.

Our remaining two questions in this series deal with immigration policies. The first was previously asked in 1995; the second was first asked in 2001.

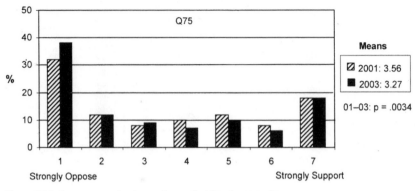

Figure 4.18. Power to restrict domestic travel within the United States

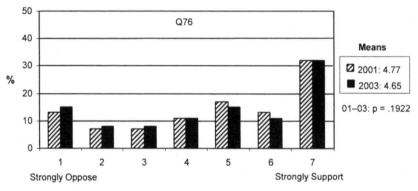

Figure 4.19. Power to restrict international travel to and from the United States

Both are shown below and graphed in figures 4.20 and 4.21.

(**Q69**) The power to quickly expel from the US any citizen of another country who is suspected of planning a terrorist act, even if the person has not been convicted of any crime

(**Q77**) How would you feel about the US government restricting immigration into the US to prevent terrorism?

Response patterns to both questions across the surveys show a relatively high public receptivity to expelling foreign visitors and preventing others from immigrating into the United States if such actions are for the purposes of preventing terrorism. Mean responses to Q69 initially increased from 1995 to the period immediately following 9/11, but declined significantly below both 2001 and 1995 levels by the time of our survey in 2003. While distributional patterns to Q77 are similar, the mean in 2003 was significantly lower

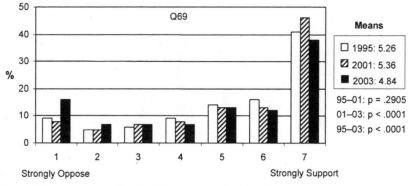

Figure 4.20. Power to expel foreign visitors suspected of planning terrorism

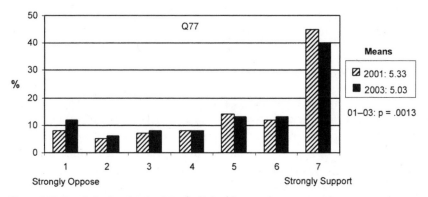

Figure 4.21. Restricting immigration into the United States to prevent terrorism

than in 2001. Together, responses to these questions suggest just some of the implications of terrorism for public support of more restrictive US immigration policies.

Next we create a domestic intrusion index consisting of combined responses to questions 69–77, and in figure 4.22 we compare distributions in 2003 with those in 2001.[6]

The patterns evident in figures 4.13–4.22 suggest that initial public support immediately following 9/11 for government actions restricting individual rights and freedoms in order to prevent terrorism declines significantly in the subsequent two years. In some cases, mean support for such measures in 2003 is even significantly below pre-9/11 levels of support. While support for restrictions on non-US citizens remains substantially higher than support for restricting the prerogatives of Americans, it seems possible that sensitivities to curtailing basic civil liberties are increasing, and that in the absence of future

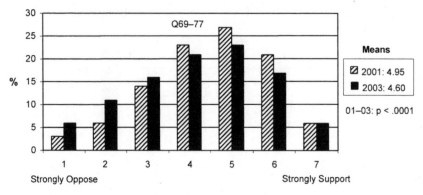

Figure 4.22. Domestic intrusion index, 2001–2003

catastrophic acts of terrorism in the United States, public support for such policies may decline further.

Responding to Terrorist Attacks

Thus far our exploration of public views of responses to terrorism have focused inward, on policies directed at the US homeland. Equally important is the external response to nations that support terrorists or external groups who are perceived to be threats. To evaluate public views on these kinds of issues, we asked participants in two distinct ways about responding to the terrorist attacks of 9/11. First we asked them to consider a range of responses when the US government determines to a high degree of certainty that a country provided personnel or training for the terrorists. Then we asked them to indicate what degree of certainty would be required of a country's complicity in the terrorist attacks before the United States should use military force against that country.

Tailoring Response Options

We posed the following question to investigate public preferences for different levels of responses to 9/11.

(Lead-in) Responding to the recent terrorist attacks on New York and Washington DC may pose difficult choices involving a range of options. If our government determines to a high degree of certainty that another country actively participated in the acts of terrorism by providing personnel or training for the terrorists, would you support the following responses by the US?

(Q78) Apply strong diplomatic and political pressures against that country

(Q79) Apply strong economic and trade sanctions against that country

(Q80) Conduct air strikes against that country using conventionally armed weapons such as bombs and cruise missiles

(Q81) Use US military forces to invade that country

(Q82) Attack that country using US nuclear weapons

We compare support in 2001 and 2003 for each response option in table 4.3.

In both surveys, more than nine out of ten participants support applying strong diplomatic and political pressures or strong economic and trade sanctions against a complicit country. The 79 percent of participants in 2001 who favor air strikes against a country that provided support to the terrorists declines significantly to 51 percent by 2003. Similarly the prospect of using US military forces to invade a country supporting the terrorists is judged acceptable by 81 percent of participants in 2001, but two years later (after beginning military operations in Afghanistan and Iraq) support drops significantly to 52 percent. About 23 percent in 2001 favor our most drastic option—using US nuclear weapons to attack the country supporting terrorism—and support for that option drops significantly to only 14 percent by 2003.

We assign a value of zero to those who express no support for any of the response options, a value of one for support of diplomatic measures, two for support of economic and trade sanctions, three for support of conventional air strikes, four for support of military invasion, and a value of five for nuclear retaliation. Using those values, we create a six-point terrorism response index representing the maximum response participants supported, ranging from no response (0) to nuclear retaliation (5). In figure 4.23, we compare index values in 2001, immediately following 9/11, with index values two years later.

Willingness to respond to terrorism by applying military force is substantially higher in 2001 than in 2003. Note the modal response in the aftermath of 9/11, when 58 percent of respondents support using US military force to invade a country determined to have supported the attacks on the United

Table 4.3. Responding to support for 9/11 terrorists

US options	2001 (%)		2003 (%)		chi sq./p-value
	No	Yes	No	Yes	
Apply strong diplomatic and political pressures against that country (Q78)	3	97	5	95	4.83/.0280
Apply strong economic and trade sanctions against that country (Q79)	5	95	8	92	6.82/.0090
Conduct air strikes against that country using conventionally armed weapons such as bombs and cruise missiles (Q80)	21	79	49	51	174.72/<.0001
Use US military forces to invade that country (Q81)	19	81	48	52	191.43/<.0001
Attack that country using US nuclear weapons (Q82)	77	23	86	14	26.27/<.0001

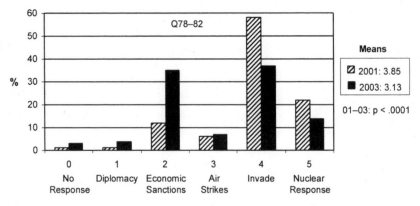

Figure 4.23. Terrorism response index, 2001–2003

States, and by 2003, support for military invasion declines to 37 percent. Conversely, while 12 percent of participants in 2001 prefer to stop at applying strong economic and trade sanctions, the percentage nearly triples by 2003 to 35 percent.

Certainty of Culpability before Responding

For the previous questions, respondents were told to assume that a country's culpability has been determined to a high degree of certainty. In our final question in this series, we ask respondents to consider the degree of certainty they would require before the United States should use military force in response to terrorist attacks.

(**Q83**) Now I would like to know how certain you think the government should be in the future that a country supported terrorist acts against the US before we take military action. Using a scale from zero to ten where zero means not at all certain, and ten means completely certain, how certain should the government be before it retaliates using military force?

As shown in figure 4.24, responses in both surveys indicate that participants expect the US government to have a very high degree of certainty that a country is culpable in supporting acts of terrorism against the United States before responding with military action. Notice that the mode for both surveys is the highest scale value (10) and that differences in means between 2001 and 2003 are not statistically significant. Implications of these findings may have been apparent in 2004, when nationwide surveys indicated that a plurality of the US public came to believe that it was a mistake to have invaded Iraq (Nagourney and Elder 2004). The invasion was justified partially on the basis of assumptions that Iraq possessed weapons of mass destruction and that it had

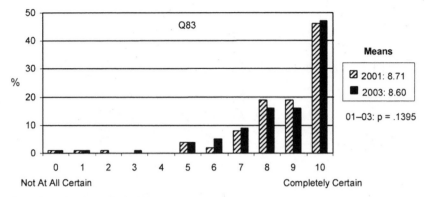

Figure 4.24. Certainty of culpability required for military response

operational ties to the Al Qaeda terrorist network. Consistent with our findings, the erosion of support for the invasion and occupation of Iraq follows extensive public discussion of the faulty intelligence underlying these claims (National Commission on Terrorist Attacks Upon the United States 2004).

Evaluating the War on Terrorism

Beginning in 2003, we included a new battery of questions to help measure implications of terrorism for ordinary citizens. Our intent was to get initial indications of public assessments of progress in the unfolding war on terrorism. One of the most readily visible and high profile initiatives in that war is the effort to improve airport security, so we began by asking the following question.

(Q94) Since the terrorist attacks on the United States in September 2001, the government has taken several actions intended to improve airport security. On a scale from zero to ten where zero means not at all effective, and ten means completely effective, how do you rate efforts to improve US airport security thus far?

We graph the distribution of responses and show the mean in figure 4.25.

On average, respondents are somewhat positive about US initiatives to improve airport security, with only about 31 percent rating efforts below midscale. Nevertheless, some ambivalence is evident, with the modal value at five, and the mean only slightly above midscale at 5.40. Less than one in five of our respondents indicated that the initiatives had been highly effective (a score of eight to ten).

We sought broader public assessments about the ongoing war on terrorism by asking respondents to rate the progress thus far, express their confidence

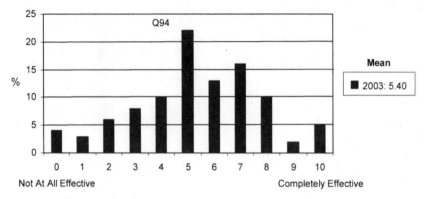

Figure 4.25. Effectiveness of US efforts to improve airport security

about eventually "winning" the war on terrorism, and estimate how long they think it may take to prevail. We start by charting responses in figure 4.26 to the following question about progress to date.

(Q95) On a scale where zero means not at all effective, and ten means completely effective, how effective do you believe US efforts in the war on terrorism have been thus far?

Here, too, respondents give mixed marks to overall US efforts to combat terrorism, with 53 percent rating progress in the war on terrorism above mid-scale. While the mean value (5.60) is above the scale midpoint, only 22 percent rated the execution of the war on terror as highly effective (a response value of eight to ten). Again, our respondents are somewhat divided about the success of the US policy response.

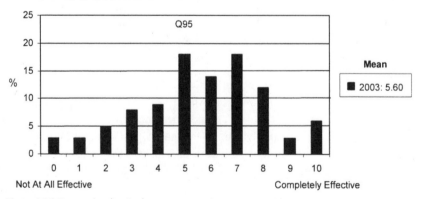

Figure 4.26. Progress to date in the war on terrorism

Next we turn to future outlooks about eventually "winning" the war on terrorism and about the likelihood of preventing all large-scale terror attacks against the United States in the near term. Because "winning" the struggle against terrorism requires a common definition or starting point, we begin with the following lead-in.

(Lead-in) For the next two questions, suppose that winning the war on terrorism is defined by a reduction in the threat of terrorism by half of that which existed immediately after the September 2001 terrorist attacks.

(Q96) First, on a scale from zero to ten, where zero means not at all confident, and ten means completely confident, how confident are you that the US eventually will win the war on terrorism?

(Q97) Next, assuming that the US can win the war on terrorism, how many years do you think it will take to win?

We chart responses to the first question in figure 4.27.

About 49 percent of respondents express some degree of confidence that the United States eventually can "win" the war on terrorism (defined as halving the threat immediately following 9/11); 17 percent pick the midpoint, indicating a fifty-fifty chance of winning or, alternatively, great uncertainty; and about 34 percent are not confident of winning.

When asked to assume that the United States eventually can win the war on terrorism, respondents estimate, on average, that it will take about twenty years to prevail. No respondents believe the war already is won, and about 12 percent believe it never can be won, and therefore do not venture an estimated time. We chart in figure 4.28 grouped estimates of those who respond, but

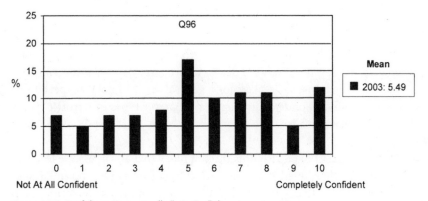

Figure 4.27. Confidence in eventually "winning" the war on terrorism

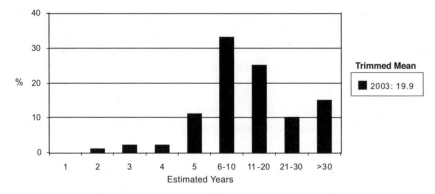

Figure 4.28. Years it will take to "win" the war on terrorism

because a few outlier estimates well beyond the range of most predictions can artificially distort the mean, we trim those responses of more than one hundred years from calculation of the mean.

Given the requirement to trim outlier responses, the distribution of responses and their mean are less important as precise judgments than as general indicators that respondents view the war on terrorism as a long-term endeavor. Only about 16 percent of respondents estimate that the threat of terrorism immediately following 9/11 can be reduced by half within five years. Note that the modal response is a range from six to ten years, and the next highest concentration of estimates are grouped in the eleven-to-twenty-year range. Clearly, our respondents do not expect a near-term conclusion to the war against terrorism.

Our final question about defending against threats asks the following:

(Q98) Using a scale from zero to ten where zero means not at all likely, and ten means extremely likely, how likely do you think it is that we will be able to prevent all large-scale attacks against the US in the next five years?

Admittedly, what "large-scale" means to respondents varies, but characterizing such an event in terms of deaths or property damage is difficult, and offensive to some. Instead, we ask for a general sense of public expectations about the likelihood of defending against whatever types of terrorist events each respondent considers to be "large-scale." We chart responses in figure 4.29.

Only 32 percent of participants think it likely that all large-scale terrorist attacks against the United States in the next five years can be prevented, suggesting that most citizens do not expect US efforts in the war on terrorism to provide an unfailing defense against future threats.

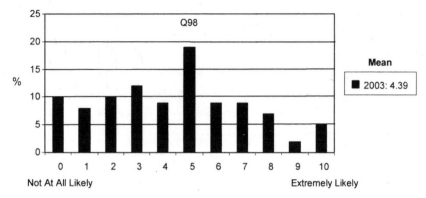

Figure 4.29. Likelihood of preventing all "large-scale" terrorist attacks against the United States in the next five years

Evaluating Behavioral Implications of Terrorism

How does the heightened sense of the threat of terrorism affect the behaviors of Americans? The initial decline in travel and economic activity following the 9/11 attacks provides ample indication that behaviors did initially change substantially in response to these threats. Our interest is in the ways in which Americans understand such threats and how they adapt to them. In this section, we describe the implications of terrorism in making Americans more cautious and fearful. We examine how members of the public describe their own changes in such activities as travel and congregation in response to the perceived threats of terrorism. We begin with the following series of questions asking respondents to reflect on the large-scale effects of the terror strikes on society.

(Lead-in) On a scale from zero to ten where zero means the terrorists who attacked the US in September 2001 were not at all successful, and ten means they were completely successful, how successful do you believe the terrorists were at bringing about each of the following?

(Q99) Causing Americans to be more suspicious of other people

(Q100) Causing Americans to give up important rights and freedoms

(Q101) Causing Americans to become more fearful in their everyday lives

In figures 4.30–4.32, we chart responses (note that vertical scales vary).

Clearly, our respondents consider the terrorist acts of 9/11 to have important consequences for Americans' outlooks about security. Notice that the modal response to each of the three questions is ten, the highest scale value. Fully 84 percent of participants think their fellow citizens are more suspicious

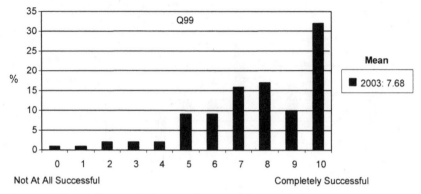

Figure 4.30. Terrorists' success in causing Americans to be more suspicious

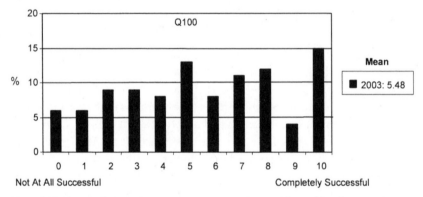

Figure 4.31. Terrorists' success in causing Americans to give up rights and freedoms

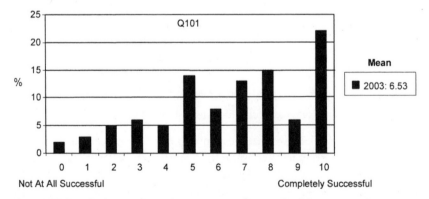

Figure 4.32. Terrorists' success in causing Americans to be more fearful

than before 9/11; half of our respondents consider important rights and freedoms to have been forfeited because of 9/11; and 64 percent think terrorism causes Americans to be more fearful. It can be argued that all are important objectives of the terrorists, and most of our participants consider the terrorists to be at least partially successful in meeting those objectives.

Next, we inquire more specifically into behavioral adaptations that respondents may make to the perceived threat of terrorism.

(Lead-in) On a scale from one to seven where one means greatly decreased, four means no change, and seven means greatly increased, how has the threat of terrorism affected your willingness to participate in the following activities?[7]

(Q103) Flying on commercial airliners in the US

(Q104) Traveling outside the US

(Q105) Attending public events or visiting public places where there are large crowds of people, such as sporting events, shopping centers, parades, and political rallies

We show response patterns and means in figures 4.33–4.35.

Despite responses to the previous set of questions (figures 4.30–4.32) suggesting that participants think the terrorist attacks of 9/11 have made Americans more suspicious and fearful and have caused the forfeit of important rights and freedoms, responses to these three more specific questions about behavior all suggest little behavioral response to threats from terrorism. Distinctive distributions having modal values of four and means very near the scale midpoint indicate that participants consider their willingness to travel domestically or overseas and their willingness to assemble among large crowds, on average, to be largely unaffected by the continuing threat of terrorism. Thus, Americans believe threats of terrorism affect *general* levels of

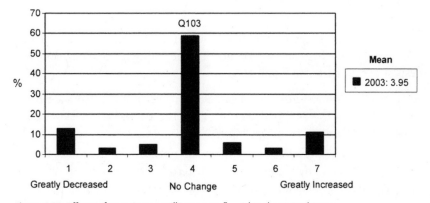

Figure 4.33. Effects of terrorism on willingness to fly within the United States

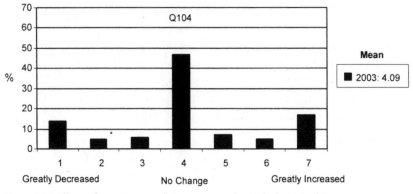

Figure 4.34. Effects of terrorism on willingness to travel outside the United States

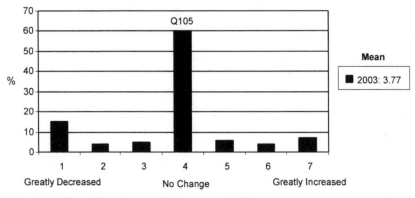

Figure 4.35. Effects of terrorism on willingness to assemble

suspicion and fear, but not their own willingness to travel and congregate in public places.

We close this chapter with a more general assessment of how 9/11 may have changed the lives of our respondents. The question is shown below, and responses are charted in figure 4.36.

(Q102) On a scale from zero to ten where zero means not at all changed, and ten means completely changed, to what degree, if any, has your way of life changed as a result of the terrorist attacks in September 2001?

While only 17 percent of participants do not consider their lives to have been changed at all by the events of 9/11, zero (no change) is the modal response, and three out of four participants rate changes in their lives as a result of the terrorist attacks on 9/11 to have been modest (at or below midscale).

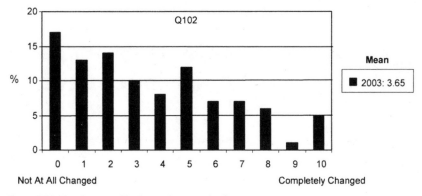

Figure 4.36. How has your life changed as a result of 9/11?

Taken together, the questions in this section suggest that while 9/11 and the continuing threat of terrorism raise concerns and anxiety in general terms, most respondents do not indicate less willingness to travel or assemble, and most rate the overall changes in their lives resulting from the threat of terrorism at relatively low levels. Coupled with the perception of widespread suspicion and fear, it appears that most Americans judge the effects of terrorism thus far to be chiefly confined to a sense of unease and insecurity but not to extend to lasting changes in the patterns of their lives.

OPINION STABILITY AT
THE INDIVIDUAL LEVEL

THUS FAR WE have explored trends over a decade in aggregate-level views of security among multiple national samples of the American public. We have shown how assessments of the security environment and preferences about security policies are related to nuclear dimensions of security and to terrorism in predictable patterns over time. In this chapter, we shift our focus from characterizing American beliefs about security to analyzing the stability of those beliefs. Are the relationships and patterns seen at aggregate levels also evident at individual levels of analysis? If the same persons are surveyed more than once, do they exhibit consistent patterns? Do personal characteristics predispose individuals to different kinds of opinions and policy preferences? Are individual-level characteristics related to security beliefs in replicable patterns over time? More broadly, we seek to identify some of the factors that help shape and anchor individual policy beliefs.

In this chapter we examine the relationships of demographic attributes to views and preferences, and in chapter 6 we investigate the nature of belief structures in predisposing and shaping opinion formation. Drawing broadly on the literature in public opinion, we argue that demographics and belief systems act at the individual level as lenses through which reality is viewed and as filters through which information passes as it is assimilated into opinions and preferences. Both are relevant to opinion stability. We begin by summarizing theoretical arguments about the volatility of mass opinions. Then we investigate the degree to which demographic characteristics may predispose individuals to policy beliefs and preferences, and their relationships to opinion stability, especially during crises. We analyze individual-level variability using panel data about terrorism collected among a subset of general public respondents who participated in our 2001 national survey, and again in a follow-up study that began exactly one year later in 2002. We also employ data from our six national surveys to investigate how individual differences and background variables anchor preference formation over time.

Debate about the Volatility of Public Opinion

Concerns about the potential volatility of mass opinions are axiomatic to traditional beliefs about public capacities. The Federalist Papers (Hamilton, Madison, and Jay [1788] 1961) are replete with cautions and structural remedies for the "passions" of the public.[1] From the Founding Fathers to today, traditional conceptions of public capacities warn against the unreliable and unstable nature of mass opinion, especially in times of national crises. Commenting on the limitations of public opinion in the post–World War II era, Almond (1950, 239) states: "Perhaps the gravest general problem confronting policymakers is that of the instability of mass moods, and cyclical fluctuations which stand in the way of policy stability." Walter Lippmann, a noted critic of public overreaction, offers the following observation of mass opinion and its influence on public policy.

The unhappy truth is that the prevailing public opinion has been destructively wrong at the critical junctures. The people have imposed a veto upon the judgments of informed and responsible officials. They have compelled the governments, which usually knew what would have been wiser, or was necessary, or was more expedient, to be too late with too little, or too long with too much, too pacifist in peace and too bellicose in war, too neutralist or appeasing in negotiation or too intransigent. . . . It [public opinion] has shown itself to be a dangerous master of decisions when the stakes are life and death. (1955, 20)

Also commenting on the implications for policymakers, Almond (1956, 376) makes the following criticism of shifting public moods: "For persons responsible for the making of security policy these *mood* impacts of the mass public have a highly irrational effect. Often public opinion is apathetic when it should be concerned, and panicky when it should be calm."[2] Converse (1964, 1975) finds public opinion to be so unstructured and unconstrained as to be devoid of consistency over time. One implication that reasonably can be drawn from Converse's research (though not explicitly stated) is that the absence of longitudinal stability of public opinion makes it susceptible to perturbations associated with exogenous and temporary events (Holsti 1996). In that tradition, Zaller (1992) suggests that members of the general public have so many different temporary constructions of views and preferences that different considerations are salient at different times, and that only the more well-informed and capable members of the public (elites) consistently constrain policy choices in accordance with organized and integrated sets of beliefs. Echoing Madison's views of two centuries ago, Mayer (1993) cautions that the public's immediate reaction to a crisis event may be very different from its considered, long-term judgment, and that changes in public attitudes produced by some crises wear off very quickly when the crises end. The implication is a warning against public overreaction in times of national stress.

Predictably, revisionists take exception to traditional models of the volatile public. Caspary (1970) challenges both Almond's premise (low and unstable public attention to foreign affairs) and conclusions (unstable support for foreign policy commitments). Analyzing a broader set of foreign policy questions, Caspary (1970, 546) concludes that "American Public Opinion is characterized by a *strong* and *stable* 'permissive mood' toward international involvements." Mueller (1973) finds that declining public support for and increasing resistance to US participation in the conflicts in Korea and Vietnam were systematically related to increasing battle deaths, reflecting a logical connection to a critical measure of associated costs. Achen (1975) concludes that when rigorous methodologies are applied, evidence shows that the US general public's foreign policy views are roughly as stable as those on domestic policy. Using a panel study, Peffley and Hurwitz (1992) find that dramatic changes in foreign policy events have predictable and reasonable effects on American public opinion, but they also document evidence of impressive stability in respondents' images of the Soviet Union and public preferences for specific foreign policies. But perhaps the largest and most comprehensive macroanalysis of empirical data on the stability of mass attitudes was conducted by Page and Shapiro (1992) and Shapiro and Page (1994). Using responses to hundreds of survey questions posed in dozens of opinion surveys collected between the 1930s and 1991, they find ample evidence of a "rational" public with highly stable views on domestic *and* foreign policy issues.

Stimson (1991, 2001) and Erikson, MacKuen, and Stimson (2002) apply an economic model and a macro approach involving multiple survey questions over many years; they find the public to have relatively stable preferences for more government or less government, and that the preferences move predictably over time relative to inflation and unemployment. They also report that while change among the better educated may be somewhat more rapid and of greater magnitude, members of the general public with lower socioeconomic attributes show controlled movement in the same directions under the same stimuli as elites.

Parallel to the policy-oriented discussions about the stability or volatility of mass opinions, a related debate is underway about the broader health of democratic processes, the degree to which they are in trouble, and what might be done to strengthen them. In this debate, "Reason is commonly portrayed as a fragile force for progress, justice, and greater democracy, which requires protection against the intrusive and destructive impulse of emotion" (Marcus 2002, 7). Language and political communication, deliberative processes, rational choice theory, decision making, media influence, and the role of elites are key elements of this discussion. The central theme is that if a more perfect and equitable space for public political discourse can be secured, a sometimes less than rational public can be helped (by elites) to derive rational policies (Habermas 1979, 1984). Fishkin (1991) suggests citizen juries, citizen conferences, and other specialized public forums to inform citizens of the scope of the issues and help educate them to the rudimentary facts in play. Others (Gutmann 1987; Nie, Junn, and Stehlik-Barry 1996) advocate a better citizenry by improving reasoning abilities. Delli Carpini and Keeter (1996) contend that one essential component for improving democratic governance is to increase the political knowledge of the electorate. Still others (Warren 1996) prefer to emphasize the ways authority is best exercised by informed elites. In common, these reforms seek to correct for deficiencies in the stability, coherence, and rationality of mass publics in collective decision making.

Much research effort has gone into investigating how the public makes political decisions (Jackson and Marcus 1975; Krouse and Marcus 1984; Lodge, Steenbergen, and Brau 1995; Marcus and Hanson 1993; Sniderman, Brody, and Tetlock 1991; Thompson 1970). An important dimension of that question having implications for opinion volatility is the interaction between reason and emotion. Marcus (2002) holds that the traditional construct in which reason and emotion are juxtaposed as polar opposites whose individual existence depends on the absence of the other (zero sum) is conceptually wrong. He argues that publics are able to be rational, in part, *because* they also have emotions. Marcus also notes that emotion—not reason—is the wellspring of public enthusiasm and the motivation for political action. In the complete absence of emotion, pure reason will almost always result in the status quo, because change depends not only on rational calculations but emotional commitments to bring about the changes they imply. According to Marcus (2002), public anxiety, such as that deriving from the traumatic events of 9/11, promotes immediate learning while diminishing reliance on the previously learned. Old habits (and old policies) did not provide the desired security, else 9/11 could not have happened; new information is needed to reevaluate the threat and understand the changed security environment. Marcus argues that, under such conditions, anxious voters may exhibit less habitual associations and may rely less on partisanship and other familiar heuristics while seeking new and more satisfying explanations of the changed circumstances. The acquisition and weighing of information also can be affected by anxiety. Marcus and MacKuen (1993) note that anxious voters learn far more about candidate positions than complacent voters. Delli Carpini and Keeter (1996) cite inadequate levels of accurate political information as a shortcoming of mass publics, and the effects of anxiety arising from events like 9/11 can stimulate public learning and information gathering.

Though anxiety does not, in itself, produce any specific decision, it profoundly affects the way people go about deciding. Bless (2000) and Schwarz and Bless (1991) report that different affective states require different information-processing strategies. They find that individuals in positive affective states rely more on general knowledge structures and familiar heuristics, while persons in negative affective states (anxiety, fear) rely less on general knowledge structures and are more likely to focus on data applicable to the situation. Thus in the absence of anxiety, complacent reliance on habit pertains, but under conditions of anxiety, publics are more willing to consider new alternatives. According to Marcus (2002), rather than fueling instability and volatility, anxiety promotes and stimulates rational processes. At the same time, the range of policy changes available for consideration can vary widely and have large implications for open societies. Anxious publics may be willing to consider new and different policy options that would not have been deliberated under more familiar conditions of status quo and complacency. This may be especially dangerous to free societies, for civil liberties may be put at risk during times of national crises and growing threats.

The terrorist attacks of 9/11 and the ongoing war on terrorism provide the kinds of security events, foreign policy challenges, and policy choices that are at the heart of the debate about public capacities. No more singularly distinctive event since the demise of the Soviet Union has received greater media attention, created more public anxiety, and posed such a wide range of options for policy change. As is evident in figure 5.1, the sheer quantitative deluge of news items about terrorism following 9/11 stands in striking contrast to prior levels—even following earlier terror events such as the Oklahoma City bombing.[3] Ample raw materials for public reactions are present for evaluating the content, coherence, and stability of the public's perceptions and reactions.

Contrasting Traditionalist and Revisionist Expectations of Public Reactions

Given the nature of the events, media attention, and the ensuing national debate about how to respond to 9/11 and how to prevent future such attacks, traditionalist theories would anticipate widespread fear and volatile public

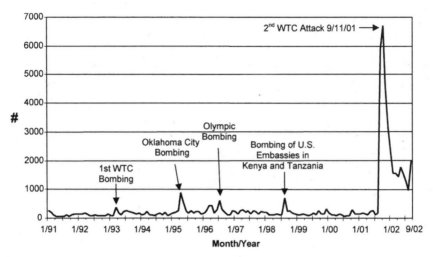

Figure 5.1. Monthly reporting on terrorist incidents, 1991–2002

moods, with mass opinion swinging widely among unrealistic assessments of the terrorist threat and its implications. In the traditionalist framework, high levels of public anxiety and a sense of vulnerability can be expected to inhibit objective evaluation of policy alternatives. Publics will be vulnerable to overreactive policies that curtail individual freedoms, justified by the need to enhance security. Public demand for retribution and the employment of coercive force are likely to pressure government to consider rapid military responses.

In contrast, revisionist theories about public opinion under such circumstances foster expectations that public assessments of the threat of terrorism will increase more realistically and without widespread fear and panic. Initial concerns and threat characterizations should dampen within the near term (depending on subsequent events and actions). Citizens will be less likely to rely solely on familiar heuristics such as ideology and partisanship and more likely to objectively assess changed circumstances. Adjustments (if any) to core beliefs about relationships between government and citizens, such as restrictions on individual prerogatives, will be temporary and transitory, leaving basic beliefs unchanged. In the absence of subsequent large-scale terrorist attacks, revisionist theory predicts declining tolerance and decreasing support over time for restrictive or intrusive domestic security measures. Initial public support for using US military force to respond is expected to be substantial, but only under limited circumstances (high degree of certainty of culpability and minimal collateral damages), and initial support will subside in the near term. These arguments are summarized in table 5.1.

Table 5.1. Contrasting expectations of public opinion following 9/11

Traditionalist expectations	Revisionist expectations
Widespread fear and panic; threat assessments veer between extremes.	Opinion responsive to events, but without panic; controlled and reasonable threat assessments.
Anxiety and vulnerability to groupthink inhibit objective analysis.	Less dependence on traditional heuristics; more willingness to examine new evidence.
Publics vulnerable to reactionary policies curtailing rights and freedoms; individual prerogatives surrendered for security.	Initial support for intrusive policies to enhance security quickly dampens. Core beliefs about individual rights do not change.
Public demands retribution; widespread support for overwhelming punitive force.	Support for use of punitive force initially increases, but soon subsides toward pre-9/11 levels.

Immediate Public Reactions to 9/11

Our survey in 2001 began on September 12 (the day following the terrorist attacks) and continued for fifty-four consecutive days, ending on November 4. To test contrasting propositions about the stability of public opinion under conditions of national stress, we separate our respondents into four sequential increments of ten days each, followed by the concluding increment of fourteen days as shown in table 5.2. In that table we also indicate the number and percent of respondents who were surveyed in each of the five time periods.[4] For our indicator variables, we employ four composite measures previously introduced to compare public reactions at ten-day intervals across the duration of the survey. The preventing terrorism index measures respondent confidence in government's abilities to stop terrorism; the domestic intrusion index reflects views about intrusive policies to prevent terrorism; and the terrorism response index measures preferences for responding to the terrorist attacks of 9/11.[5] This approach allows us to examine volatility among our respondents during what arguably was the most fluid and changing period immediately following the attacks. In table 5.2 we compare mean values for each of the four indices across the five time periods beginning the day following 9/11.

Over the course of the first fifty-four days following 9/11, combined assessments of the threat of all kinds of terrorism expressed on a scale from zero (no threat) to ten (extreme threat) varies from a high of 7.83 in the first time period (days 1–10) to a low of 7.21 in the fourth period (days 31–40). Though the variation across periods is statistically significant ($p = .0067$), it represents a reasonable assessment of a modestly declining (but still high in absolute terms) threat as early expectations of additional terrorist attacks in the days following 9/11 diminished. Note that none of our remaining three indices

Table 5.2. Mean indicators at post-9/11 intervals, 2001

	T-1 9/12– 9/21	T-2 9/22– 10/01	T-3 10/02– 10/11	T-4 10/12– 10/21	T-5 10/22– 11/04	
Number of Respondents	199	247	297	258	225	1,226
% sample	16.2	20.1	24.2	21.0	18.5	100
Dependent variables	*Mean values*					ANOVA *p-values*
Terrorism threat index (0 = no threat↔10 = extreme threat)	7.83	7.65	7.48	7.21	7.26	*.0067*
Preventing terrorism index (1 = minimum confidence↔7 = maximum confidence)	4.82	4.67	4.85	4.71	4.58	.2522
Domestic intrusion index (1 = strongly oppose↔7 = strongly support)	4.92	5.00	5.02	4.99	4.80	.4841
Terrorism response index (0 = no action; 1 = diplomatic; 2 = economic; 3 = air strikes; 4 = invasion; 5 = nuclear)	3.81	3.78	3.93	3.85	3.86	.5702

Note: p-values are shown in italics for differences in means that are statistically significant at the 95 percent confidence level ($p < .05$).

changes significantly across the measurement periods. This is particularly noteworthy in regard to the terrorism response index, which reflects mean preferences for US actions should a country be determined to a high degree of certainty to have provided personnel or training to those responsible for the attacks of 9/11. Note that mean preferences do not spike in the first time period, which might be expected of a vengeful public. On average, participants exhibit steady support for responding with diplomatic and economic measures and employing conventional military force, but a large majority (from 74 to 82 percent) consistently rejects nuclear retaliation in each time period.

The data we collected over the course of the first fifty-four days following the most deadly attack against the United States in history do not show the wild public volatility and emotional mood swings that traditionalist theory predicts. Changes during this period for three of our composite measures are small and statistically insignificant, and for the one index that does vary significantly, the threat of terrorism is judged to decrease modestly as no follow-on attacks occur. These kinds of stable, measured views are more in accordance with revisionist expectations of public opinion.

Panel Views over the First Year Following 9/11

Of the 1,226 respondents to our survey in 2001, 935 agreed to be called again to participate in a future survey. One year later, beginning on September 12, 2002, we surveyed 474 of these participants constituting a "panel" of respondents who participated in both 2001 and 2002. In this section, we continue the analysis of the same dependent variables, but we focus more intently on our 474 panel members and relationships between individual attributes and opinion stability. We present a table for each of the same four dependent variables about terrorism. In the columns, these tables illustrate unpaired comparisons of means within each measurement period across demographic categories of age, gender, education, income, and race/ethnicity. In addition to the mean values for our panel members in 2001 and 2002, we include pre-9/11 values (where possible) and values in 2003 for baseline comparisons. Moving horizontally across each table, the middle three columns show paired comparisons of means among panel members within the same demographic and belief categories that illustrate change across the two measurement periods (2001 vs. 2002).

If traditional expectations of public volatility hold, we should find large changes immediately following the events of 9/11 that vary substantially from earlier or later central tendencies, and we should find substantial differences between assessments of our panel members in 2001 and 2002. If revisionist expectations of public stability hold, we should expect changes following 9/11 in each of our indices, but not the kind of volatile swings in public moods that would constrain or compel policymakers to undertake ill-advised policies. We begin in table 5.3 with comparisons of central tendencies in public judgments of the threat of terrorism.

Looking first at the averages for all members of each sample (top row), it is not surprising that panel members rate our composite measure of the threat of terrorism significantly higher in 2001 (7.40) than do our pre-9/11 respondents in 1997 (6.75). A threat that is already seen as serious by the public in 1997 is seen as still more serious—by an average of 0.65 on an eleven-point scale—immediately after the attacks in 2001. This mirrors increases of most expert and nonexpert judgments following 9/11, and is indeed a relatively modest jump in perceived threats given the deluge of media reports following the events (see figure 5.1). But also note that one year after 9/11, the same panel members place the mean composite assessment of terrorism within four one-hundredths of their mean rating in 2001. By the time of our survey of a new national sample in 2003, the mean composite rating declines by three tenths to 7.14. Thus composite mean ratings of the threat of terrorism are well above midscale four years before 9/11, rise significantly but moderately in the aftermath of 9/11, remain almost unchanged among the same panel members for the first year following 9/11, and decline modestly by the time of our survey in 2003. These overall changes reflect judgments that appear both reasonable and relatively stable, even in the aftermath of the traumatic events of 9/11.

To examine individual-level implications for composite assessments of

Table 5.3. Mean terrorism threat index by demographic attributes
(scale: 0 = no threat↔10 = extreme threat)

Grouping variables	Means 1997 all	Means 2001 panel	Means 2002 panel	2001, 2002 paired p-value	Means 2003 all
All	6.75	7.40	7.44	.6028	7.14
Age					
18–30 (1)	6.62	7.26	6.78	.2088	7.00
31–50 (2)	6.84	7.38	7.55	.3493	7.25
>50 (3)	6.72	7.45	7.49	.4999	7.09
Unpaired t-tests	1,2 p = .1201	1,2 p = .6596	1,2 p = .0084		1,2 p = .1046
	1,3 p = .5196	1,3 p = .5199	1,3 p = .0153		1,3 p = .5679
	2,3 p = .3583	2,3 p = .7197	2,3 p = .7418		2,3 p = .1841
Gender					
Women (0)	7.04	7.63	7.71	.6355	7.43
Men (1)	6.42	7.15	7.16	.8062	6.79
Unpaired t-tests	0,1 p < .0001	0,1 p = .0048	0,1 p = .0015		0,1 p < .0001
Education					
No college (1)	6.97	7.51	7.30	.3378	7.26
College (2)	6.73	7.41	7.57	.1822	7.14
Graduate work (3)	6.38	7.25	7.34	.9664	6.93
Unpaired t-tests	1,2 p = .0586	1,2 p = .6696	1,2 p = .2293		1,2 p = .3693
	1,3 p = .0006	1,3 p = .3324	1,3 p = .8673		1,3 p = .0422
	2,3 p = .0223	2,3 p = .4393	2,3 p = .2639		2,3 p = .1105
Income ($)					
0–50K (1)	6.75	7.42	7.57	.6599	7.22
51–100K (2)	6.72	7.37	7.45	.3518	6.97
>100K (3)	6.50	7.22	7.37	.3414	7.21
Unpaired t-tests	1,2 p = .8295	1,2 p = .7864	1,2 p = .5515		1,2 p = .0761
	1,3 p = .2828	1,3 p = .4440	1,3 p = .4430		1,3 p = .9770
	2,3 p = .3521	2,3 p = .5718	2,3 p = .7759		2,3 p = .2240
Racial/ethnic minority					
All others (0)	6.69	7.35	7.44	.3428	7.07
Grouped minorities (1)	7.00	7.73	7.54	.5465	7.48
Unpaired t-tests	0,1 p = .0642	0,1 p = .1781	0,1 p = .7113		0,1 p = .0248

Note: p-values are shown in italics for differences in means that are statistically significant at the 95 percent confidence level (p < .05).

the threat of terrorism, we move vertically within each column to compare central tendencies among various categories of individual attributes. In most cases, mean values among differing categories of age, income, and race are not significantly differentiated in any of the surveys. Note, however, that women rate the composite threat of terrorism significantly higher, on average, than do men in each of the surveys. Note also that mean threat ratings tend to decline in absolute terms with increasing education. Respondents with the highest levels of formal education (more than a bachelor's degree) rate the composite threat of terrorism significantly lower than do their counterparts without college educations in 1997 and in 2003, but the mean threat of terrorism is not differentiated by education among panel members in either 2001 or 2002. By 2003, the most highly educated respondents again perceive the lowest levels of threat, although these remain well above the level of threat perceived prior to 9/11.

To compare individual-level judgments among our panel members, we move horizontally across the middle columns (years 2001 and 2002). Mean panel assessments of the composite threat of terrorism do not vary significantly between 2001 and 2002 for any of the demographic categories. This reflects a high degree of opinion stability during the first year following 9/11 among each of the demographic categories and subdivisions. Clearly, these findings do not support traditionalist expectations of high volatility during a time of unprecedented national crisis.

In tables 5.4–5.6, we show the same types of demographic comparisons for three other dependent variables described in chapter 4 (preventing terrorism index; domestic intrusion index; and terrorism response index).

As to public confidence that government can prevent future acts of terrorism, the top row of table 5.4 suggests that in the immediate aftermath of 9/11, there is a counterintuitive increase in public confidence. That may be influenced by an initial tendency to rally together against the new threat, or an initial impression based on news reports and statements by officials that the government has focused on addressing the threat. But the initial increase in confidence is temporary, and two years after the attacks, public confidence is comparable to pre-9/11 levels.

Looking vertically in table 5.4, mean levels of confidence in government abilities to stop terrorism are not consistently differentiated by age, education, income, or minority membership, but in 1995 and in 2003, women are systematically more confident than are men. Moving horizontally across the middle columns, we find that, with only two exceptions, panel members in each demographic category and subgroup are significantly less confident that government can stop terrorism in 2002 than they are in 2001.

In table 5.5, we compare mean levels of support for intrusive domestic measures intended to prevent future acts of terrorism. Support for trade-offs between individual rights and security from terrorism is more of a mixed story, with some demographic categories showing high levels of differentiation. While age is not a strong discriminator, mean support for intrusive measures to prevent terrorism generally increases in absolute terms with age, and

Table 5.4. Preventing terrorism index by demographic attributes
(scale: 1 = minimum confidence government can stop terrorism↔7 = maximum confidence
government can stop terrorism)

Grouping variables	Means 1995 all	Means 2001 panel	Means 2002 panel	2001, 2002 paired p-value	Means 2003 all
All	4.34	4.78	4.43	<.0001	4.27
Age					
18–30 (1)	4.27	4.69	4.26	.0174	4.13
31–50 (2)	4.31	4.75	4.50	.0251	4.33
>50 (3)	4.43	4.84	4.40	<.0001	4.26
Unpaired *t*-tests	1,2 p = .7422	1,2 p = .7661	1,2 p = .2095		1,2 p = .0949
	1,3 p = .2135	1,3 p = .4471	1,3 p = .5095		1,3 p = .3054
	2,3 p = .3186	2,3 p = .4706	2,3 p = .4072		2,3 p = .4154
Gender					
Women (0)	4.53	4.89	4.44	<.0001	4.35
Men (1)	4.13	4.66	4.42	.0272	4.18
Unpaired *t*-tests	0,1 p < .0001	0,1 p = .0584	0,1 p = .9107		0,1 p = .0444
Education					
No college (1)	4.40	4.63	4.31	.0664	4.29
College (2)	4.24	4.75	4.49	.0058	4.28
Graduate work (3)	4.50	4.98	4.40	<.0001	4.27
Unpaired *t*-tests	1,2 p = .1049	1,2 p = .4593	1,2 p = .2555		1,2 p = .9079
	1,3 p = .5070	1,3 p = .0742	1,3 p = .6199		1,3 p = .8695
	2,3 p = .0630	2,3 p = .1142	2,3 p = .5457		2,3 p = .9370
Income ($)					
0–50K (1)	4.42	4.61	4.36	.0452	4.15
51–100K (2)	4.21	4.69	4.43	.0021	4.32
>100K (3)	4.42	5.28	4.52	.0003	4.47
Unpaired *t*-tests	1,2 p = .0597	1,2 p = .6032	1,2 p = .6293		1,2 p = .0824
	1,3 p = .9924	1,3 p = .0009	1,3 p = .3542		1,3 p = .0200
	2,3 p = .3574	2,3 p = .0023	2,3 p = .5815		2,3 p = .2812
Racial/ethnic minority					
All others (0)	4.39	4.80	4.45	<.0001	4.28
Grouped minorities (1)	4.04	4.52	4.21	.1013	4.27
Unpaired *t*-tests	0,1 p = .0100	0,1 p = .1740	0,1 p = .2522		0,1 p = .9122

Note: p-values are shown in italics for differences in means that are statistically significant at the 95 percent confidence level (p < .05).

some differences in age-group preferences are statistically significant in 2003 when respondents below thirty years of age are significantly less supportive of such measures than are either of the two older age groups. Women are significantly more supportive of intrusive prevention measures than are men among

Table 5.5. Domestic intrusion index by demographic attributes
(scale: 1 = strongly oppose intrusive policies to prevent terrorism↔7 = strongly support
intrusive policies to prevent terrorism)

Grouping variables	Means 1995 all	Means 2001 panel	Means 2002 panel	2001, 2002 paired p-value	Means 2003 all
All	4.76	4.84	4.59	<.0001	4.57
Age					
18–30 (1)	4.72	4.77	4.48	.1780	4.07
31–50 (2)	4.70	4.75	4.59	.0099	4.56
>50 (3)	4.88	4.97	4.63	.0001	4.76
Unpaired *t*-tests	1,2 p = .8807	1,2 p = .9446	1,2 p = .5951		1,2 p = .0002
	1,3 p = .2759	1,3 p = .3547	1,3 p = .4865		1,3 p < .0001
	2,3 p = .1685	2,3 p = .1136	2,3 p = .7799		2,3 p = .0519
Gender					
Women (0)	5.02	4.96	4.73	.0011	4.72
Men (1)	4.46	4.71	4.45	.0005	4.39
Unpaired *t*-tests	0,1 p < .0001	0,1 p = .0456	0,1 p = .0316		0,1 p = .0005
Education					
No college (1)	5.04	5.17	5.33	.5106	5.17
College (2)	4.59	4.89	4.49	<.0001	4.49
Graduate work (3)	4.49	4.44	4.19	.0371	4.07
Unpaired *t*-tests	1,2 p < .0001	1,2 p = .0774	1,2 p < .0001		1,2 p < .0001
	1,3 p = .0005	1,3 p = .0001	1,3 p < .0001		1,3 p < .0001
	2,3 p = .5061	2,3 p = .0036	2,3 p = .0494		2,3 p = .0002
Income ($)					
0–50K (1)	4.85	4.87	4.77	.1568	4.64
51–100K (2)	4.60	4.74	4.40	<.0001	4.42
>100K (3)	4.62	4.97	4.53	.0519	4.49
Unpaired *t*-tests	1,2 p = .0362	1,2 p = .4012	1,2 p = .0130		1,2 p = .0472
	1,3 p = .3382	1,3 p = .6139	1,3 p = .1844		1,3 p = .3716
	2,3 p = .9351	2,3 p = .2714	2,3 p = .4743		2,3 p = .6315
Racial/ethnic minority					
All others (0)	4.74	4.84	4.61	<.0001	4.56
Grouped minorities (1)	4.92	4.87	4.54	.0840	4.86
Unpaired *t*-tests	0,1 p = .2353	0,1 p = .8977	0,1 p = .7606		0,1 p = .0335

Note: p-values are shown in italics for differences in means that are statistically significant at the 95 percent
confidence level (p < .05).

each sample. Support for such measures declines with education, but patterns
of support are less clearly differentiated by income or racial minority status.[6]

Table 5.6, the final in this series, compares preferences for responding to
countries suspected of facilitating the 9/11 attacks. As shown in the top row,

Table 5.6. Terrorism response index by demographic attributes
(scale: 0 = oppose all responses; 1 = strong diplomatic and political pressures; 2 = strong economic and trade sanctions; 3 = conventional air strikes; 4 = military invasion; 5 = use nuclear weapons)

Grouping variables	Means 2001 panel	Means 2002 panel	2001, 2002 paired p-value	Means 2003 all
All	3.81	3.56	*< .0001*	3.13
Age				
18–30 (1)	3.73	3.42	.1030	2.94
31–50 (2)	3.88	3.73	*.0173*	3.24
>50 (3)	3.75	3.41	*< .0001*	3.10
	1,2 *p* = .3047	1,2 *p* = .0602		1,2 *p* = .0069
Unpaired *t*-tests	1,3 *p* = .8939	1,3 *p* = .9810		1,3 *p* = .1642
	2,3 *p* = .1925	2,3 *p* = .0027		2,3 *p* = .0848
Gender				
Women (0)	3.71	3.42	*.0004*	2.94
Men (1)	3.92	3.70	*.0004*	3.36
Unpaired *t*-tests	0,1 *p* = .0272	0,1 *p* = .0062		0,1 *p* < .0001
Education				
No college (1)	3.86	3.75	.0538	3.47
College (2)	3.93	3.61	*< .0001*	3.08
Graduate work (3)	3.51	3.33	.0600	2.88
	1,2 *p* = .5288	1,2 *p* = .2691		1,2 *p* < .0001
Unpaired *t*-tests	1,3 *p* = .0229	1,3 *p* = .0056		1,3 *p* < .0001
	2,3 *p* < .0001	2,3 *p* = .0202		2,3 *p* = .0358
Income ($)				
0–50K (1)	3.76	3.64	*.0409*	3.11
51–100K (2)	3.79	3.56	*.0031*	3.11
>100K (3)	4.08	3.45	*.0002*	3.30
	1,2 *p* = .7887	1,2 *p* = .5167		1,2 *p* = .9722
Unpaired *t*-tests	1,3 *p* = .0279	1,3 *p* = .2187		1,3 *p* = .1517
	2,3 *p* = .0309	2,3 *p* = .4467		2,3 *p* = .1220
Racial/ethnic minority				
All others (0)	3.81	3.56	*< .0001*	3.12
Grouped minorities (1)	3.92	3.62	*.0184*	3.18
Unpaired *t*-tests	0,1 *p* = .4453	0,1 *p* = .7329		0,1 *p* = .6395

Note: p-values are shown in italics for differences in means that are statistically significant at the 95 percent confidence level (*p* < .05).

overall mean support for forceful response declines significantly among our panel members during the first year after 9/11, and drops even lower by the time of our survey in 2003. Preferences are not clearly distinguished by age, income, or racial minority, but they are more highly differentiated by gender and education. Women are significantly less supportive of forceful responses in each measurement period, and support for the use of force declines systematically with increasing levels of education.

Among panel members, support for military actions declines in each demographic category and subgroup over the course of the first year following 9/11, and the change is statistically significant for all but two subgroups. The same pattern of declining support continues among our respondents in 2003.

Together, the comparisons of mean preferences in tables 5.3–5.6 suggest that some demographic attributes are providing predispositions that help anchor opinions about terrorism before, during, and after the national crisis presented by the events of 9/11. For these issues, the two most discriminating demographic categories are gender and education. On average, women report systematically higher assessments of the threat of terrorism, greater levels of confidence in government abilities to prevent terrorism, more willingness to accept intrusive measures to prevent terrorism, and less support of forceful military responses to 9/11. Though less pervasive in its effects, education also is associated with clear patterns of preferences. Composite assessments of the threat of terrorism tend to decrease with higher levels of formal education, and support of intrusive preventive measures and support for more forceful responses to 9/11 clearly decline as education increases.

In summary, the overall stability of views among the same individuals over the tumultuous first year after 9/11 is quite remarkable. Rather than the panicky and volatile swings traditional theory anticipates, we find much more stable and predictable patterns and measured change over time. Moreover, such characteristics as gender, education, age, and race or ethnicity appear to systematically, albeit modestly, anchor the variations in how Americans perceive and respond to security concerns over time.[7] And now, having looked at individual-level attributes and central tendencies about terrorism within a panel of the same individuals, in the following sections we turn again to our multiple surveys over the period 1993–2003 to examine dynamic relationships between key individual-level attributes and persistent views and preferences about a broader range of security issues.

Age and Beliefs about Security over Time

In this section, we examine the relationship of age to views about nuclear security and terrorism by employing age as a continuous independent variable in separate bivariate regressions to explain variations in domain-level beliefs about the risks and benefits of nuclear weapons, our terrorism threat index, our preventing terrorism index, and related policy preferences.[8] In table 5.7,

Table 5.7. Relating age to domain beliefs about nuclear security and terrorism, 1993–2003 (bivariate regression coefficients: *p < .05; †p < .01; ‡p < .001)

Dependent variable	1993	1995	1997	1999	2001	2003
External nuclear risk index (0 = no risk↔10 = extreme risk)	.003	.002	−.005	.001	.000	−.010†
Domestic nuclear risk index (0 = no risk↔10 = extreme risk)	.003	−.011‡	−.012‡	−.012‡	−.002	−.010†
External nuclear benefit index (0 = not at all beneficial↔10 = extremely beneficial)	.023‡	.025‡	.016‡	.018‡	.013‡	.013‡
Domestic nuclear benefit index (0 = not at all beneficial↔10 = extremely beneficial)	.009*	.009†	.016‡	.016‡	.012†	.010†
Terrorism threat index (0 = no threat↔10 = extreme threat)	NA	NA	.001	NA	.003	−.004
Preventing terrorism index (1 = minimum confidence↔ 7 = maximum confidence)	NA	.004	NA	NA	.004	.000

we show the regression coefficients when age is used to predict each of the nuclear security risk and benefit indices and the two terrorism indices over time.[9]

As these regression coefficients show, age is related systematically to public assessments of external nuclear risks (risks from others' nuclear weapons) only in our 2003 survey. Age is related negatively to assessments of the domestic risks associated with maintaining the US nuclear arsenal in our 1995, 1997, 1999, and 2003 surveys, but is not systematically related in our 1993 or 2001 surveys. However, age is related positively both to external and domestic nuclear benefits in each of the six surveys spanning a decade. Though the power of age for explaining nuclear weapons benefits is small (from 1–4 percent of overall variation in perceptions), the direction is consistent, and the relationships all are statistically significant. Older respondents tend to rate domestic nuclear risks lower and external and domestic nuclear benefits higher than do younger respondents. Age is not related systematically to either the threat of terrorism or to assessments of the government's abilities to stop terrorism.

Turning to relationships between age and specific security policy preferences, in table 5.8 we compare coefficients for bivariate regressions in which age is used as the independent variable to predict preferences for three key nuclear policy issues, the domestic intrusion index, and the index for responding to terrorism.

Age is related positively to the importance of retaining US nuclear weapons and to support for investing in nuclear infrastructure in each of our six surveys. Age is not related to preferences for building ballistic missile defenses. For our two terrorism policy measures, age is not related systematically to our

Table 5.8. Relating age to key security policy preferences, 1993–2003
(bivariate regression coefficients: $^*p < .05$; $^\dagger p < .01$; $^\ddagger p < .001$)

Dependent variable	1993	1995	1997	1999	2001	2003
Importance of retaining US nuclear weapons (Q36: 0 = not at all important ↔10 = extremely important)	.033‡	.031‡	.017‡	.028‡	.013†	.025‡
Spending for maintaining the ability to develop and improve US nuclear weapons in the future (Q44: 1 = substantially decrease↔7 = substantially increase)	.021‡	.010‡	.018‡	.023‡	.014‡	.015‡
Should US build a system of ballistic missile defenses? (Q59: 1 = definitely should *not*↔7 = definitely *should*)	NA	NA	NA	.003	−.006	.005
Domestic intrusion index (1 = strongly oppose↔7 = strongly support)	NA	NA	NA	NA	.008†	.015‡
Terrorism response index (0 = no response↔5 = nuclear retaliation)	NA	NA	NA	NA	−.001	−.002

index of response options, but age is related positively in both measurement periods to our index of intrusive policies for preventing terrorism (tolerance for intrusive measures increases with age). For all measures, explanatory power is small, with variation in age explaining about 1–3 percent of variation in the dependent variables. However, we note that although coefficients representing change for one year of increase in age are small, when projected over the course of an average adult lifespan, age can account for appreciable change in support for these policy preferences. For example, a forty-year age difference is estimated to result in a full point difference in the average rating of the importance of retaining the nuclear stockpile (Q36).

Age and Nuclear Deterrence

Beliefs about the efficacy of nuclear deterrence are critical to nuclear security, and key questions concern (a) how individual citizen's perceptions of deterrence change with age, and (b) how aggregate public attitudes about nuclear deterrence may evolve as the portion of the public having personally experienced the nuclear tensions of the Cold War decreases. Will younger individuals with less chronological maturity (or perhaps, on average, simply less extensive experience in observing human wisdom and folly) view the value of deterrence differently than their elders? If so, we should expect to see age have a continuous (though not necessarily linear) effect on perceptions of deterrence. But age might also have a more discrete influence, in which individuals who did not live through the Cold War as adults perceive nuclear deterrence substantially differently than those who experienced the nuclear dangers of that era. If so, age cohorts—as distinct from chronological age—might be-

Table 5.9. Relating age to importance of nuclear deterrence, 1995–2003
(bivariate regression coefficients: $^*p < .05$; $^\dagger p < .01$; $^\ddagger p < .001$)

Dependent variable	1995	1997	1999	2001	2003
Importance of nuclear deterrence in preventing nuclear conflict during the Cold War (Q23: 0 = not at all important↔10 = extremely important)	.024‡	.015‡	.016‡	.011*	.012‡
Importance of nuclear deterrence for preventing nuclear conflict today (Q24: 0 = not at all important↔10 = extremely important)	.020‡	.009*	.017‡	.014†	.019‡
Effectiveness of nuclear deterrence for preventing nuclear conflict if more countries acquire nuclear weapons (Q25: 0 = not at all effective↔10 = extremely effective)	.023‡	.014†	.015†	.007	.022‡
Importance of nuclear deterrence for preventing countries from using chemical or biological weapons against the US today (Q26: 0 = not at all important↔10 = extremely important)	NA	NA	.019‡	.006	.022‡

come a demographic factor importantly related to future public valuation of nuclear security. Such an effect would be evident in differences across cohorts of those who experienced the Cold War as adults as compared to those who did not.

We asked several questions about nuclear deterrence in each of our security surveys beginning in 1995, and we graph mean responses and trends over time in chapter 3, figures 3.7–3.10. In table 5.9, we summarize results of bivariate regressions in which age is used as the independent variable to predict responses over time to each of four deterrence questions.[10]

Results show that, with one exception in 2001, assessments of the importance of deterrence for preventing nuclear conflict systematically increase with age, whether the frame of reference is the Cold War, or today, or a more proliferated future. Also, in two of three surveys, age is related positively to the importance of nuclear deterrence for preventing countries from using chemical or biological weapons against the United States today.

In order to distinguish between the effects of age (maturity) and cohorts (experience of the Cold War), we analyze combined data from 1995–2003 employing measures of both characteristics as independent variables to predict the importance of deterrence today. To measure the cohort effect, we create a dummy variable identifying those who experienced the Cold War as adults, coding respondents who were eighteen years of age or older in 1991 (end of Cold War) with a value of one, and all others as zero. The cohort dummy variable is then regressed onto the deterrence measure along with the measure of respondent age. Results in table 5.10 show that when age is held constant, the effect of cohort group (respondents who experienced some portion of the

Table 5.10. Using age and adult Cold War experience to predict importance of nuclear deterrence today (Q24)

	Coefficient	Std. error	Std. coeff.	t-value	p-value	Adj. R²
Intercept	6.804	.093	6.804	73.347	<.0001	.011
Age	.014	.094	.094	7.214	<.0001	
Experienced Cold War as adult	.128	.017	.017	1.268	.2048	

Cold War as adults) is not statistically significant. Age, on the other hand, remains highly statistically significant and is related positively to the perceived importance of deterrence.

We conclude that although it still is early in the post–Cold War era, our data do not yet suggest that persons who did not experience the Cold War as adults systematically value nuclear deterrence differently than persons who were adults during the Cold War years. At the same time, increasing age is associated with a modestly rising sense of the importance of deterrence.

Gender and Beliefs about Security over Time

In tables 5.11 and 5.12 we compare mean values for our external and domestic nuclear risk indices among women and men in each of our security surveys.

In each of our six surveys, women perceive greater risks from others' nuclear weapons (external nuclear risks) than do men, and assign greater risks to managing our own nuclear arsenal (domestic nuclear risks). Differences

Table 5.11. Mean external nuclear risk index by gender, 1993–2003
(scale: 0 = no risk↔10 = extreme risk)

	1993	1995	1997	1999	2001	2003
Women	6.63	6.41	6.46	6.77	6.75	6.75
Men	6.26	6.28	6.16	6.53	6.29	6.25
Difference	−0.37	−0.13	−0.30	−0.24	−0.46	−0.50
p-value	.0003	.1004	.0020	.0086	<.0001	<.0001

Table 5.12. Mean domestic nuclear risk index by gender, 1993–2003
(scale: 0 = no risk↔10 = extreme risk)

	1993	1995	1997	1999	2001	2003
Women	6.68	7.37	5.67	5.92	5.24	5.47
Men	5.41	5.88	4.45	4.69	4.27	4.28
Difference	−1.27	−1.49	−1.22	−1.23	−0.97	−1.19
p-value	<.0001	<.0001	<.0001	<.0001	<.0001	<.0001

in mean external nuclear risks are statistically significant in each year except 1995, and differences in mean domestic nuclear risks all are statistically significant. These data show substantial gender-related differences in beliefs about risks associated with nuclear security over time, with women consistently assessing those risks significantly higher than do their male counterparts.

We do not find systematic differences over time in views among men and women about the *benefits* of US nuclear weapons for achieving national security objectives (external nuclear benefits), or for economic and technical benefits deriving from investments in nuclear security capabilities (domestic nuclear benefits). Though men tend to rate nuclear security benefits somewhat higher, differences generally are not significant.[11]

In tables 5.13 and 5.14 we compare mean values for the terrorism threat index and the preventing terrorism index in available surveys among women and men.

As was the case with nuclear risks, our composite index of threats posed by terrorism are differentiated systematically by gender in each of the three surveys in which all component questions are asked. Note that men rate the threat of terrorism significantly lower than do women in each survey, and the difference is consistent whether measured before 9/11, immediately after 9/11, or two years later. As to our index reflecting respondent beliefs about the potential for government to prevent terrorism, even if doing so intrudes on some individual prerogatives, women are more confident about efforts to prevent future terrorism in 1995 and 2003 than are men. Note that opinions statistically are not differentiated by gender in the immediate aftermath of

Table 5.13. Mean terrorism threat index by gender, 1997, 2001, 2003
(scale: 0 = no threat⟷10 = extreme threat)

	1997	2001	2003
Women	7.04	7.77	7.43
Men	6.42	7.14	6.79
Difference	−0.62	−0.63	−0.64
p-value	<.0001	<.0001	<.0001

Table 5.14. Mean preventing terrorism index by gender, 1995, 2001, 2003
(scale: 1 = minimum confidence⟷7 = maximum confidence)

	1995	2001	2003
Women	4.53	4.78	4.35
Men	4.12	4.67	4.18
Difference	−0.41	−0.11	−0.17
p-value	<.0001	.1927	.0444

9/11.[12] Gender differences for these two terrorism indices are consistent with those previously reported among our panel members.

Gender and Security Policy Preferences

In table 5.15, we compare mean responses by women and men to the same three key nuclear security policy items and the two terrorism policy measures previously used. Within each cell, we display mean values reported by women participants in the first line, followed by mean values of men (shown in italics) in the second line, and the *p*-value of differences in means is provided in the third line.

On average, men rate the importance of retaining nuclear weapons higher in each survey than do women, but differences in means are statistically significant in only half the surveys (1995, 1999, and 2003). Responses to the question of how spending should change for nuclear infrastructure are not consistently differentiated by gender, nor are responses to our question about whether the United States should build a national system for defense against ballistic missiles. For our two terrorism indices, men average significantly higher on the terrorism response index (more willing to use force against other countries that aid terrorists) in both years, and women are significantly more accepting of intrusive domestic efforts to prevent terrorism in both surveys. Both findings are consistent with those reported for our panel members.

Table 5.15. Mean security policy preferences by gender, 1993–2003

Policy issue	Women / Men / p-value					
	1993	1995	1997	1999	2001	2003
Importance of retaining US nuclear weapons today (Q36: 0 = not at all important↔10 = extremely important)	6.43 *6.75* .0666	6.61 *6.98* .0047	7.11 *7.27* .2405	7.33 *7.72* .0064	7.80 *7.71* .5253	7.13 *7.49* .0136
Spending for maintaining the ability to develop and improve US nuclear weapons in the future (Q44: 1 = substantially decrease↔7 = substantially increase)	3.62 *3.74* .3289	4.05 *3.95* .2598	4.60 *4.27* .0025	4.74 *4.84* .3671	5.18 *4.85* .0054	4.54 *4.38* .1616
Should US build a system of ballistic missile defenses? (Q59: 1 = definitely should *not*↔7 = definitely *should*)	NA	NA	NA	5.05 *5.27* .0487	5.28 *5.08* .1139	5.04 *4.94* .3914
Domestic intrusion index (1 = strongly oppose↔7 = strongly support)	NA	NA	NA	NA	5.11 *4.78* <.0001	4.74 *4.34* .0012
Terrorism response index (0 = no response↔5 = nuclear retaliation)	NA	NA	NA	NA	3.78 *3.94* .0123	2.94 *3.36* <.0001

Education and Beliefs about Security over Time

In table 5.16, we compare mean beliefs among respondents with college degrees or higher levels of formal education with those of participants without college degrees about the risks and benefits of nuclear weapons, the terrorism threat index, and the preventing terrorism index. Within each cell of the table, mean values for those who are not college graduates are shown in the first row, followed by means for college graduates shown in italics in the second row, and *p*-values for differences in means in the third row.

Respondents with a bachelor's degree or higher educational attainment rate composite external and domestic nuclear risks and composite external and domestic nuclear benefits significantly lower than do participants without college educations. Similarly, college graduates judge composite measures of the threat posed by all forms of terrorism to be lower than do those without college degrees, except in 2001 immediately following 9/11. Conversely, our preventing terrorism index is significantly differentiated by education only in 2001, when those with college educations are significantly (and temporarily) more confident that government can prevent future terrorism.

Turning to more specific policy positions, in table 5.17, we compare mean values for selected nuclear security and terrorism policy issues between those with and without college educations.

Table 5.16. College education and mean domain beliefs about nuclear security and terrorism, 1993–2003

	Non-college graduate / *College graduate or higher* / p-value					
Dependent variable	*1993*	*1995*	*1997*	*1999*	*2001*	*2003*
External nuclear risk index (0 = no risk↔10 = extreme risk)	6.64 *6.14* <.0001	6.70 *6.37* <.0001	6.37 *6.24* .2009	6.83 *6.37* <.0001	6.61 *6.43* .1176	6.63 *6.37* .0078
Domestic nuclear risk index (0 = no risk↔10 = extreme risk)	6.40 *5.50* <.0001	5.80 *4.98* <.0001	5.29 *4.77* <.0001	5.65 *4.92* <.0001	5.05 *4.39* <.0001	5.15 *4.63* <.0001
External nuclear benefit index (0 = not at all beneficial↔10 = extremely beneficial)	6.73 *6.18* <.0001	7.07 *6.77* .0002	7.03 *6.71* .0026	7.29 *6.86* <.0001	7.34 *7.12* .0456	7.35 *6.78* <.0001
Domestic nuclear benefit index (0 = not at all beneficial↔10 = extremely beneficial)	5.25 *4.51* <.0001	6.29 *5.97* .0004	6.70 *6.37* .0042	6.80 *6.34* <.0001	6.88 *6.30* <.0001	6.74 *6.30* .0002
Terrorism threat index (0 = no threat↔10 = extreme threat)	NA	NA	6.92 *6.43* <.0001	NA	7.53 *7.40* .3238	7.29 *6.92* .0008
Preventing terrorism index (1 = minimum confidence↔7 = maximum confidence)	NA	4.35 *4.32* .8024	NA	NA	4.61 *4.93* .0002	4.31 *4.24* .3823

Table 5.17. College education and mean policy preferences about nuclear security and terrorism, 1993–2003

Dependent variable	Non-college graduate / *College graduate or higher* / p-value					
	1993	*1995*	*1997*	*1999*	*2001*	*2003*
Importance of retaining US nuclear weapons today (Q36: 0 = not at all important↔10 = extremely important)	6.90	6.89	7.23	7.60	7.83	7.55
	6.06	*6.57*	*7.11*	*7.33*	*7.64*	*6.97*
	<.0001	.0183	.4332	.0589	.2025	<.0001
Spending for maintaining the ability to develop and improve US nuclear weapons in the future (Q44: 1 = substantially decrease↔7 = substantially increase)	3.79	4.07	4.55	4.97	5.20	4.78
	3.50	*3.89*	*4.26*	*4.47*	*4.77*	*4.09*
	.0168	.0585	.0125	<.0001	.0003	<.0001
Should US build a system of ballistic missile defenses? (Q59: 1 = definitely should *not*↔7 = definitely *should*)	NA	NA	NA	5.37	5.50	5.55
				4.79	*4.72*	*4.32*
				<.0001	<.0001	<.0001
Domestic intrusion index (1 = strongly oppose↔7 = strongly support)	NA	NA	NA	NA	5.15	4.91
					4.67	*4.21*
					<.0001	<.0001
Terrorism response index (0 = no response↔5 = nuclear retaliation)	NA	NA	NA	NA	3.88	3.32
					3.81	*2.90*
					.2361	<.0001

Consistent with the previous relationships between education and domain-level beliefs, education also is associated with more specific policy preferences about nuclear security and terrorism. As shown in table 5.17, participants who are college graduates (shown in italics) rate the importance of retaining US nuclear weapons lower (statistically significantly lower in 1993, 1995, and 2003), and are significantly less supportive of investing in nuclear weapons infrastructure than respondents without college educations in all but one survey year. College graduates also are significantly less supportive of building missile defenses in each of the three measurement periods. Turning to preferences about terrorism, support for forceful responses to terrorism are not differentiated by education in the immediate aftermath of 9/11, but by 2003, college graduates are less supportive of using military force to respond to terrorist acts, and they are significantly less accepting of intrusive domestic methods for preventing terrorism in both measurement periods.

Income and Beliefs about Security over Time

We asked participants in each of our surveys to identify their combined household income for the previous calendar year within a range of 10,000-dollar increments from zero to more than 100,000 dollars. In table 5.18, we compare coefficients of bivariate regressions in which income is used as the

Table 5.18. Relating annual household income to domain beliefs
about nuclear security and terrorism, 1993–2003
(bivariate regression coefficients: $^*p < .05$; $^\dagger p < .01$; $^\ddagger p < .001$)

Dependent variable	1993	1995	1997	1999	2001	2003
External nuclear risk index (0 = no risk↔10 = extreme risk)	−.081†	−.040†	.008	−.035	−.064†	−.031
Domestic nuclear risk index (0 = no risk↔10 = extreme risk)	−.163‡	−.132‡	−.086‡	−.136‡	−.169‡	−.120‡
External nuclear benefit index (0 = not at all beneficial↔10 = extremely beneficial)	−.014	−.010	.017	−.019	−.011	−.010
Domestic nuclear benefit index (0 = not at all beneficial↔10 = extremely beneficial)	−.060*	.009	.009	−.066†	−.051*	−.014
Terrorism threat index (0 = no threat↔10 = extreme threat)	NA	NA	−.040	NA	−.059†	−.027
Preventing terrorism index (1 = minimum confidence↔7 = maximum confidence)	NA	−.012	NA	NA	.055‡	.030*

independent variable to predict our measures of domain-level beliefs about nuclear security and terrorism.

Income is most consistently related to beliefs about the domestic risks of managing US nuclear weapons, where assessments of domestic nuclear risks decline with increasing levels of income in each of our surveys. Similarly, but less systematically, income is related negatively to beliefs about external nuclear risks in half the surveys. Income is not related to estimates of the external benefits of US nuclear weapons and is weakly related to beliefs about the domestic benefits of US nuclear weapons. Income also is weakly and inconsistently related to beliefs about the threat of terrorism, but is related positively in both post-9/11 surveys to beliefs about the abilities of government to prevent terrorism.

We follow in table 5.19 with regression outcomes when annual household income is used as the independent variable in separate bivariate regressions to predict key policy preferences.

Income is not systematically related to the importance of retaining US nuclear weapons or to preferences for how spending should change for nuclear weapons infrastructure. As income increases, support for building national missile defenses declines (at an increasing rate) in each of the three surveys in which that issue is addressed. Income is related weakly and inconsistently to the index of intrusive domestic measures for preventing terrorism, and income is not predictably related in either year to preferences for responding to terrorism.

Table 5.19. Relating annual household income to policy preferences about nuclear security and terrorism, 1993–2003 (bivariate regression coefficients: $^*p < .05$; $^\dagger p < .01$; $^\ddagger p < .001$)

Dependent variable	1993	1995	1997	1999	2001	2003
Importance of retaining US nuclear weapons today (Q36: 0 = not at all important↔10 = extremely important)	−.062	−.003	.051	.014	.030	.043
Spending for maintaining the ability to develop and improve US nuclear weapons in the future (Q44: 1 = substantially decrease↔7 = substantially increase)	−.034	−.023	−.008	−.008	−.036	−.035
Should US build a system of ballistic missile defenses? (Q59: 1 = definitely should *not*↔7 = definitely *should*)	NA	NA	NA	−.049*	−.072†	−.109‡
Domestic intrusion index (1 = strongly oppose↔7 = strongly support)	NA	NA	NA	NA	−.021	−.037*
Terrorism response index (0 = no response↔5 = nuclear retaliation)	NA	NA	NA	NA	.016	.017

Race/Ethnicity and Beliefs about Security over Time

Because of the relatively small numbers of respondents in any category other than white (non-Hispanic), we limit our analysis of racial/ethnic implications to comparing means between combined respondents from three minority groups and all others. American Indians, African Americans, and Hispanics in the United States historically have been subject to force and institutional discrimination, and many social and economic indicators suggest that, on average, citizens of these minorities continue to be disadvantaged. In tables 5.20 and 5.21, we compare mean assessments of nuclear security risks and benefits over time by grouped participants from these three racial/ethnic minorities with those of all other respondents.

Mean assessments of external nuclear risks are differentiated by race/ethnicity only in 1993 and 2001, but respondents from racial and ethnic minorities judge domestic nuclear risks to be significantly higher than their counterparts in the majority.

Table 5.20. Mean external nuclear risk index by racial/ethnic minority and majority groupings, 1993–2003 (scale: 0 = no risk↔10 = extreme risk)

	1993	1995	1997	1999	2001	2003
Grouped minorities	6.85	6.76	6.38	6.83	7.02	6.76
All others	6.40	6.55	6.37	6.66	6.48	6.52
Difference	0.45	0.21	0.01	0.17	0.54	0.24
p-value	.0041	.0629	.9580	.2041	.0011	.1365

Table 5.21. Mean domestic nuclear risk index by racial/ethnic minority and
majority groupings, 1993–2003
(scale: 0 = no risk↔10 = extreme risk)

	1993	1995	1997	1999	2001	2003
Grouped minorities	6.65	5.99	5.22	6.11	5.59	5.36
All others	5.97	5.45	5.00	5.12	4.62	4.81
Difference	0.68	0.54	0.22	0.99	0.97	0.55
p-value	.0002	<.0001	.2045	<.0001	<.0001	.0055

Neither external nor domestic nuclear benefit assessments are systematically differentiated over time by race/ethnicity.

In table 5.22 we compare mean values for our terrorism threat index in 2001 and 2002, and in table 5.23, we show comparisons by race/ethnicity for our preventing terrorism index for the same years.

In both measurement periods, respondents who are members of the three racial or ethnic minority groups rate our combined measures of the threat of all kinds of terrorism significantly higher, on average, than do other respondents. In 2001, immediately following 9/11, racial/ethnic minorities are less confident that government can prevent future terrorist acts than are their counterparts in the majority, but that difference disappears by 2003.

A comparison of preferences between the racial/ethnic majority and minority portions of our respondents for the same five nuclear security and terrorism issues previously used reveals that mean responses to each of the following items are not statistically significantly differentiated by racial group-

Table 5.22. Mean terrorism threat index by racial/ethnic minority
and majority groupings, 2001–2003
(scale: 0 = no threat↔10 = extreme threat)

	2001	2003
Grouped minorities	8.00	7.48
All others	7.48	7.07
Difference	0.52	0.41
p-value	.0027	.0248

Table 5.23. Mean preventing terrorism index by racial/ethnic minority
and majority groupings, 2001–2003
(scale: 0 = minimum confidence↔10 = maximum confidence)

	2001	2003
Grouped minorities	4.50	4.27
All others	4.78	4.28
Difference	0.28	0.01
p-value	.0246	.9122

ing: (1) the importance of retaining US nuclear weapons today; (2) spending for maintaining the ability to develop and improve nuclear weapons in the future; and (3) preferences for responding to acts of terrorism against the United States. Support for intrusive domestic measures for preventing future terrorism are not statistically differentiated by racial/ethnic categories in 2001 (immediately following the attacks of 9/11). By 2003, support for such measures declines among all groups, but support among minority participants declines substantially less than it does among others. Minority members are significantly more supportive of building national missile defenses than are other respondents.

In sum, using surveys that span a decade, we have been able to show that the effects of individual characteristics—age, gender, education, income, and race/ethnicity—tend to have consistent relationships with security policy beliefs. That consistency is quite remarkable and survives (or in some cases reemerges after) the shock of the terrorist attacks on 9/11. Acting in concert, it is quite plausible that the consistent effects of individual demographic attributes contribute to the overall stability and structure of public attitudes about security.

Relating Combined Demographics to Security Beliefs

We have examined independent relationships over time among separate demographic categories and beliefs about nuclear security and terrorism, but we have yet to analyze relationships of predictor variables when other independent variables are held constant. We do that by examining the interaction of demographics using the following attributes as independent variables simultaneously in multivariate regressions to predict domain-level beliefs about nuclear security and terrorism and related policy preferences: (1) age; (2) gender (using a dummy variable in which a value of one represents men); (3) education (using a dummy variable in which a value of one represents those with a bachelor's degree or higher); (4) annual household income; and (5) racial/ethnic status (using a dummy variable in which a value of one represents native Americans, African Americans, and Hispanic minorities).[13] In table 5.24, we summarize results of multiple regressions in which respondents' demographic characteristics are used as independent variables to explain beliefs and preferences about nuclear security and terrorism in 2003. These results show relationships between each demographic attribute and the dependent variable when all other demographic characteristics are held constant.

Assessments of external and domestic nuclear risks are systematically lower among men and those with college educations. Views of domestic nu-

Table 5.24. Relating combined demographics to beliefs about security, 2003
(multiple regression coefficients: $*p < .05$; $^†p < .01$; $^‡p < .001$)

Nuclear security measure	Age	Gender	Education	Income	Race/ethnicity	Adj. R²
External nuclear risk index (0 = no risk⟷10 = extreme risk)	−.006	−.439‡	−.328†	.006	.320	.025
Domestic nuclear risk index (0 = no risk⟷10 = extreme risk)	−.015‡	−1.174‡	−.284*	−.082‡	.497*	.112
External nuclear benefit index (0 = not at all beneficial⟷10 = extremely beneficial)	.018‡	.302*	−.754‡	.040	.486†	.066
Domestic nuclear benefit index (0 = not at all beneficial⟷10 = extremely beneficial)	.012†	.149	−.607‡	.021	.187	.024
Terrorism threat index (0 = no threat⟷10 = extreme threat)	.001	−.517‡	−.465‡	.023	.547†	.031
Preventing terrorism index (1 = minimum confidence⟷7 = maximum confidence)	.000	−.118	−.122	.034*	−.001	.001
Importance of retaining nuclear weapons (0 = not at all important⟷10 = extremely important)	.028‡	.492†	−.912‡	.102‡	.400	.062
Spending for ability to develop/improve nuclear weapons in future (1 = substantially reduce⟷7 = substantially increase)	.015‡	−.095	−.758‡	.014	.287	.047
Build missile defenses (1 = definitely should not⟷7 = definitely should)	.006	−.020	−1.197‡	−.031	.754‡	.107
Domestic intrusion index (1 = strongly oppose⟷7 = strongly support)	.016‡	−.204*	−.694‡	.013	.442†	.081
Terrorism response index (0 = no response⟷5 = nuclear retaliation)	.001	.457‡	−.467‡	.037*	.080	.062

clear risks decrease with age and income and are higher among racial/ethnic minorities.

Judgments of external and domestic nuclear benefits increase with age and are lower among the college educated. Men and racial/ethnic minorities rate external benefits higher.

Assessments of the importance of retaining US nuclear weapons and support for investing in nuclear infrastructure increase with age and are systematically lower among college graduates. Support for the retain issue increases with annual household income and is higher among men.

Support for building missile defenses is lower among college graduates and higher among racial/ethnic minorities. The missile defense issue is not systematically differentiated by age, gender, or income.

The threat of terrorism is rated higher by women, those without college educations, and members of racial/ethnic minorities. Confidence in government abilities to prevent future terrorism increases with income but is not related systematically to other demographic characteristics. Support for intrusive domestic measures to prevent terrorism increases with age and is higher among women and racial/ethnic minorities, but it is lower among college graduates. Support for forceful responses to terrorism increases with income and is higher among men, but it is lower among those with college educations.

The combined explanatory power of demographic attributes is strongest for predicting domestic nuclear risks, external nuclear benefits, acceptance of intrusive antiterrorism measures, and support for building national missile defenses, where demographics explain about 7–11 percent of variation.

As contributing evidence to the continuing debate about public capacities, these data suggest that individual characteristics consistently help anchor public views about security. While modest, the effects of these characteristics are robust over time and when controlling for possible overlapping or confounding influences in a multivariate model. These results are consistent with and contribute to our findings that individual-level changes in beliefs about security have been measured over the period of our surveys, and the levels of change observed following a dramatic national crisis are more consistent with revisionist theory about public capabilities than with traditional assumptions about the volatility of mass opinions.

Using the demographic influences on policy beliefs and preferences analyzed here as a point of departure, we turn to exploring the integrated effects of demographic predispositions for belief structures by modeling demographics and key beliefs about nuclear security and terrorism in chapter 6.

MASS BELIEF
STRUCTURES

IF OPINIONS OF the mass public about policy issues largely are disjointed and poorly structured, expressions of such opinions will be incoherent as well. For that reason, understanding how mass beliefs are organized and structured is central to the debate about public capacities. It is widely accepted that coherence of policy beliefs depends on a stable and systematic structure within which dispositions deriving from abstract values and general beliefs predictably constrain more specific policy-relevant beliefs. Traditional theory asserts that structured beliefs observable among members of elite groups are lacking among mass publics. Revisionists disagree, arguing that mass beliefs are hierarchically structured in ways similar to elite belief systems, though less tightly. Thus the degree to which structured beliefs exist among ordinary citizens is considered key to the coherence of their policy preferences and to the public's capacity for usefully contributing to issue debates and policy processes. In chapters 2 and 3, we describe trends in public views of nuclear risks and benefits and trends in preferences about a number of specific issues such as minimum numbers of US nuclear weapons, investments in nuclear weapons capabilities, and arms control. In chapter 4, we describe public assessments of the threats of terrorism and alternative measures for its prevention, and in chapter 5, we analyze some of the ways in which demographic attributes and experience contribute to the stability of public opinion. In this chapter, we integrate the elements of public beliefs to analyze the underlying structures and evaluate the coherence of mass beliefs.

Our focus is on the relationship between broad beliefs and values, on the one hand, and more specific policy preferences on the other. Following our analytical framework as described in chapter 1 and employing a hierarchical model of belief structures (Fiske and Taylor 1992; Hurwitz and Peffley 1987; Hurwitz, Peffley, and Seligson 1993; Sabatier and Jenkins-Smith 1993, 1999), we investigate three levels of beliefs and their relationships. The most general and abstract of these beliefs are dubbed *core beliefs*, consisting of fundamental underlying normative dispositions that transcend specific policy issue areas. Examples include ideology, political culture, beliefs about nature, justice, equity, and other deeply held values.[1]

Domain beliefs are those reflecting fundamental orientations and strategies that apply across a given policy domain. Examples include assessments of the security environment, beliefs about risks and benefits of technologies, beliefs about militarism or internationalism in foreign affairs, and trade-offs between security and individual prerogatives.[2]

Policy preferences are beliefs that reflect specific choices applicable to an issue area. Preferences about whether and in what numbers the United States should retain nuclear weapons, whether the United States should participate in specific treaties, and which policies the United States should employ in the struggle against terrorism are examples of security policy preferences.[3]

If beliefs are structured hierarchically among mass publics, we should find systematic connections, persistent over time, among different levels of beliefs. We expect to find core beliefs helping directly to shape domain beliefs and indirectly to influence policy preferences, and we expect domain beliefs to most powerfully and consistently predict policy preferences.[4] Interacting with all three levels of beliefs are the kinds of individual demographic attributes we examined in chapter 5. These attributes are widely understood to influence fundamental predispositions for belief structures and their relationships. At the end of this chapter we will model causal relationships among demographics, core beliefs, domain beliefs, and policy preferences about key nuclear security and terrorism issues and discuss their implications for the debate over the coherence of public views. We begin our discussion with measures of core beliefs.

Core Beliefs

We analyze core beliefs and their relationships to other levels of mass beliefs in two different but complementary ways. In the first method, we include measures of political beliefs (ideology and partisanship) worded exactly the same in each of our six surveys. Responses to those questions allow us to investigate linkages between core political beliefs, mid-level domain beliefs, and lower-level policy preferences. In 1993 and 1995, we included additional measures of core beliefs by asking an extensive series of questions designed to identify respondents' worldviews in terms of political culture. We then analyzed how different cultural types are related to policy beliefs and preferences. By employing both approaches, we are able to present reinforcing evidence about the functions of core beliefs in mass belief structures.

Ideology and Partisanship

Hinich and Munger (1996, 10) identify three core functions of ideology. First, political ideologies provide "collections of ideas with intellectually derivable normative implications for behavior and for how society should be organized" (see also Converse 1964; Higgs and Twight 1987; Lodge 1976; North 1981; and Reichley 1981). Second, ideologies provide "economizing devices by which individuals understand and express ideas about politics" (see also Congleton 1991; Downs 1957; Enelow and Hinich 1984; Macridis 1980; and North 1994). Finally, ideologies can be conceived as "dogmatic belief systems by which individuals interpret, rationalize, and justify behavior and institutions" (see also Christenson et al. 1975; Domhaff 1983; Jovrasky 1970; North 1990; and Sartori 1969).

Various methodologies have been employed to measure ideology, but none are without limitations. Some techniques involve asking participants to define the concept in their own words, which are then related to textbook definitions (usually as evidence to show how poorly most individuals understand the concept). Critics of such methods note that inability to fully and correctly articulate a concept does not necessarily mean people cannot approximate meaning and apply the concept in political behaviors such as voting. Other methods infer ideological positions based on voter registration, party membership, or voting records, but they incur difficulties of documentation, and they do not adequately address political independents. Still others ask a series of questions about policy orientations from which political ideology is inferred from responses, but these approaches suffer from selection bias and lack of comprehensiveness.

One of the oldest and most widely used methods is to ask participants to self-rate their personal ideology on a unidimensional scale from strongly liberal (left) to strongly conservative (right), but this method also is contestable. Critics of such a continuum note that positions considered liberal by some may be perceived as conservative by others, and that apolitical attitudes sometimes can be construed as partisan. Some people are reluctant to place themselves at either end of the continuum, because they may associate the polar positions with extremism. Also, there is some evidence that liberal and conservative labels do not always represent the opposite poles of a spatial relationship, and that people differ in their self-defined assumptions about what is liberal and what is conservative (Conover and Feldman 1981). Others argue that ideological beliefs can vary widely between economic and social policy domains, and both dimensions must be measured separately (Asher 1980; Weisberg and Rusk 1970).

Those who see utility in a unidimensional ideology metric argue that it is parsimonious, widely used in the common language of public political discourse, and that it allows the individual who theoretically is most knowledgeable about the complex spectrum of beliefs comprising such a characterization to locate the center of gravity of his or her own personal beliefs along the scale. And there is substantial evidence indicating that the terms "liberal" and "conservative" provide an important symbolic framework for simplifying societal conflict and debate in the United States. In their analysis of American voter behavior, Holm and Robinson (1978, 242) report that "ideology's impact on vote overlaps strongly with issue position, as would be expected given the role of ideology in guiding specific policy orientations on some issues. Still, ideology continues to retain a very significant independent predictive effect, explaining its own variance independent of and not as a surrogate for issue or party."[5]

As our data illustrate, we find considerable evidence that ordinary citizens consistently can place themselves along an ideological continuum and that placement is predictably related to domain-level beliefs and specific policy preferences. To measure ideological self-placement, we asked participants in each of our surveys to respond to the following question:

(Q145) On a scale of political ideology, individuals can be arranged from strongly liberal to strongly conservative. Which of the following categories best describes your views? Would you say that you are (1) strongly liberal, (2) liberal, (3) slightly liberal, (4) middle of the road, (5) slightly conservative, (6) conservative, or (7) strongly conservative?

In table 6.1, we compare distributions of self-rated ideology values for each of our biennial surveys between 1993 and 2003, and in table 6.2 we compare unweighted mean ideology values with means weighted to national demographic data for race and gender in each reporting period.

These data illustrate how the liberal-conservative metric, applied in six separate national samples of the US general public, provides quite comparable estimates of political ideology over a decade. Distributions and mean self-ratings of ideology are remarkably stable at the aggregate level, with both unweighted and weighted means varying only 0.12 points across ten years. It is, of course, possible that these aggregate measures mask volatility at the individual level. To test for stability at the individual level, we conducted a

Table 6.1. Distributions of self-rated ideology, 1993–2003 (%)

Year	Strongly liberal (1)	Liberal (2)	Slightly liberal (3)	Middle of road (4)	Slightly conservative (5)	Conservative (6)	Strongly conservative (7)
1993	4	12	12	28	17	19	9
1995	2	10	11	28	21	20	7
1997	4	10	11	28	17	24	7
1999	4	13	8	29	17	20	8
2001	4	12	11	27	18	19	9
2003	6	12	10	27	18	19	9

Table 6.2. Mean ideology ratings, unweighted and weighted
(1 = strongly liberal↔7 = strongly conservative)

Means	1993	1995	1997	1999	2001	2003	All
Unweighted	4.34	4.46	4.43	4.37	4.35	4.34	4.39
Weighted	4.31	4.43	4.41	4.36	4.31	4.37	4.38

panel study in which 474 respondents to our survey in 2001 participated in a follow-on survey with identical content one year later. In that study, fully 51.5 percent of our panel members report no change in their ideological self-placement during the twelve months between our 2001 and 2002 surveys, and 88.1 percent move one point or less on the seven-point scale (chi-square 618.44, $p < .0001$). These results are quite striking: nearly nine out of ten of our respondents indicate that their ideological self-placement shifts only modestly, if at all, over a full calendar year. Thus, contrary to traditional assumptions, our data indicate that at both aggregate and individual levels of analyses, ordinary American citizens are able consistently to locate quite stable ideological beliefs along a unidimensional continuum.

Another aspect of the public's abilities to employ ideology relates to the degree to which citizens consistently associate ideology with attachments to political parties and gradations of partisanship. Sensible understandings of ideological implications should be manifested in organized associations between positions on the ideology continuum and varying levels of identity with major political parties. To examine this association, we measured partisanship using the following two questions in each of our surveys.

(Q143) With which political party do you most identify? (1) Democratic Party; (2) Republican Party; (3) Independent; (4) other

(Q144) Do you (3) completely, (2) somewhat, or (1) slightly identify with that political party?

By combining responses to these questions, we create a partisanship scale having the following values: (1) identify completely with the Democratic Party; (2) identify somewhat with the Democratic Party; (3) identify slightly with the Democratic Party; (4) identify slightly with the Republican Party; (5) identify somewhat with the Republican Party; (6) identify completely with the Republican Party; (7) all others. In table 6.3 we chart the distribution by partisanship category of respondents to each of our surveys, and in table 6.4 we compare mean ideology values with partisan preferences.

With two exceptions, mean self-rated ideology relates monotonically to affinity for the two major political parties across the surveys. The only relationships not predictably ordered occur in 1999 and 2003 between those identifying completely or somewhat with the Democratic Party. Clearly, these relationships show that our respondents are able systematically to organize political ideology along a liberal-conservative continuum within the context of partisan political orientations.[6] Our findings do not support traditional assumptions about citizens' inabilities to form an integrated ideology, or to express ideological perspectives with reasonable consistency, nor are they

Table 6.3. Distribution of respondents by political partisanship, 1993–2003 (% identifying with major political parties)

Year	Completely Democratic	Somewhat Democratic	Slightly Democratic	Slightly Republican	Somewhat Republican	Completely Republican	All others
1993	12	23	8	7	23	9	18
1995	7	21	9	7	22	8	27
1997	9	26	8	8	27	9	13
1999	11	28	8	8	25	8	12
2001	16	25	3	4	21	20	10
2003	15	22	4	5	25	15	14
All	11	23	7	7	24	11	18

Table 6.4. Mean ideology values by political partisanship, 1993–2003

Year	Completely Democratic	Somewhat Democratic	Slightly Democratic	Slightly Republican	Somewhat Republican	Completely Republican	All others
1993	3.35	3.53	4.17	4.81	5.17	6.03	4.23
1995	3.67	3.77	4.14	5.00	5.15	5.88	4.19
1997	3.41	3.60	3.94	4.73	5.34	5.54	4.22
1999	3.60	3.49	3.79	5.12	5.40	5.77	4.04
2001	3.25	3.54	3.89	4.73	4.95	5.85	4.13
2003	3.36	3.25	4.34	4.52	5.20	6.00	4.09
All	3.44	3.57	4.05	4.86	5.21	5.85	4.17

consistent with crude two-party aggregations cueing publics incapable of high-order abstraction.

In order for structured systems of beliefs to provide a basis for public engagement in the policy processes concerning nuclear security and terrorism, meaningful relationships should exist between political ideology, political partisanship, and views on security issues. We begin that analysis by focusing on relationships between core political beliefs and domain-level beliefs represented by our nuclear risk and benefit indices introduced in chapter 2.[7] In table 6.5, we compare coefficients of separate bivariate regressions in which self-rated ideology is used as the independent variable to predict assessments of external and domestic nuclear benefits and external and domestic nuclear risks for each of our six national surveys.

Assessments of external and domestic benefits from US nuclear weapons increase predictably with increasingly conservative ideological views. Similarly, views of the risks deriving from maintaining and managing our own nuclear weapons decrease as ideology values increase (more conservative). However, political ideology is a weak predictor of risks associated with others' nuclear weapons. These differences in relationships between ideology and assessments of the benefits and risks of nuclear weapons are replicated when respondents are grouped by expressed partisanship. In figures 6.1–6.4, we graph trends in mean nuclear weapons benefit and risk assessments over time among strong Democrats (respondents who identify completely or somewhat with the Democratic Party) and strong Republicans (those who identify completely or somewhat with the Republican Party). To provide a comparative baseline, we also show mean values of all respondents in each survey. (Note that vertical scales vary and are truncated for better illustration.)

These graphs show that respondents identifying completely or somewhat with the Democratic Party rate mean external and domestic nuclear benefits significantly lower and mean domestic nuclear risks significantly higher than

Table 6.5. Relating ideology to nuclear risks and benefits, 1993–2003 (coefficients of separate bivariate regressions: $^*p < .05$; $^\dagger p < .01$; $^\ddagger p < .001$)

Year	External nuclear benefit index (Adj. R^2)	Domestic nuclear benefit index (Adj. R^2)	External nuclear risk index (Adj. R^2)	Domestic nuclear risk index (Adj. R^2)
1993	$.363^\ddagger$ (.073)	$.145^\dagger$ (.009)	$.090^\dagger$ (.005)	$-.166^\ddagger$ (.016)
1995	$.283^\ddagger$ (.050)	$.235^\ddagger$ (.019)	.043 (.000)	$-.250^\ddagger$ (.023)
1997	$.320^\ddagger$ (.065)	$.104^\dagger$ (.006)	.046 (.000)	$-.134^\ddagger$ (.009)
1999	$.295^\ddagger$ (.070)	$.149^\ddagger$ (.013)	$.069^*$ (.003)	$-.150^\ddagger$ (.012)
2001	$.227^\ddagger$ (.043)	$.211^\ddagger$ (.029)	.011 (.000)	$-.165^\ddagger$ (.014)
2003	$.421^\ddagger$ (.137)	$.316^\ddagger$ (.058)	$-.005$ (.000)	$-.264^\ddagger$ (.040)

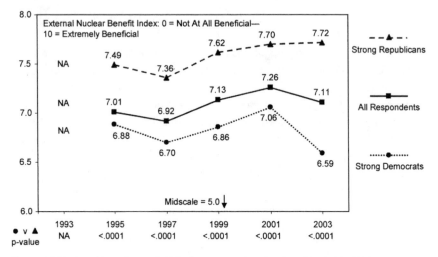

Figure 6.1. Partisanship and mean beliefs about external nuclear benefits, 1995–2003

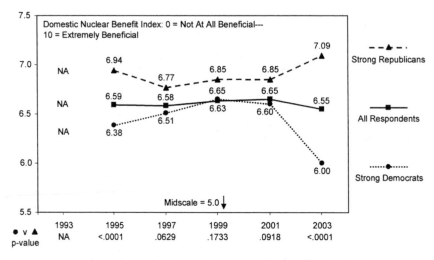

Figure 6.2. Partisanship and mean beliefs about domestic nuclear benefits, 1995–2003

respondents identifying completely or somewhat with the Republican Party. As with ideology, differences in political partisanship are not systematically related to assessments of external nuclear risks.[8] These trends in relationships over a decade illustrate how political beliefs are predictably associated with some domain beliefs about nuclear security, whether the predictor variable is political ideology or party preferences.

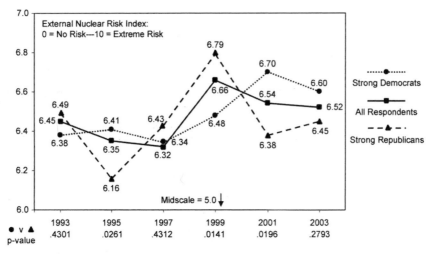

Figure 6.3. Partisanship and mean beliefs about external nuclear risks, 1993–2003

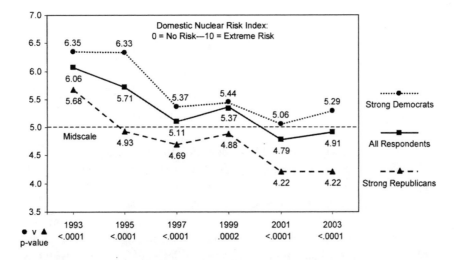

Figure 6.4. Partisanship and mean beliefs about domestic nuclear risks, 1993–2003

Next, we analyze how political ideology and partisanship relate to preferences for specific nuclear security policy choices. In table 6.6, we compare regression coefficients where political ideology is used as the independent variable in separate bivariate regressions to explain variation in eight nuclear security policy issues across the six surveys.[9]

Increasing conservatism is related systematically, over time, with each of

Table 6.6. Relating ideology to nuclear security policy preferences, 1993–2003 (coefficients of separate bivariate regressions: $^*p < .05$; $^\dagger p < .01$; $^\ddagger p < .001$)

Issue	Coefficients (Adj. R^2)					
	1993	1995	1997	1999	2001	2003
Feasible to eliminate all nuclear weapons in next 25 years (Q34: 1 = strongly disagree↔7 = strongly agree)	−.082 (.000)	−.230‡ (.021)	−.247‡ (.024)	−.184‡ (.014)	−.205‡ (.018)	−.271‡ (.033)
Comprehensive nuclear test ban (Q31: 1 = strongly oppose↔7= strongly support)	NA	−.161‡ (.016)	−.165‡ (.014)	−.264‡ (.039)	−.296‡ (.049)	−.278‡ (.045)
Importance of retaining US nuclear weapons today (Q36: 0 = not at all important↔10 = extremely important)	.449‡ (.055)	.522‡ (.058)	.448‡ (.070)	.424‡ (.070)	.406‡ (.074)	.579‡ (.134)
Spending for developing/testing new US nuclear weapons (Q40: 1 = substantially decrease↔7 = substantially increase)	.204‡ (.027)	.185‡ (.021)	.176‡ (.023)	.252‡ (.055)	.222‡ (.039)	.362‡ (.115)
Spending for maintaining existing US nuclear weapons (Q41: 1 = substantially decrease↔7 = substantially increase)	.127‡ (.010)	.171‡ (.014)	.176‡ (.019)	.254‡ (.053)	.245‡ (.055)	.289‡ (.072)
Spending for US nuclear weapons infrastructure (Q44: 1 = substantially decrease↔7 = substantially increase)	.239‡ (.033)	.216‡ (.020)	.266‡ (.040)	.333‡ (.074)	.276‡ (.053)	.416‡ (.117)
Minimum acceptable number of US nuclear weapons (Q27 *reversed*: increments of 500 with 1 = zero↔15 = 6,500–7,000)	NA	NA	.434‡ (.019)	.338‡ (.012)	.584‡ (.034)	.636‡ (.047)
Building US ballistic missile defenses (Q59: 1 = strongly oppose↔7 = strongly support)	NA	NA	NA	.232‡ (.038)	.360‡ (.081)	.558‡ (.188)

the following: disagreement with the assertion that it is feasible to eliminate all nuclear weapons worldwide in the next twenty-five years; opposition to US participation in a comprehensive nuclear test ban treaty; increasing importance of retaining US nuclear weapons today; increased spending for developing and testing new nuclear weapons, reliably maintaining existing nuclear weapons, and maintaining the ability to develop and improve nuclear weapons in the future; higher minimum acceptable levels of US nuclear weapons; and greater support for building US missile defenses. The results in table 6.6 also suggest that the strength of the association between ideology and nuclear security policy preferences grows over the decade of our surveys. For virtually every measure, the estimated effect of ideology on policy beliefs grows over time, while the proportion of explained variance doubles (or more).

In table 6.7, we compare mean preferences over time for these issues among political partisans, finding predictable differences between the policy preferences of partisan Democrats and partisan Republicans. Within each cell of the table, values for strong Democrats are shown in the first row, values for

Table 6.7. Partisanship and nuclear security policy preferences, 1993–2003

Issue	Comparing mean preferences among strong Democrats vs. *strong Republicans* (differences in means)					
	1993	*1995*	*1997*	*1999*	*2001*	*2003*
Feasible to eliminate all nuclear weapons in next 25 years (Q34: 1 = strongly disagree↔7 = strongly agree)	4.03	4.13	4.16	3.99	3.77	4.12
	3.51	*3.31*	*3.22*	*2.95*	*2.92*	*3.03*
	(−0.52)	(−0.82)	(−0.94)	(−1.04)	(−0.85)	(−1.09)
Comprehensive nuclear test ban (Q31: 1 = strongly oppose↔ 7 = strongly support)	NA	5.46	5.61	5.78	5.51	5.78
		5.18	*5.23*	*4.77*	*4.46*	*4.52*
		(−0.28)	(−0.38)	(−1.01)	(−1.05)	(−1.26)
Importance of retaining US nuclear weapons today (Q36: 0 = not at all important↔10 = extremely important)	6.20	6.36	6.96	7.16	7.38	6.60
	7.10	*7.52*	*7.72*	*8.15*	*8.32*	*8.14*
	(0.90)	(1.16)	(0.76)	(0.99)	(0.94)	(1.54)
Spending for developing/testing new US nuclear weapons (Q40: 1 = substantially decrease↔7 = substantially increase)	2.63	2.42	2.89	3.19	3.54	2.92
	2.99	*2.88*	*3.32*	*3.98*	*4.16*	*3.93*
	(0.36)	(0.46)	(0.43)	(0.79)	(0.62)	(1.01)
Spending for maintaining existing US nuclear weapons (Q41: 1 = substantially decrease↔7 = substantially increase)	4.35	4.11	4.48	4.85	5.07	4.42
	4.71	*4.73*	*4.93*	*5.54*	*5.63*	*5.22*
	(0.36)	(0.62)	(0.45)	(0.69)	(0.56)	(0.80)
Spending for US nuclear weapons infrastructure (Q44: 1 = substantially decrease↔7 = substantially increase)	3.45	3.91	4.28	4.52	4.65	3.84
	3.99	*4.40*	*4.71*	*5.37*	*5.36*	*5.13*
	(0.54)	(0.49)	(0.43)	(0.85)	(0.71)	(1.29)
Building US ballistic missile defenses (Q59: 1 = strongly oppose↔7 = strongly support)	NA	NA	NA	4.80	4.56	4.27
				5.58	*5.81*	*5.70*
				(0.78)	(1.25)	(1.43)

strong Republicans are italicized in the second row, and differences are shown in parentheses in the third row.

In each survey, strong Democrats are less likely to disagree with the assertion that it is feasible to eliminate all nuclear weapons and more supportive of a comprehensive nuclear test ban than are their Republican counterparts. Conversely, strong Republicans consistently rate the importance of retaining US nuclear weapons higher and are more supportive of investing in nuclear weapons capabilities. Republican partisans also are more supportive of US missile defenses. Differences in means between partisan Democrats and partisan Republicans are statistically significant ($p < .05$) for each policy issue. Our remaining security issue measure concerning the minimum acceptable number of US nuclear weapons has been asked in each of our biennial surveys since 1997. It has response categories representing ranges of values for which comparisons of means are not appropriate. Comparisons of median ranges using combined data for the years 1997–2003 show that strong Republicans prefer significantly higher minimum numbers (with a median preferred range of 2,500–3,000) nuclear weapons than do their Democrat counterparts (with a median preferred range of 500–1,000). As these data indicate, political partisanship is related systematically in each of our surveys over ten years to policy preferences about nuclear weapons.

The relationship between partisanship and security preferences grows stronger over the decade of our surveys. Over that period, the magnitude of the gap between self-identified strong Republicans and strong Democrats doubles for nearly every measure (the smallest increase across our measures is 70 percent). As with the ideology measures, these changes indicate that the linkages between more general political beliefs and specific nuclear policy preferences grew tighter over time. Moreover, the change in magnitude of the relationship between party identification and policy preferences is statistically significant for six of the seven variables.[10] We should note that observation of a trend of this kind—even if statistically significant—is not tantamount to confirmation of such a relationship.[11] Nevertheless, the results indicate that mass belief system structures can and do change, even in relatively short time spans. We return to this issue in chapter 7.

Political Culture

Political culture is a less intuitive construct than is political orientation, but as we will show, it can be useful in understanding and predicting the public's policy views. The term does not refer to culture in the common vernacular. *Political* culture, as we employ it, is not defined by nationality, ethnicity, tradition, language, history, political system, or any of the other attributes we commonly relate to culture in its broadest sense. While many variants exist, theories of political culture typically have been developed by anthropologists, sociologists, and political scientists in order to find general explanations for the patterns evident in the relationships among very different peoples living in very different circumstances. One particularly fruitful theoretical approach grounds culture in the twin concepts of group inclusion and social distinction.[12]

The central thesis in cultural theory is that adults (regardless of ethnicity, nationality, demographics, etc.) can be usefully classified according to two variables. One, termed "group" by Mary Douglas, is the degree to which individuals understand themselves to be incorporated into bounded units or social groups. Douglas named the other dimension "grid." It refers to the degree to which the patterns of interactions in individual lives are circumscribed by externally imposed prescriptions, such as rules, laws, and traditions. Douglas explains that the group dimension taps the extent to which "the individual's life is absorbed in and sustained by group membership" (Douglas 1982, 206). She defines grid as "an explicit set of institutionalized classifications [that] keeps [individuals] apart and regulates their interactions" (Douglas 1982,

192). When the two continuums of group and grid are overlaid, they produce a matrix of four primary cultural types (Douglas 1982; Ellis and Coyle 1994; Jenkins-Smith and Smith 1994).

Hierarchists are persons with high group identity and binding prescriptions (high group, high grid). They tend to place the welfare of the group before their own and usually are aware of whether other individuals are members of the group or outsiders. They prefer organizations to be stratified, with individuals having unequal roles based on status in the hierarchy. Hierarchists value procedures, lines of authority, social stability, and order. They are predisposed to trust experts and those in authority and to have faith in technologies that are sanctioned by experts.

Individualists are persons with little if any group identity who feel bounded by few structural prescriptions (low group, low grid). They prefer a libertarian society with few rules and regulations and feel little obligation to define themselves in terms of group memberships. Individualists perceive themselves to be involved in bidding and bargaining with others to transact their own terms for social relations. Intrusions on or restrictions to the bargaining process are seen as threats to charting their own courses in life.

Egalitarians seek strong group identities and prefer minimal external prescriptions (high group, low grid). One of the important values of egalitarianism is equality of outcome. Egalitarians fear concentration of powers and distrust experts and those in positions of authority. Potentially hazardous technologies controlled by organizations that are not open to public scrutiny pose particularly high risks. The "establishment" is not trusted by most egalitarians.

Fatalists consider themselves subject to binding external constraints, yet they feel excluded from membership in important social groups (low group, high grid). Believing they have little control over their lives, equity is an unreachable goal; one's fate is much more a matter of chance than choice. Fatalists suffer the social isolation of individualism without the freedom of autonomy; the constraint of hierarchy without the benefits of group belonging. Of the four principal cultural types, fatalists are presumed to be the fewest in number and the least likely to be active in policy processes.

The theoretical framework provided by grid-group analysis and its resulting cultural types provides a cosmology of worldviews that can be used to test relationships between core and other levels of beliefs. Because of the number of questions required for classifying respondents, our investigations of political culture among mass publics are limited to surveys in 1993 and 1995 in which we classify the four cultural types by averaging multiple measures for each type.[13] We calculate a mean score for each cultural category and classify those respondents whose average scores are higher in one of the categories

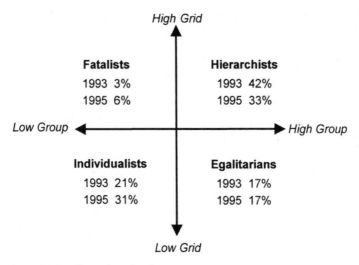

Figure 6.5. Distribution by cultural type

than in each of the other three categories in accordance with their highest mean score. Participants who do not clearly score higher in one category than in the other three are not culturally typed. Figure 6.5 shows the distribution of respondents according to their identification with the four cultural types.

The majority of our respondents in each survey are typed as hierarchists or individualists. About 17 percent in each survey are predominately egalitarian, and only three to six percent of participants are fatalists. The remaining 17 percent in 1993 and 13 percent in 1995 did not exhibit a dominant worldview or did not respond to all the classification questions.

Given the attributes of each cultural type, cultural theory predicts that the sharpest policy-relevant cultural distinctions will occur between hierarchists (who place great trust in experts and the establishment) and egalitarians (who are suspicious of experts and distrust establishment processes). The second most conspicuous difference should be between individualists and egalitarians, who share dislike for societal constraints but differ in affinities for group membership. Because of their small numbers and because they do not feel they have influence over policy choices, fatalists are not expected to demonstrate consistent patterns of preferences. We compare mean values in 1993 and 1995 for domain-level beliefs among hierarchists, egalitarians, and individualists in table 6.8, and in table 6.9 we compare selected policy preferences among the same cultural types. In each table, p-values reflect the statistical significance of differences in means.

These data show our indicators of political culture are linked systematically to beliefs about nuclear security. As table 6.8 shows, the largest differ-

Table 6.8. Political culture and mean domain level beliefs, 1993–1995

Domain belief measures (0–10)	Means (p-values)				
	Hierarchists		Egalitarians		Individualists
1993					
External nuclear benefit index	6.76		5.71		6.49
		(<.0001)		(.0002)	
Domestic nuclear benefit index	5.18		4.50		4.68
		(.0003)		(.4225)	
External nuclear risk index	6.30		6.50		6.53
		(.1954)		(.8373)	
Domestic nuclear risk index	5.79		6.62		5.77
		(<.0001)		(<.0001)	
1995					
External nuclear benefit index	7.09		6.48		7.10
		(<.0001)		(<.0001)	
Domestic nuclear benefit index	6.69		6.07		6.82
		(<.0001)		(<.0001)	
External nuclear risk index	6.22		6.59		6.26
		(.0017)		(.0064)	
Domestic nuclear risk index	5.73		6.34		5.12
		(<.0001)		(<.0001)	

ences in mean beliefs about domain-level nuclear risks and benefits are found between hierarchists and individualists, on the one hand, and egalitarians on the other. Egalitarians rate nuclear weapons benefits significantly lower and domestic nuclear risks significantly higher than do hierarchists or individualists. Views about risks from others' nuclear weapons are less clearly distinguishable, which is consistent with relationships between political beliefs and external nuclear risks previously shown.

As shown in table 6.9, predictable differences also are evident among cultural types and nuclear security policy preferences, with egalitarians more in agreement that nuclear weapons can be eliminated and more supportive of a nuclear test ban. Egalitarians also assign less importance to retaining US nuclear weapons and are less supportive of investing in nuclear weapons capabilities than are hierarchists and individualists.

To summarize our discussion thus far, core beliefs—whether measured as ideology, partisanship, or more abstract political culture—substantively and systematically act over time to constrain the nuclear security policy beliefs of the American public. We have not argued for the primacy of any specific conceptualization of core beliefs, in part because such an exercise is beyond the scope of this book. Also, more generally, we would not be surprised to learn that in a complex, postindustrial society there exist a montage of partially reinforcing, partly conflicting patterns of core beliefs that act as guides and

Table 6.9. Political culture and mean policy preferences, 1993–1995

Policy preferences	Means (p-values)					
	Hierar-chists		Egalita-rians		Individ-ualists
1993						
Feasible to eliminate all nuclear weapons in next 25 years (Q34: 1 = strongly disagree↔7 = strongly agree)	3.54	(.0005)	4.24	(.0001)	3.35
Comprehensive nuclear test ban (Q31: 1= strongly oppose↔7 = strongly support)	NA		NA		NA
Importance of retaining US nuclear weapons today (Q36: 0 = not at all important↔10 = extremely important)	6.97	(<.0001)	5.51	(.0002)	6.63
Spending to develop/test new US nuclear weapons (Q40: 1 = substantially decrease↔7 = substantially increase)	3.01	(<.0001)	2.10	(.0007)	2.69
Spending for maintaining existing US nuclear weapons (Q41: 1 = substantially decrease↔7 = substantially increase)	4.63	(.0207)	4.24	(.0602)	4.60
Spending for US nuclear weapons infrastructure (Q44: 1 = substantially decrease↔7 = substantially increase)	3.90	(<.0001)	3.06	(.0023)	3.65
1995						
Feasible to eliminate all nuclear weapons in next 25 years (Q34: 1 = strongly disagree↔7 = strongly agree)	3.81	(.0041)	4.47	(<.0001)	3.40
Comprehensive nuclear test ban (Q31: 1 = strongly oppose↔7 = strongly support)	5.28	(<.0001)	5.80	(.0011)	5.45
Importance of retaining US nuclear weapons today (Q36: 0 = not at all important↔10 = extremely important)	6.90	(<.0001)	6.12	(<.0001)	6.96
Spending to develop/test new US nuclear weapons (Q40: 1 = substantially decrease↔7 = substantially increase)	2.67	(.0018)	2.33	(.0636)	2.53
Spending for maintaining existing US nuclear weapons (Q41: 1 = substantially decrease↔7 = substantially increase)	4.37	(.1424)	4.19	(.0052)	4.54
Spending for US nuclear weapons infrastructure (Q44: 1 = substantially decrease↔7 = substantially increase)	4.15	(.0033)	3.77	(.1000)	3.99

channels for public beliefs about policies. We expect that the relative force of these core beliefs can vary over time and place, in part as events (such as the collapse of the Soviet Union or the 9/11 terrorist attacks) and the actions of political elites serve to evoke or suppress the norms, fears, or values embedded in these core beliefs in public discourse. Indeed, the growing and reinforcing linkages between ideology and partisanship over the last decade of the twentieth century that we document in this chapter appear to be evidence for such variation. But whatever the ontology and dynamic of core beliefs, it is clear that citizens draw on them in shaping their perceptions of the policy domain and in the formulation of specific policy preferences.

Domain-Level Beliefs

As noted earlier, theories of the structure of belief systems posit a hierarchy of beliefs in which core beliefs constrain domain-level policy beliefs, which in turn constrain more specific policy preferences. Recall that domain beliefs concern fundamental orientations and strategies that apply across a given policy domain. We measure domain-level beliefs about nuclear security in two ways. The most extensive method is to construct the composite external and domestic nuclear weapons risk and benefit indices described in chapter 2 for each of our six national surveys. In 1999 and 2001, we also incorporated a second approach that allows us to create an additional nuclear belief index consisting of different domain-level measures of nuclear views. In the following discussions we summarize our findings about how each of these two different ways of measuring domain beliefs are related to more specific security policy choices.

Nuclear Risk and Benefit Indices

In chapter 2, we describe how we construct composite indices of assessments of the risks posed by others' nuclear weapons capabilities (external nuclear risks) and the risks posed to US society by maintaining our own nuclear arsenal (domestic nuclear risks). Similarly, we develop indices measuring assessments of the benefits of US nuclear weapons for international influence and status (external nuclear benefits) and public views of economic and technological benefits deriving from US nuclear weapons research (domestic nuclear benefits). Earlier in this chapter, we show how core political beliefs and worldviews based on political culture are related to these domain beliefs about the risks and benefits of nuclear weapons. Following a hierarchical model of belief structures, we now investigate how these same domain-level beliefs about risks and benefits predict more specific policy preferences. We begin by calculating multiple regressions in which our four risk and benefit indices are used together as independent variables to predict beliefs about the importance of retaining US nuclear weapons expressed on a continuous scale where zero means "not at all important," and ten means "extremely important" (Q36). We summarize regression coefficients and explanatory values for each of our

Table 6.10. Relating domain beliefs about nuclear risks and benefits to importance of retaining US nuclear weapons, 1993–2003 (multiple regressions)

Importance of retaining US nuclear weapons (0–10)	Multivariate coefficients: $^*p < .05$; $^\dagger p < .01$; $^\ddagger p < .001$				
	External nuclear risk index	Domestic nuclear risk index	External nuclear benefit index	Domestic nuclear benefit index	Adj. R^2
1993	.520‡	−.256‡	.624‡	.155‡	.42
1995	.304‡	−.193‡	.809‡	.101‡	.34
1997	.128‡	−.134‡	.668‡	.130‡	.30
1999	.081*	−.103‡	.791‡	.143‡	.39
2001	.079*	−.091†	.751‡	.101‡	.36
2003	.047	−.167‡	.785‡	.122‡	.41

six surveys in table 6.10.[14] Each coefficient represents the change in importance of retaining US nuclear weapons associated with a one-unit change in each risk/benefit index when the other three indices are held constant.

Note the consistency of relationships in several respects. First, the directions of relationships in each of the six surveys over a ten-year period are consistent. Second, with one exception, each of the four indices is statistically significantly related to the importance of retaining nuclear weapons in each of the surveys. (The coefficient for the external nuclear risk index falls below statistical significance only in 2003.) Third, note the substantial explanatory values (R^2) indicating that these measures of domain beliefs explain from about 30 to 40 percent of variation in the retain issue. Finally, note that in each of the surveys, assessments of external nuclear benefits consistently are more powerful (larger regression coefficients) than the other indices for predicting preferences for retaining US nuclear weapons.

It also is interesting to note the declining importance of the external risk index as a predictor variable. In 1993, about eighteen months after the end of the Cold War, public beliefs about external nuclear risks are second only to beliefs about external benefits in explaining variation in the perceived importance of retaining nuclear weapons. Over subsequent surveys, the magnitude of the relationship steadily dwindles such that by the 2001 and 2003 surveys, the external risk measure is the weakest among the four indices. This decline in the power of external nuclear risks for justifying the retention of US nuclear weapons parallels what many see as a decline in the Soviet nuclear threat to the United States. This trend indicates that the mix of domain-level considerations used by Americans to reach conclusions about the importance of the US nuclear arsenal is evolving, giving less weight to perceived external risks and greater weight to whether the arsenal provides external benefits in the form of international leadership, influence, and deterrence, and domestic

Table 6.11. Relating domain beliefs about nuclear risks and benefits to support for nuclear weapons infrastructure, 1993–2003 (multiple regressions)

Investing in nuclear weapons infrastructure (1–7)	Multivariate coefficients: $^*p < .05$; $^\dagger p < .01$; $^\ddagger p < .001$				
	External nuclear risk index	Domestic nuclear risk index	External nuclear benefit index	Domestic nuclear benefit index	Adj. R^2
1993	.114‡	−.133‡	.295‡	.154‡	.20
1995	−.021	−.080‡	.368‡	.138‡	.15
1997	−.027	−.022	.405‡	.142‡	.19
1999	.002	−.021	.399‡	.193‡	.22
2001	−.038	.013	.476‡	.148‡	.25
2003	.025	−.046	.415‡	.178‡	.26

benefits in terms of positive economic implications and technology transfers.

In table 6.11, we employ the same domain beliefs about the risks and benefits of nuclear weapons as independent variables in multiple regressions to explain variance in beliefs about how spending should change for maintaining the ability to develop and improve US nuclear weapons in the future, expressed on a continuous scale where one means "substantially reduce," and seven means "substantially increase" (Q44).

The much larger predictive power of nuclear weapons benefits as compared to nuclear weapons risks is even more apparent when analyzing preferences for how spending should change for nuclear weapons infrastructure. External nuclear risks are systematically related to preferences for spending only in 1993, and domestic nuclear risks are predictive only in 1993 and 1995. In contrast, external and domestic nuclear benefits are related systematically to investing in future nuclear weapons capabilities in each measurement period, explaining about 15 to 25 percent of variation. Relationships are similar when risk and benefit assessments are used to predict preferences about eliminating nuclear weapons, participating in a nuclear test ban treaty, and funding other categories of nuclear weapons investments. In most cases, beliefs about the benefits of US nuclear weapons are related more predictably to preferences about nuclear security policies than are beliefs about nuclear risks.

Other Measures of Domain Beliefs

To examine other measures of domain-level security policy beliefs, in 1999 and 2001 we presented starkly contrasting pairs of statements representing different beliefs about security and asked respondents to indicate with which statement in each pair they most agreed. As illustrated below, each component of the nine pairs of contrasting statements is coded zero or one, and when responses are combined, they allow us to situate participants along a continuum of domain-level beliefs from "nuclear doves" (those who see the world as having become safer, who prefer less aggressive military policies and want less reliance on nuclear deterrence) to "nuclear hawks" (those who see the world as increasingly dangerous, who prefer more aggressive military policies and greater reliance on nuclear deterrence).[15] We introduced the series with the following lead-in:

For the next series, I will read several pairs of opposing statements, and I want you to tell me which statement you agree with the most. It is OK if you do not completely agree with either statement. I just need to know which statement you agree with the most.

In tables 6.12–6.14 we show responses to three pairs of statements that contrast beliefs about the current security environment, the relative importance of military power, and the use of US military force.[16]

As shown in table 6.12, two out of three participants in 1999 and three out of four respondents in 2001 agree more with the assertion that the security en-

Table 6.12. The current security environment

Which of these statements that contrast views about world security do you agree with the most?	1999 %	2001 %	Code
a. Today the world is a less dangerous place for the US than it was during the Cold War.	36	24	0
b. Today the world is a more dangerous place for the US than it was during the Cold War.	64	76	1

Table 6.13. Importance of military power

Which of these statements that contrast views about US military power do you agree with the most?	1999 %	2001 %	Code
a. US military power is less important today than it was during the Cold War.	28	19	0
b. US military power is more important today than it was during the Cold War.	72	81	1

Table 6.14. Using US military force

Which of these statements that contrast views about US foreign policy do you agree with the most?	1999 %	2001 %	Code
a. Unless it is directly attacked, the US should use military force only when it is authorized by the United Nations.	53	46	0
b. The US should use military force when the US thinks it is necessary, even if the United Nations does not authorize it.	47	54	1

vironment at the time of the survey was more dangerous for the United States than that which existed during the Cold War.[17] And, as shown in table 6.13, almost three out of four in 1999 and more than eight out of ten in 2001 consider US military power to be more important at the time of the survey than during the Cold War. A small majority of respondents in 2001 agree more with the statement that the United States should use military force when it considers force necessary, even if the United Nations does not authorize it. This was a change from 1999, when the proportions identifying with each statement in table 6.14 are reversed. The changes in proportions for each of the three pairs of questions between 1999 and 2001 are statistically significant.[18]

Our next two pairs of statements contrast views about the efficacy of nuclear deterrence and the utility of nuclear weapons. We compare the statements and responses to them in tables 6.15 and 6.16.

Six out of ten participants in 1999 and in 2001 agree most with the statement in table 6.15 that nuclear deterrence helps prevent large-scale wars. Similar proportions in both years also identify most with the statement in table 6.16 that in addition to deterring the use of nuclear weapons by others, US nuclear capabilities are useful for winning wars should deterrence fail. While these statements represent majority affinities, there are sizable minorities of approximately 40 percent who disagree, and public views about the efficacy of US nuclear weapons for deterrence and for winning wars clearly are divided. Differences across the two time periods for each pair of statements are not statistically significant.

In table 6.17 we compare reactions to opposing statements about comparative risks and benefits of US nuclear weapons, and in table 6.18 we con-

Table 6.15. Efficacy of nuclear deterrence

Which of these statements that contrast views about nuclear deterrence do you agree with the most?	1999 %	2001 %	Code
a. Nuclear deterrence is dangerous, unstable, and does not prevent war.	40	40	0
b. Nuclear deterrence is safe, stable, and prevents large conflicts like World Wars I and II.	60	60	1

Table 6.16. Utility of US nuclear weapons

Which of these statements that contrast views about the uses of nuclear weapons do you agree with the most?	1999 %	2001 %	Code
a. US nuclear weapons have no use except for deterring others from using their nuclear weapons against us.	42	40	0
b. US nuclear weapons are useful both for deterring others from using their nuclear weapons against us and for winning wars if necessary.	58	60	1

Table 6.17. Risks vs. benefits of the US nuclear arsenal

Which of these statements that contrast views about risks and benefits of the US nuclear arsenal do you agree with the most?	1999 %	2001 %	Code
a. The US nuclear arsenal deters attacks and ensures our security, and these benefits far outweigh any risks from US nuclear weapons.	73	79	1
b. The US nuclear arsenal threatens civilization and cannot be safely managed, and these risks far outweigh any benefits from US nuclear weapons.	27	21	0

Table 6.18. Nuclear weapons and US values

Which of these statements that contrast views about US nuclear weapons and personal values do you agree with the most?	1999 %	2001 %	Code
a. US nuclear weapons threaten institutions that support freedom, self-determination, and human rights.	28	19	0
b. US nuclear weapons protect institutions that support freedom, self-determination, and human rights.	72	81	1

trast responses to conflicting statements about whether US nuclear weapons threaten or protect key societal values.

Substantial majorities of respondents in each period agree most with the statements that the benefits of US nuclear weapons outweigh associated risks and that US nuclear weapons protect rather than threaten key societal values. For each question, increases in majority views between 1999 and 2001 are statistically significant.

Our final two pairs of statements contrast important but conceptually distinct dimensions of the issue of nuclear abolition. In table 6.19, we show responses to two contrasting statements about the desirability of eliminating all nuclear weapons; in table 6.20, we show preferences for contrasting statements about the feasibility of eliminating all nuclear weapons.

More than 60 percent of participants in both surveys agree that a world without nuclear weapons would be safer than one with nuclear weapons, and the percentage agreeing with that assertion is statistically significantly lower in 2001 than in 1999. When the issue shifts to the *feasibility* of eliminating all nuclear weapons, more than 80 percent of participants in both surveys agree

Table 6.19. Desirability of eliminating all nuclear weapons

Which of these statements that contrast views about the desirability of a world without nuclear weapons do you agree with most?	1999 %	2001 %	Code
a. If all nuclear weapons were eliminated, the world would be safer, because wars would be less likely to destroy civilization.	69	63	0
b. If all nuclear weapons were eliminated, the world would be more dangerous, because large conflicts like World Wars I and II would be more likely.	31	37	1

Table 6.20. Feasibility of eliminating all nuclear weapons

Which of these statements that contrast views about eliminating nuclear weapons worldwide do you agree with the most?	1999 %	2001 %	Code
a. Eliminating all nuclear weapons worldwide can be achieved if the US sets the example and uses its influence to persuade other countries.	16	13	0
b. Eliminating all nuclear weapons worldwide cannot be achieved, because knowledge about them is too widespread, and the US cannot prevent others from acquiring them.	84	87	1

most with the statement that nuclear abolition cannot be achieved because knowledge about nuclear weapons is too widespread. Though the proportion in 2001 choosing that statement is somewhat higher than in 1999, the difference does not reach statistical significance at the 95 percent confidence level.

The above nine pairs of contrasting statements are designed to present opposing views about a range of domain beliefs we hypothesize to be related to nuclear security policy preferences. When the scores associated with responses to each pair of statements are summed, they provide a policy score for each respondent on a ten-point scale (zero to nine). A score of zero indicates a "nuclear dove" preference for each of the following statements.

Today the world is a *less* dangerous place for the US than it was during the Cold War.

US military power is *less* important today than it was during the Cold War.

Unless it is directly attacked, the US should use military force only when it is authorized by the United Nations.

Nuclear deterrence is dangerous, unstable, and does not prevent war.

US nuclear weapons have no use except for deterring others from using their nuclear weapons against us.

The US nuclear arsenal threatens civilization and cannot be safely managed, and these *risks* far outweigh any *benefits* from US nuclear weapons.

US nuclear weapons *threaten* institutions that support freedom, self-determination, and human rights.

If all nuclear weapons were eliminated, the world would be safer, because wars would be less likely to destroy civilization.

Eliminating all nuclear weapons worldwide can be achieved if the US sets the example and uses its influence to persuade other countries.

A score of nine indicates a "nuclear hawk" preference for each of the following statements.

Today the world is a *more* dangerous place for the US than it was during the Cold War.

US military power is *more* important today than it was during the Cold War.

The US should use military force when the US thinks it is necessary, even if the United Nations does not authorize it.

Nuclear deterrence is safe, stable, and prevents large conflicts like World Wars I and II.

US nuclear weapons are useful both for deterring others from using their nuclear weapons against us and for winning wars if necessary.

The US nuclear arsenal deters attacks and ensures our security, and these *benefits* far outweigh any *risks* from US nuclear weapons.

US nuclear weapons *protect* institutions that support freedom, self-determination, and human rights.

If all nuclear weapons were eliminated, the world would be more dangerous, because large conflicts like World Wars I and II would be more likely.

Eliminating all nuclear weapons worldwide cannot be achieved, because knowledge about them is too widespread, and the US cannot prevent others from acquiring them.

Each participant who expresses a preference for one of the statements in each of the nine pairs of contrasting beliefs is placed on the nuclear security policy scale ranging from those most critical of establishmentarian beliefs about nuclear security (a "nuclear dove" with a value of zero) to those most supportive of conventional beliefs about nuclear security (a "nuclear hawk" with a value of nine).[19] We compare distributions of scores and mean values for 1999 and 2001 in figure 6.6.

Response patterns in 2001, immediately following the terrorist attacks of 9/11, clearly are more heavily weighted toward the hawkish end of the scale than responses in 1999. Though the modal values for both surveys is seven, the three highest scale values (7–9) are selected by 51 percent of participants in 2001, compared to 39 percent of their predecessors in 1999.

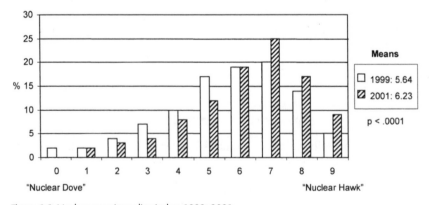

Figure 6.6. Nuclear security policy index, 1999–2001

Table 6.21. Relating the nuclear security policy index to policy preferences, 1999–2001 (separate bivariate regressions: $^*p < .05;$ $^\dagger p < .01;$ $^\ddagger p < .001$)

Issue (dependent variable)	1999 coefficients (R^2)	2001 coefficients (R^2)
Support for US participating in comprehensive test ban (Q31: 1 = strongly oppose↔7 = strongly support)	−.254‡ (.060)	−.307‡ (.073)
Importance of retaining US nuclear weapons today (Q36: 0 = not at all important↔10 = extremely important)	.575‡ (.211)	.548‡ (.186)
Spending for developing/testing new US nuclear weapons (Q40: 1 = substantially decrease↔7 = substantially increase)	.279‡ (.111)	.259‡ (.074)
Spending for maintaining existing US nuclear weapons (Q41: 1 = substantially decrease↔7 = substantially increase)	.324‡ (.147)	.340‡ (.151)
Spending for US nuclear weapons infrastructure (Q44: 1 = substantially decrease↔7 = substantially increase)	.389‡ (.173)	.349‡ (.122)
Minimum acceptable number of US nuclear weapons (Q27: scale reversed: 1 = none↔15 = 6,500–7,000)	.613‡ (.068)	.517‡ (.038)
Preference for building US ballistic missile defenses (Q59: 1 = definitely should not build↔7 = definitely should build)	.271‡ (.089)	.300‡ (.084)

The nuclear security policy index of hawks and doves provides a broad policy core measure for evaluating the structure of public opinion. We employ the index as the independent variable in separate bivariate regressions to predict specific preferences about nuclear security policy options. We summarize regression results in table 6.21.

Note the consistency with which the nuclear security policy index predicts specific policy preferences in both surveys. As scores increase (become more hawkish), support for a nuclear test ban treaty declines, while support for investments in nuclear weapons capabilities, the minimum acceptable number of US nuclear weapons, and support for ballistic missile defenses grow.

Thus, whether we use domain-level beliefs about risks and benefits of nuclear weapons or we employ an index of a wider array of domain-level views about nuclear security, results show systematic relationships between domain beliefs and lower-level beliefs about specific policy choices. These results are consistent with revisionist arguments that mass publics employ hierarchically organized beliefs to shape policy preferences.

Mapping Mass Belief Structures

In this section, we integrate public beliefs about nuclear security and terrorism into structural patterns by employing causal modeling techniques to measure standardized linkages among respondents' demographic characteristics, core beliefs, domain beliefs, and policy preferences about nuclear security and terrorism.

Modeling Beliefs about Nuclear Security

To provide the highest level of integration, we combine the data from our six national surveys of the US general public between 1993 and 2003 into a single database used to examine overall relationships among hierarchical patterns of beliefs relating to nuclear security. The results, graphically depicted in figures 6.7 and 6.8, show direct and indirect effects over time of different levels of dispositions on two key dependent variables: the importance of retaining US nuclear weapons today (Q36) and willingness to invest in nuclear weapons infrastructure for the future (Q44).

Based on demographic relationships reported in chapter 5, we expect individual respondent attributes of age, gender, education, income, and race/ethnicity to provide a predispositional context influencing core beliefs such as ideology and domain beliefs about relative risks and benefits of nuclear weapons. For example, data from each of our surveys show that women attribute statistically significantly greater external and domestic risks to nuclear weapons than do men. Based on bivariate regressions, we also expect that some demographic influences may be strong enough to affect specific policy preferences directly.

The bivariate and multivariate relationships shown above between core beliefs about ideology, domain beliefs about benefits and risks associated with nuclear security, and specific policy preferences suggest patterns of causal influences. For example, assessments of benefits associated with US nuclear weapons increase systematically with increasingly conservative ideological views. We also find positive bivariate relationships between political conservatism and increasing support for US nuclear weapons. We anticipate similar causal patterns in our modeling.

In each of our surveys we find that domain-level beliefs about nuclear weapons risks and benefits relate systematically, but not proportionally, to policy and spending preferences about nuclear security. For example, beliefs about benefits associated with US nuclear weapons are more strongly related to policy preferences than are beliefs about risks associated with others' nuclear weapons or our own nuclear arsenal.

Based on these findings, we construct a causal model integrating demographic influences, core ideological beliefs, and domain beliefs about nuclear benefits and risks to help explain beliefs about the importance of retaining US nuclear weapons. Using combined data from all six national surveys, we calculate sequential multivariate regressions and identify standardized coefficients among those relationships that are statistically significant. In the first stage, we use age, gender (a dummy variable measuring the influence of being male), education (a dummy variable measuring the influence of a college education), income, and race/ethnicity (a dummy variable measuring the influence of being Native American, African American, or Hispanic) as independent variables in multiple regressions to explain variation in core beliefs about political ideology.[20] In the second stage, we combine the same demographic predispositions with core ideological beliefs as independent variables to explain domain beliefs about risks and benefits of nuclear weapons. In the third stage, we complete the model by combining demographic attributes, ideology, and our nuclear risk and benefit indices as independent variables to explain beliefs about retaining nuclear weapons (figure 6.7) and support for investing in nuclear weapons infrastructure (figure 6.8). This iterative process allows us to see which independent variables act through intermediate variables and which act directly on our final dependent variables.

Both causal models show only those statistical relationships that are significant at the 95 percent confidence level. The direction and size of the

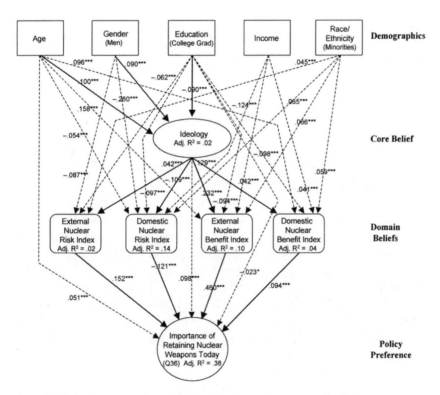

Figure 6.7. Estimating causes of variation in beliefs about retaining US nuclear weapons (combined data, 1993–2003)

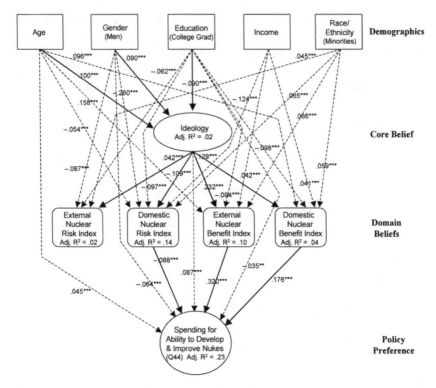

Figure 6.8. Estimating causes of variation in preferences for nuclear weapons investments (combined data, 1993–2003)

standardized regression coefficients are interpreted as follows: a change of one standard deviation in the independent variable produces the fractional change of a standard deviation in the dependent variable represented by the standardized coefficient. For example, a standardized coefficient of 0.25 means that a change of one standard deviation in the independent variable results in a change of 0.25 standard deviations in the dependent variable. In the case of a dummy variable, the coefficient represents the effect of the attribute coded as a value of one on the dependent variable. Because the coefficients are all standardized, they can be compared. Explanatory powers are shown as adjusted R^2 values. Solid lines represent first-order relationships between independent and dependent variables in adjacent echelons of the models; dashed lines depict relationships extending beyond adjacent echelons. We begin in figure 6.7 by graphically modeling beliefs about the importance of retaining US nuclear weapons today.

The model is consistent with the argument that public belief systems are structured in a hierarchical pattern, with core beliefs influencing (or constraining) policy domain beliefs which, in turn, influence more specific policy preferences. The causal paths evident in the model suggest the following conclusions.

Age

The direct effects of an increase of one standard deviation in respondent age causes increases of 0.100 standard deviations in ideology (more conservative), 0.158 in external nuclear weapons benefits, 0.096 in beliefs about the domestic benefits of nuclear weapons, and 0.051 in assessed importance of retaining US nuclear weapons. Also, as age increases one standard deviation, assessed domestic risks of managing the US nuclear arsenal decline by −0.054 standard deviations.

Gender

Direct effects of gender are limited to ideological beliefs and beliefs about external and domestic nuclear risks. Being male is associated with an increase of 0.090 standard deviations in conservatism, a decrease of −0.087 in external risk beliefs, and a decrease of −0.260 in beliefs about domestic nuclear risks.

Education

Level of education exerts unique effects on belief structures by being the only predictor variable that has a direct influence on all higher-level beliefs in the model. Having a college degree results in reductions of the following magnitudes in each of the belief items: −0.090 standard deviations in ideology (more liberal); −0.062 in external nuclear risk assessments; −0.097 in beliefs about domestic nuclear risks; −0.094 in external nuclear benefits; −0.098 in domestic nuclear benefits; and the importance of retaining US nuclear weapons declines by −0.023 standard deviations.

Income

An increase of one standard deviation in annual household income is associated with an increase of 0.042 standard deviations on our external nuclear benefit index, and 0.041 on our index of domestic nuclear benefits. Finally, as income increases, assessments of domestic nuclear risks decrease by −0.124 standard deviations.

Race

Being American Indian, African American, or Hispanic is positively related to beliefs about external (0.045) and domestic (0.065) nuclear risks, as well as external (0.066) and domestic (0.059) nuclear benefits.

Ideology

As ideological beliefs increase one standard deviation (more conservative), assessments of external nuclear risks increase 0.042 standard deviations, external nuclear benefits increase 0.232, domestic nuclear benefits increase 0.129, and the importance of retaining nuclear weapons increases 0.098 standard deviations. Increasing conservatism is related negatively to beliefs about domestic nuclear weapons risks (−0.109).

Domain Beliefs about Nuclear Weapons Risks and Benefits

As our index of estimates about external risks stemming from others' nuclear weapons capabilities increases one standard deviation, the importance of retaining nuclear weapons increases 0.152 standard deviations. Conversely, as estimates of domestic risks from managing our own nuclear arsenal increase, support for retaining nuclear weapons declines −0.121. The importance of retaining nuclear weapons increases with both nuclear benefit indices (0.460 for external benefits and 0.094 for domestic benefits).

This model illustrates how different levels of selected beliefs are structured in relationship to a specific policy issue. Together, demographics and our measures of core and domain beliefs explain about 38 percent of variation in the importance respondents place on retaining US nuclear weapons today.

To assess another kind of policy issue, in figure 6.8 we illustrate the same belief structure as it relates to public judgments of how spending should change for maintaining the ability to develop and improve US nuclear weapons in the future (investment in nuclear weapons infrastructure).

Of course, standardized relationships among demographics, ideology, and domain beliefs remain the same, but standardized relationships between those categories and the dependent variable shift noticeably. Whereas in the previous model, gender is not directly related to the final dependent variable, in this model, being male is associated negatively (−0.064) with support for increasing spending for nuclear weapons infrastructure. At the domain level of beliefs, external nuclear risk is not predictive of willingness to invest in future nuclear weapons capabilities. Overall, this model explains about 23 percent of the variation in the dependent variable.

Modeling Beliefs about Terrorism

Next we analyze causal relationships among respondent beliefs about terrorism. Though we did not broadly investigate terrorism in all of our surveys, we made extensive inquiries in our 2001 and 2003 studies, and we combine data from those surveys for modeling beliefs about terrorism. Following our previous models of predispositions, we begin with demographic attributes and core beliefs about ideology. For measures of domain beliefs, we employ two indices described in chapter 4. Our terrorism threat index (figure 4.4) combines assessments of the current and future threat of nuclear terrorism anywhere in the world with views of the overall threat of all kinds of terrorism occurring in the United States (questions 17, 18, and 65). The terrorism threat index is expressed on a scale from zero (no threat) to ten (extreme threat). Our second measure of domain beliefs about terrorism is provided by composite assessments of the potential for government to prevent future acts of terrorism. As described in chapter 4 (figure 4.12), our preventing terrorism index is composed of responses to questions 66–68, and is expressed on a scale from one (minimum confidence that government can stop terrorism) to seven (maximum confidence that government can and must stop terrorism).

Employing our measures of core dispositions and our two indices of domain beliefs about the threat of terrorism and the potential for preventing it, we analyze causal relationships among two dependent variables: an index of beliefs about foreign policies for responding to acts of terrorism, and an index of beliefs about domestic policies for preventing terrorism.

The dependent variable for our first model is the terrorism response index described in chapter 4 and shown in figure 4.23. It is predicated on the determination, to a high degree of confidence, that the target country actively participated in the 9/11 attacks by providing personnel or training to the terrorists. Respondents considered a range of possible response options represented by the following scale values: (0) no response; (1) strong diplomatic and political pressures; (2) strong economic and trade sanctions; (3) air strikes using conventionally armed weapons such as bombs and cruise missiles; (4) military invasion; and (5) nuclear retaliation. We model combined responses from 2001 and 2003 in figure 6.9.

Causal paths suggest the following conclusions.

Age

An increase of one standard deviation in age causes an increase of 0.100 standard deviations in ideology (more conservative) and a decrease of −0.058 standard deviations in the dependent variable; age is not linked directly to either measure of domain beliefs.

Gender

Gender exerts direct causal effects on each of our measures of core and domain beliefs as well as preferences for responding to terrorism. Being male causes an increase of 0.081 standard deviations in ideology, a reduction of −0.154 standard deviations in composite assessments of the threat of terrorism, a decrease of −0.072 in our index of beliefs about preventing terrorism,

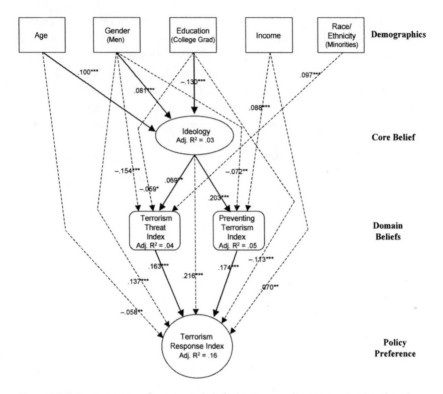

Figure 6.9. Estimating causes of variation in beliefs about responding to terrorism (combined data, 2001–2003)

and an increase of 0.137 standard deviations in the terrorism response index (more willing to use force).

Education

Level of education is linked directly to ideology, measures of the threat of terrorism, and preferences for responding. Having a college education causes ideology to decline by –0.130 (more liberal), the terrorism threat index to decrease by –0.059 (lower assessed threat), and the terrorism response index to decline by –0.113 standard deviations (less willing to use force).

Income

Annual household income is linked directly only to the preventing terrorism index and the response index. As income increases one standard deviation, confidence that government can stop terrorism increases by 0.088, and willingness to use more forceful responses to terrorism increases 0.070 standard deviations.

Race

Being American Indian, African American, or Hispanic is linked directly in our model only to assessments of the threat of terrorism, which increases 0.097 standard deviations.

Ideology

More politically conservative views are linked directly to greater assessments of the threat of terrorism (0.069), greater confidence in government's abilities to stop terrorism (0.203), and support for more forceful responses to acts of terrorism (0.216).

Domain Beliefs

Both domain measures exert systematic causal effects on our dependent variable. As composite assessments of the threat of terrorism increase one standard deviation, the terrorism response index increases 0.163, and as confidence in government's abilities to prevent terrorism increases one standard deviation, the response index increases 0.174 standard deviations. Together, demographic attributes and our core and domain belief measures explain about 16 percent of variation in preferences for how to respond to acts of terrorism.

This model addresses preferences about external policies in response to terrorism, but does not address preferences about domestic policies to prevent terrorism. We turn to that issue in our final causal model shown in figure 6.10 where the dependent variable is our index of support for domestic measures for preventing future terrorist acts. As described in chapter 4 and illustrated in figure 4.22, our domestic intrusion index incorporates preferences for nine policy options encompassing varying levels of intrusiveness, and is expressed on a continuous scale where one means the options are strongly opposed and seven means they are strongly supported.

Unlike the previous model, age is linked directly to the final dependent variable, which increases by 0.081 standard deviations. Gender again is linked directly with all three levels of beliefs, with men being more politically conservative, perceiving lower threats, being less confident about stopping terrorism, and being less willing to trade off individual prerogatives for more security (−0.067). Again, education is negatively linked to ideology, estimates of terrorist threats, and willingness to tolerate intrusions (−0.157). Income exerts positive effects on confidence in preventing terrorism, and being a member of a minority is related positively to the terrorism threat index and to the dependent variable (0.042). Increasing conservatism is related positively to threat assessments, confidence in preventing terrorism, and willingness to accept intrusive measures to prevent terrorism (0.248). Similarly, both do-

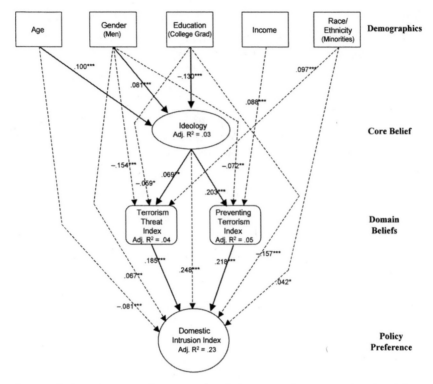

Figure 6.10. Estimating causes of variation in beliefs about preventing terrorism (combined data, 2001–2003)

main measures exert positive causal influence on the dependent variable. The greater the perceived threat of terrorism, or the more optimistic one is that government can successfully fight terrorists, the greater the willingness to accept an array of intrusive measures to reduce the threat of terrorism.

The Coherence of Public Beliefs

We began this chapter by noting the critical importance of coherence in public opinion. One of the key points of agreement between traditional and revisionist theories is that coherence is partially a function of systematic structures of beliefs, and that coherence is a requisite for reasoned opinions. To a significant extent, theoretical arguments about the abilities of mass publics to contribute to making collective decisions in complex policy domains, such as nuclear security or terrorism, depend on evidence about the coherence of mass opinions. Rather than the confused and disjointed ramblings of disinterested and disengaged publics characterized by traditional assumptions about mass opinions, we document a high degree of consistency and connectedness among the views of Americans about nuclear security and terrorism. Several dimensions of public coherence are particularly noteworthy.

Temporal Coherence

The stability of public views about nuclear security over time is remarkable. That is not to suggest that mass views do not evolve, but changes in views about nuclear security largely are consistent in direction and similar in magnitude during a turbulent period of great change in international relationships and threats. The changes we measure appear to be logically and rationally connected to the evolving post–Cold War security environment, and they parallel changes in elite views on the same issues.[21] During the period of our measurements (1993–2003), we find little evidence of erratic and volatile changes. The consistency of composite measures of nuclear weapons risks and benefits and valuations of nuclear deterrence reported in chapters 2 and 3 illustrate the stability of public views over time. The directional consistency and magnitude of changes in views about nuclear security policies reported in chapter 3 provide reliable indications about key trends in evolving sentiments. Overall, we find that public beliefs about nuclear security exhibit a high degree of temporal coherence.

Within that stability, however, there appear to be two notable exceptions in which significant underlying changes become apparent in the structure of public beliefs over the past decade. First, the strength of ideology and partisanship as predictors of nuclear security policy preferences increases markedly over the period of our analysis. These are evident in the growing magnitudes of the estimated relationships, and the changes themselves are statistically significant. Second, the ways in which the mass public relates domain beliefs and policy preferences has evolved. Perceptions of external nuclear risks (risks posed by others' nuclear weapons) have diminishing predictive power for an array of policy preferences, while assessments of external nuclear benefits (benefits of US nuclear weapons for achieving national objectives) remain positive and predictive of policy preferences. In part, we believe, this latter change reflects growing public understanding of the complexity of coming to terms with external nuclear risks: to some, high risks imply the need for greater nuclear deterrence, while to others they bring greater urgency to reducing the US nuclear arsenal. In short, the lens through which the public views nuclear security has become both more partisan and more subtle.

Topical Coherence

We also document persistent connections among views about complex security topics. For example, we find logically consistent linkages between assessments of risks and benefits of nuclear weapons and policy judgments about issues such as retaining and investing in US nuclear weapons capabilities, preferences for the size of the US nuclear arsenal, and support for strategic arms control. In another example, most respondents are not confused about the two dimensions of nuclear abolition. Many think a world free of nuclear weapons is desirable, but most remain unconvinced that it is feasible in the foreseeable future. They support reducing the size of the nuclear weapons stockpile, but going to zero is a qualitatively different proposal currently not supported by most Americans we surveyed. Similarly, when the topic is terrorism, we find the same kinds of logical linkages between assessments of the threat of terrorism, preferences for responding to terrorist acts, and support for domestic measures to prevent future acts of terrorism. Though not discussed in this book, our research into public opinions on energy issues, another complex topic, reveals the same kinds of coherence in views on the risks and benefits of nuclear energy and preferences for future energy development (Jenkins-Smith and Herron 2002a; Jenkins-Smith and Herron 2002b; Jenkins-Smith, Mitchell, and Herron 2004). In these and other areas, we find a logical consistency among views about related dimensions of different issue domains that indicates strong topical coherence.

Integrative Coherence

The systematic connections we document between and among individuals' demographic characteristics, their hierarchically structured beliefs, and their preferences about complex security issues show how ordinary citizens coherently integrate predispositions, assessments, beliefs, and policy choices. In addition to measuring and reporting policy-relevant views about specific issues, we also investigate statistical relationships among key variables that give insights into why and how views about nuclear security and terrorism are shaped. Our findings indicate a high degree of coherence in the ways in which publics integrate different dimensions that affect opinion formation and change at the individual level. For example, women consistently assess risks and threats higher than do men, and men consistently are more willing to employ military force. Assessments of threats and policy preferences for prevention or response are systematically differentiated by levels of formal education. Ideological beliefs are predictably related to views about security and related policy preferences. At the individual level, most of our respondents exhibit the ability to integrate personal predispositions, beliefs, experience, assessments of reality, and evaluations of policy alternatives with a coherence that provides reasonable and stable preferences. These abilities are much more in line with revisionist theory about public capacities than with traditional assumptions.

Certainly we have not been able to definitively map all these relationships. But for those we have studied, the consistency with which key elements are integrated suggests that even though most members of the general public do not possess technical knowledge about nuclear weapons designs, nuclear deterrence, delivery systems, foreign policy, terrorism, and many other aspects of security, they nevertheless manage to connect important "dots" that form a security picture with a high degree of integrative coherence.

7 ‖ MAKING SENSE OF PUBLIC BELIEFS AND PREFERENCES ABOUT SECURITY POLICY

THIS BOOK HAS presented a description of the American public's beliefs and preferences concerning nuclear security and terrorism, and analyzed the consistency and coherence of these beliefs over a decade bridging the 1990s to the new century. Our objectives have been twofold. First, we sought to describe the evolution of American citizens' thinking about strategic security issues over the seminal decade that immediately followed the collapse of the Soviet Union and the end of the Cold War and that encompassed the emergence of terrorism as a potent and highly salient threat to the US homeland. Second, we attempted to use our measures of public beliefs on security issues to address some of the most fundamental questions about the characteristics of public belief systems, with implications for the role of public opinion in democratic governance. In an era in which American foreign policy aggressively seeks to spread democracy and its benefits across the globe, arguments about the capacities of publics to constructively engage in setting the course of public policy loom large. For that reason, attending to the trenchant and persistent criticisms of the prospects for meaningful democratic participation in our own backyard is of no small importance.

Trends in Public Opinion on Nuclear Security

The complexity of nuclear security policy, compounded by a history of elite dominance in policymaking conducted largely under a shroud of secrecy, might seem to negate the utility of attending to mass beliefs and opinions on the subject. Worse yet, uninformed and poorly considered opinions might prove dangerous, particularly in the face of national threats such as those posed by rogue nations with nuclear arms or aggressive transnational terror organizations. Indeed, in the modern security environment, policymakers can ill afford to be stampeded by the "trampling and the roar of a bewildered herd," as Walter Lippmann characterized public opinion at its worst (1925, 155).

In our view, these concerns naturally call for an assessment of public opinion over the past turbulent decade and how it has changed over that time. With that in mind, we detail the evolution of public beliefs and preferences about security in chapters 2 through 4. In this closing chapter, we briefly recap the primary trends as we have identified them in our series of six biennial surveys of the American public. We then seek to place the substance of public beliefs within the context of the debate among policy experts about policy decisions concerning nuclear security and terrorism.

Trends in Assessments of the Strategic Environment

Most participants in our surveys do not consider US or international security to have improved substantially since the end of the Cold War. An opposite trend is apparent as mean ratings of US and international security decrease significantly between 1995 and 2003. Public estimates of the threats posed by Russia's nuclear weapons decline significantly, but overall perceptions of systemic nuclear threats do not lessen over the decade of our surveys. Current and projected nuclear threats to US security posed by China are judged to be significantly higher than nuclear threats from Russia, and in the views of the American public, China has replaced Russia as the chief state-level nuclear protagonist.

Trends in Views of Nuclear Weapons Risks and Benefits

Employing an index of six questions measuring risks of nuclear conflict, nuclear proliferation, and nuclear terrorism, composite measurements confirm that mean public judgments of external nuclear risks have not declined appreciably thus far in the post–Cold War era. Public assessments of external nuclear risks remain well above midscale and are quite steady across the six surveys. The absence of a substantial decline in external nuclear risk assessments twelve years into the post–Cold War period indicates that the end of the nuclear standoff between the United States and the Soviet Union has not reduced appreciably the American people's concerns about other external nuclear threats. Over the same period, public estimates of the risks associated with managing our own nuclear arsenal decline approximately 19 percent to an average that is below midscale.

Contrary to our initial expectations, composite measures of public beliefs about the benefits of US nuclear weapons for achieving national objectives and deterring nuclear threats hold relatively steady during our decade of surveys. Thus far into the new security environment, Americans have yet to devalue the benefits of the US nuclear arsenal. Domestically, trends in mean assessments of trade-offs between US nuclear and conventional military capabilities, economic benefits of defense-related jobs, and benefits of transferring defense technologies vary little, and our index of domestic nuclear benefits remains statistically unchanged over the decade of measurements.

Relevance of Nuclear Weapons

While many Americans consider a world without nuclear weapons to be desirable, most members of the public do not think it is feasible, and support for participating in an agreement to eliminate all nuclear weapons declines 9 percent during the course of our surveys. When asked to assess the importance of nuclear deterrence for preventing nuclear conflict during the Cold War, mean ratings are significantly higher in 2003 than when first measured in 1995. When asked to assess the importance of nuclear deterrence for preventing interstate nuclear conflict today, mean ratings in 2003 are statistically unchanged from 1995. When told to assume further nuclear proliferation in the future, mean assessments of the effectiveness of future nuclear deterrence are more modest (though they remain, on average, statistically unchanged from 1995 to 2003). Overall, while these measures reflect a continuing valuation by the American public of the importance and efficacy of US nuclear weapons for deterring the use of nuclear weapons by other countries, they also show that public views of the relative value of deterrence now versus that in the early Cold War period are changing. Given a world with increased nuclear proliferation, public perception of the importance of deterrence for preventing nuclear conflict between states has eroded slightly (but statistically significantly) over the decade of our surveys.

Changes in the mix of threats to which the nuclear arsenal may be applied as a deterrent and changes in potential substitutes for nuclear weapons as a means of deterrence have also registered with the public. In 1999, 2001, and 2003, we measured public evaluations of the importance of nuclear weapons for deterring other countries from using chemical or biological weapons against the United States. Though mean valuations are well above midscale, they decline significantly over the course of the surveys. In addition, the growing effectiveness of US precision-guided munitions ("smart bombs") seems to be increasing the view among some members of the public that conventionally armed precision munitions may partially offset or supplement nuclear weapons for purposes of deterrence. Though mean assessments of that potential remain below midscale, they increase significantly between 1999 and 2003.

Minimum Numbers of US Nuclear Weapons

In the view of most experts, US nuclear weapons must be considered in terms of capabilities, not just numbers, but most of our survey respondents support reducing the size of the US nuclear arsenal. When asked to identify the minimum number of US nuclear weapons they consider acceptable in the context of mutual and verifiable US and Russian reductions, about 15 to 20 percent consider zero US nuclear weapons to be acceptable, and between 10 to 15 percent want no reductions. The majority of respondents are distributed across the remaining thirteen categories representing increments of 500, with the median range falling between 1,500–2,000 in 1997 and 1999, jumping to 2,500–3,000 in 2001 immediately following 9/11, and declining to 500–1,000 by 2003. These median ranges suggest that most Americans are supportive of a much smaller US nuclear arsenal, but most do not favor eliminating all US nuclear weapons. Our findings also suggest that nonnuclear attacks such as 9/11 that extract a heavy toll in American lives may temporarily strengthen public valuation of US nuclear weapons, even though most Americans do not support their use in retaliation.

Nuclear Weapons Testing

We measure two dimensions relating to public views of underground nuclear weapons testing. In 1995 we began asking respondents to indicate whether the United States should participate in a treaty to ban nuclear testing, and we include the same question in each of our subsequent surveys. Responses show that while average public support for an international treaty to comprehensively ban all nuclear test explosions remains well above midscale in each survey, the level of support declines significantly between 1995 and 2003. The last US nuclear test explosion was conducted in 1992, and large investments have been made in a stockpile stewardship program to maintain the reliability of the US nuclear arsenal without full operational testing. In our 2001 and 2003 surveys, we asked participants to assess the importance of underground nuclear testing for assuring the safety and reliability of US nuclear weapons. Responses in both surveys are below midscale, on average, and the mean declines significantly between 2001 and 2003. These results suggest that as time elapses without US nuclear testing, members of the American public place less significance on a nuclear test ban treaty and, in the absence of contrary evidence, seem confident in US abilities to ensure stockpile reliability without testing.

National Missile Defenses

In 1999 we began asking a series of questions on national missile defenses that are repeated in 2001 and 2003. Roughly two-thirds of respondents in each of the three surveys did not know that at the time of the surveys the United States did not have national defenses against long-range ballistic missiles. After advising participants that the United States did not then have an operational system to shoot down such missiles, we presented brief, balanced arguments for and against missile defenses, followed by a short series of questions. Large pluralities of participants in each of our surveys agree with the statement that the US government has a responsibility to build a national missile defense system, but opinion is much more divided on whether money for such defenses would be better spent on other programs, and whether US missile defenses will lead to a new arms race with Russia and China. Despite countervailing considerations, when asked to make an overall judgment, more than two out of three respondents in each survey support building missile defenses.

Trends in Preferences for Nuclear Investments

We expected to chart declining support for nuclear investments paralleling what we predicted would be decreasing public valuation of nuclear weapons, but results were somewhat different. On average, the public prefers to decrease spending to develop and test new nuclear weapons over the entire decade, but the percentage supporting an increase in these expenditure rises from about 20 percent in 1993 and 1995 to nearly 30 percent in 2003. Initially, the public also prefers to decrease spending for maintaining the ability to develop and improve US nuclear weapons in the future, but by 2003 this shifts such that 55 percent support increasing such expenditures. And over the entire decade, a gradually growing majority supports increasing expenditures for maintaining and increasing the safety of the stockpile, and for training those who manage it. Substantially larger (and growing) majorities support increasing expenditures for preventing the spread of nuclear weapons and preventing nuclear terrorism. These trends are consistent with the evolving assessments of the risks and benefits of nuclear weapons discussed above.

Developing New Smaller-Yield Penetrating Warheads

Because of emerging debate about the need for new smaller-yield nuclear warheads that can penetrate to destroy deeply buried targets, we included a series of questions in 2003 to sample public reactions. Opinion is divided about whether new small-yield nuclear warheads would enhance deterrence, but most participants think such weapons would reduce attempts by others to protect high-value targets by burying them underground. While the survey shows initial support for new deep penetrating nuclear warheads (53 percent support, 38 percent oppose), support declines significantly (41 percent support, 49 percent oppose) when respondents are told to assume a need for underground testing of such warheads. This suggests that developing new US nuclear warheads may engender substantially more public resistance if nuclear test explosions are required.

Public Views on Terrorism

We examine public attitudes, beliefs, and preferences with regard to security from terrorism in chapter 4. Some of these measures are employed before and after the 9/11 terror attacks in New York and Washington, and therefore they permit examination of the change in public views associated with an unquestionably traumatic public event. We highlight those findings here.

Assessing the Threat of Terrorism

In absolute terms, mean assessments since 1993 of the current and future threat of *nuclear* terrorism register above 6.8 on a continuous scale from zero (no threat) to ten (extreme threat), and they remain comparatively stable over the series in relative terms. Compared to 1997, the mean threat of all forms of terrorism is rated significantly higher in 2003, but significantly lower than that reported immediately following 9/11.

Preventing Terrorism

Compared to measurements from 1995, respondents in 2003 are less likely to agree with assertions that government can stop determined terrorists only with unacceptable intrusions into individual rights and privacy, and that government must try to stop terrorism even if it does intrude on some people's rights. On average, participants support government actions to infiltrate and spy on organizations in the United States that are suspected of planning terrorist acts, and seizing weapons from such groups, even if they have not been convicted of any crime. Mean support for both measures is significantly higher in 2003 than when first asked in 1995, but significantly lower than that recorded in 2001 immediately following 9/11. Respondents differentiate between support for restrictions on speech and restrictions on the flow of information, with mean support for suppressing the advocacy of violence on radio or television placed below midscale, while mean support for banning bomb-making information from computer networks is above midscale. Interestingly, support for both options is lower in 2003 than in 2001 *or* 1995.

Support for domestic measures by government that intrude on privacy and other liberties varies significantly before, immediately following, and in the years after the 9/11 crisis. Support for national identification cards for all US citizens increases from 52 percent in 1995 to 67 percent in 2001, and then declines to 56 percent in 2003. Only 34 percent (down from 38 percent in 2001) of participants in 2003 support restricting domestic travel within the United States in an effort to prevent terrorism, while 58 percent (down from 62 percent in 2001) support restricting international travel to and from the United States if necessary. Mean support for expelling from the United States any citizen of another country suspected of planning a terrorist act, even if the person has not been convicted of any crime, declines significantly in 2003 from previous levels. Similarly, mean support for restricting immigration into the United States to prevent terrorism declines significantly between 2001 and 2003. In general, support in 2003 for a range of restrictions to individual prerogatives for the purposes of preventing terrorism declines substantially from the levels reported immediately following 9/11.

Responding to Terrorism

Support for US actions against countries that support terrorism varies from almost unanimous approval of diplomatic and economic sanctions, to majority support for air strikes and military invasion, to little support for using US nuclear weapons. Overall, support for military options declines significantly in 2003 from levels recorded in the aftermath of 9/11. Respondents consistently prefer that the United States have a very high degree of certainty of culpability before using military force against a country suspected of supporting terrorists.

Evaluating the War on Terrorism

On average, participants in 2003 give positive marks to US efforts to improve airport security and to overall progress in the war on terrorism to date, but are less sure about whether the government can prevent all large-scale terrorist attacks against the United States in the next five years. Most respondents are optimistic about eventually "winning" the war on terrorism, but consider it a long-term struggle in which it could take twenty years to prevail.

Behavioral Implications of Terrorism

Most respondents in 2003 agree that terrorism causes Americans to be more fearful and suspicious and to forfeit certain rights and freedoms. However, most participants deny that terrorism influences their willingness to travel or to assemble.

Evaluating Public Opinion

In what way can the observed content and trends in public opinion inform the debate over the role of public opinion in democratic governance? Such an evaluation is necessarily somewhat treacherous, in part because distributions of beliefs from samples of the public over a decade provide an enormous canvas from which to find confirmation for competing positions, and in part because consensus on definitive criteria for evaluating public beliefs is quite elusive.[1]

Some support for the traditionalist perspective can be found in the data and trends discussed in this book. On some critical issues, the public is badly and persistently misinformed.[2] The issue of ballistic missile defenses, which has garnered considerable policy attention over the period preceding the 2000 presidential campaign through the present, provides a prime example. In our 1999 survey, 63 percent of respondents wrongly believe that the United States has an operational defensive system for shooting down long-range ballistic missiles. In both the 2001 and 2003 surveys, approximately 60 percent of respondents persist in this incorrect belief despite substantial press coverage to the contrary.[3] One can also point to the "soft" or labile quality of public preferences on other important issues, in which substantial variation in expressed opinion results from changing considerations or the introduction of counterarguments. Consider stated preferences for developing new nuclear weapons designed for attacking deeply buried bunkers and weapons sites. When asked in our 2003 survey whether, on balance, the United States should build such weapons, a majority of 53 percent say it should. But when asked to consider that such development might require the resumption of nuclear testing, support for developing new nuclear weapons drops to 41 percent. This kind of instability in policy preferences, and susceptibility to substantial change as alternative considerations are raised, underlies much of the traditionalists' concerns about the role of public opinion in policy formation. Indeed, in assessing the prospects for a meaningful public role in complex democratic decisions, Yankelovich (1991) argues that the *quality* of public beliefs can be assessed in part by the firmness and consistency of public views, and he identifies different stages in issue maturation as opinions solidify. Thus, malleable public responses to the questions on new and more specialized nuclear weapons might be taken as evidence of poor-quality public opinion, or they might reflect the early stages of opinion formation.

Ample grounds also can be found for reaffirming the traditionalist perspective based on the substantive content of public opinion, though on these grounds the evaluation necessarily takes on a more overtly normative tone. A security "hawk," for example, might be alarmed at the broad willingness of the public to reduce substantially the size of the US nuclear stockpile despite growing agreement that the stockpile provides significant security and foreign policy benefits. Moreover, declining support for domestic and international measures to fight terrorism, as 9/11 fades from immediate memory, might be taken as evidence of an irresolute and even irresponsible public unwilling to bear the costs and inconveniences of assuring security. A security "dove," on the other hand, would likely find persistent public pessimism about the feasibility of nuclear abolition to be unwise. The widely held public view that it is important to retain a nuclear arsenal (even if a smaller one), and the eroding support for treaty provisions that call for eventual abolition of nuclear weapons and weapons testing, could all be taken by some elites as evidence of ill-considered opinion.

In combination, the identification of "defective" substantive policy positions, evidence of policy ignorance, and malleable preferences would seem to justify skepticism about the contributions of the public to reasoned policymaking. But in our view, such a judgment would be inaccurate and misleading.

A reasonable and balanced evaluation of public opinion on security policy over the measured decade requires at least three distinct strands of analysis. First, on the tricky issue of substantive credibility, one needs to compare the weight (or central tendency) of public opinion with a valid external criterion. Second, one would evaluate change over time in public beliefs relative to both stability and measured change in response to policy-relevant events. And third, one would look for reasonable structure within public beliefs, such that core values, policy core beliefs, and policy preferences are related in consistent and sensible ways. We undertake each of these analyses in turn.

Comparing Elite and Mass Beliefs about Nuclear Security

Given that security policy choices are strongly contested even among policy specialists, it makes little sense to compare what the public believes with a preferred or ideal set of policy positions. Instead, we opt to compare the central tendencies of public beliefs and preferences with the range of positions taken by informed specialists on the central nuclear policy issue: the retention and role of US nuclear weapons. If beliefs of contending policy experts bracket those of the public, then it is difficult to argue that public opinion is unreasoned or irresponsible. In the following discussion, we briefly set the context of a critical debate, sketch two paths of elite arguments, and orient public views on the central issue of the future of US nuclear weapons.

The Nuclear Security Policy Context

The end of the Cold War, formalized by the dissolution of the USSR on December 31, 1991, marked the beginning of a new international security environment warranting renewed examination of US nuclear security policies. Nuclear restructuring in the early post–Cold War years was presaged by the Strategic Arms Reduction Treaty (START), signed in July 1991, which called for the elimination of almost half of the nuclear warheads carried by US and Soviet ballistic missiles. By January 1993, it was supplanted by the START II treaty that committed the United States and Russia to reduce long-range nuclear weapons to 3,000–3,500 and phase out all missiles with multiple warheads. The 1991 Presidential Nuclear Initiative unilaterally eliminated the entire inventory of US ground-launched "nonstrategic" (tactical) nuclear weapons, removed all tactical nuclear weapons from surface ships, attack submarines, and land-based naval aircraft bases, removed US strategic bombers from alert, and took several other steps to reduce nuclear forces and their alert postures. A second Presidential Nuclear Initiative in January 1992 took further unilateral steps to curtail production of US nuclear bombers and land- and sea-based strategic missiles.

Elsewhere, South Africa announced in 1991 that it had successfully developed nuclear weapons and subsequently destroyed them. The newly independent states of Kazakhstan, Ukraine, and Belarus cooperatively removed all nuclear weapons to the possession and control of Russia. In May 1995, 178 nations (including the United States) renewed the Nuclear Non-proliferation Treaty and extended its provisions indefinitely into the future. In October of that year, President Clinton signed the Comprehensive Test Ban Treaty (CTBT).[4]

The Nuclear Abolition Path

During and subsequent to this period, advocates of nuclear abolition conducted a vigorous campaign for nuclear disarmament and binding steps leading to the complete worldwide elimination of all nuclear weapons. Key elements of the movement included such highly publicized actions as an official opinion by the International Court of Justice, issued in July 1996, that the use of nuclear weapons would generally be contrary to the rules of international law and that an international obligation exists to pursue complete nuclear disarmament. A month later, the Canberra Commission on the Elimination of Nuclear Weapons issued a report calling for specific steps and processes leading to verifiable elimination of the world's nuclear arsenals.[5] The Canberra report was followed in December 1996 with a public statement signed by sixty-one retired generals and admirals from seventeen countries calling for nuclear abolition. In October 1997, Archbishop Renato Martino, United Nations Permanent Observer of the Holy See, stated to the United Nations the official position of the Roman Catholic Church that nuclear weapons cannot be justified morally and must be eliminated. In early 1998, more than one hundred international civilian leaders, including some fifty current or past heads of state or heads of government, also joined in the call for eliminating nuclear arsenals. In June of that year, seventy-five US Catholic Bishops issued a condemnation of nuclear deterrence and called for the complete elimination of nuclear weapons. These and many other advocates have publicly challenged the United States and all other nuclear-capable states to abandon such weapons in the post–Cold War era.

The Nuclear Realism Path

Also during this period, US nuclear security policy underwent two formal Nuclear Posture Reviews (NPR) in 1994 and 2001. These reports, required by Congress and conducted by the Department of Defense, established the framework for US nuclear policy for the succeeding five to ten years. The 1994 NPR was the first of its kind in fifteen years, and the first of the post–Cold War period. This formal policy guidance reaffirmed the central importance of nuclear deterrence in US strategic planning and committed the United States to retaining a reduced number of nuclear weapons as a cornerstone of national defense. The 2001 NPR shifted US nuclear policy from its threat-based focus on a massive nuclear strike against the United States to a capabilities-based posture to meet immediate, potential, or unexpected contingencies with a mix of conventional and nuclear weapons. In May 2002, the United States and Russia signed the Strategic Offensive Reductions Treaty (Moscow Treaty) limiting each side to 1,700 to 2,200 strategic nuclear weapons by the year 2012. While some of these policies have been criticized in terms of requirements for specific numbers and types of nuclear weapons, the advisability of modernizing the US nuclear arsenal, the need for nuclear testing, and requisite funding levels, the large majority of security policy elites in the United States have not challenged the core decision to retain US nuclear weapons in some number and configuration for the foreseeable future.[6]

The Path Preferred by the Public

Thus, the US public was presented with arguments for two alternative nuclear security paths in the early post–Cold War era. The nuclear abolitionist path argued for international agreements and controls leading to the verified elimination of all nuclear weapons worldwide, while the nuclear realist path argued for deep reductions in the US nuclear stockpile, but a continued, if modified, role of nuclear weapons for maintaining US national security. These were the reasoned positions taken by well-informed policy elites, as articulated in the public press and policy debates over the 1990s and early 2000s. They provide one criterion by which we can evaluate public opinion: does the central tendency of public opinion on nuclear security fall within the bounds of the corresponding elite policy debate?

Chapters 2 and 3 detail the evolution of public preferences on these issues, and summaries are presented above in this chapter. While majorities of the public have consistently viewed elimination of nuclear weapons as a desirable goal, they also believe that achieving and sustaining a disarmed world is not feasible. As our data show, the US public, on average, consistently supports retaining US nuclear weapons, though at substantially reduced numbers. Indeed, in public views, the importance of US nuclear weapons *increases* during the decade of our surveys. Overall, while the public clearly shares some of the concerns of nuclear abolitionists, the weight of public opinion falls nearer the positions of nuclear realists. The broader implication is that, in the central issues of the utility of US nuclear weapons and whether they should be retained, the average positions of the public fall well within the parameters of the policy debate as waged by security experts and policymakers. Similar assessments can be made with respect to other critical security issues, such as the application of military force in responding to state-sponsored terrorism. Therefore, if the comparison with informed elite opinion is used as the external criterion for evaluation, the substance of the aggregate view of the public cannot be seen as a disqualification for consideration in policymaking.

Stability and Change in Public Beliefs

A second strand of analysis by which we can evaluate change over time in public beliefs is to look for a combination of stability coupled with measured change in response to policy-relevant events. Recall that a consistent traditionalist critique of public opinion is that, given the expected ignorance, emotionalism, and susceptibility to demagoguery, the public will be prone to inconsistency and—in the rather scathing indictment by Walter Lippmann— will compel policymakers "to be too late with too little, or too long with too much, too pacifist in peace and too bellicose in war, too neutralist or appeasing in negotiation or too intransigent" (1955, 20). The challenge for those who would make a revisionist argument for serious consideration of public opinion in the making of security policy is to demonstrate that, in the aggregate, the public has stable policy beliefs and preferences that show reasonable adjustments over time in response to evolving policy contexts. Even more, we would want such a demonstration to hold under challenging conditions, such as those that would arouse strong emotions and fears and in which vital state interests are at stake.

In chapters 2 to 4, we present detailed descriptions of the changes over time in public beliefs concerning nuclear security and the threat of terrorism. In chapter 5, we focus specifically on the matter of the stability of public opinion. Our general finding is that, contrary to traditionalists' expectations, public beliefs about security issues are remarkably stable, and yet they also are responsive to some of the complex changes occurring in the international security policy environment. We will not recount these findings in detail here, but rather will focus on trends that are particularly revealing for different reasons. The first concerns the manner in which members of the public understand the relative effectiveness of US nuclear weapons for purposes of deterrence in the post–Cold War era. The matter is of particular concern because the context of deterrence has so radically changed. The former USSR, with its strident ideological hostility to the United States and its massive nuclear weapons capabilities, has collapsed. Over the same period, the efficacy of deterrence has been seriously challenged as additional countries achieved nuclear capabilities, the threat of attacks by chemical and biological weapons has received wider attention, and substate terror groups have sought weapons of mass destruction with which to attack the United States and its interests. To what extent has the American public apprehended these changes?

As we discuss in chapter 3, our surveys since 1995 measure public perceptions of the importance of deterrence for preventing nuclear conflict both retrospectively, as deterrence applied in the Cold War, and currently. In the 1999, 2001, and 2003 surveys, we also ask participants to indicate how important nuclear weapons are for deterring the use of chemical and biological weapons against the United States. The average responses are shown in figure 7.1.

Like historians, the public appears to revise its assessment of historical events such as the Cold War. The perceived mean importance of deterrence for having prevented nuclear conflict during the Cold War rises modestly (but statistically significantly) over the 1995–2003 period. This historical assessment by the public provides a useful backdrop for evaluating the public sense of the effectiveness of deterrence in today's multipolar world. By comparison, the perceived importance of deterrence for preventing nuclear attacks today is relatively flat over the decade of our measures. The result is that *relative* importance of deterrence now, compared to deterrence in the Cold War, declines over the series of surveys. More striking still is the comparison with public sense of the importance of deterring the use of other weapons of mass destruction, such as chemical and biological weapons. In 1999, the year of our

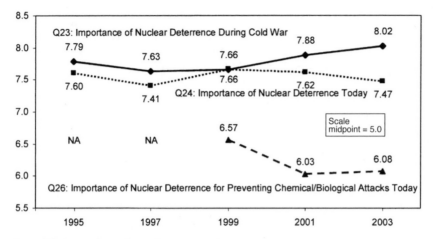

Figure 7.1. Comparisons of mean importance of deterrence

first measure, the public rates the importance of nuclear weapons for deterring these kinds of attacks above midscale but more than a full point below
that for nuclear attacks. After the 9/11 attacks, and after anthrax was used
and widely discussed, the public further downgrades its assessment of the
importance of nuclear deterrence for these kinds of weapons. Thus our data
are consistent with a substantial and reasonably subtle public reassessment of
the importance of deterrence, in which its utility in preventing nuclear attacks
remains important but declines relative to the Cold War, and its importance
against other weapons of mass destruction is significantly lower.

We also call attention to a trend that focuses more directly on the issue
of the potential for emotive instability and recklessness on the part of public
opinion that has been of particular concern to some traditionalists. Rarely has
there been a period in which the potential for intense public animosity to be
directed in dangerous and indiscriminant ways than that following the terrorist attacks in New York and Washington in September of 2001. Indeed, the
popular culture reflected that potential in music[7] and raised concerns about
the safety of Muslim Americans. In that context, what actions did the public
prefer in responding to states that supported terrorism?

As we describe in detail in chapter 4, our measures of public support for
retaliatory actions against countries determined to have assisted terrorists in
strikes against the United States were taken initially in the weeks following
the September 2001 attacks and subsequently in the autumn months of 2002
and 2003. In the immediate aftermath of the terror strikes, public support for
military invasion was high (81 percent) and remained so over the five weeks

in which our 2001 data were collected, then declined to 52 percent by 2003. Over that same period, support for the strongest option, nuclear retaliation, reached 23 percent in 2001 but fell off markedly by 2003 to only 14 percent. Through the entire period, the public consistently preferred very high levels of certainty that a country is culpable in supporting the terror attacks before condoning retaliatory strikes. Overall, during one of the most traumatic periods in modern US history, public support for military retaliation did indeed rise to high levels, but opposition to nuclear retaliation was overwhelming (more than three out of four) and consistent demands were made for high levels of certainty before retaliation. Over time, as the appropriateness of the 2003 invasion of Iraq became a central issue, support for military intervention declined to just over 50 percent.

Does this pattern reveal emotional overreaction? While one can readily debate the wisdom of invading Afghanistan or Iraq, at no time do as many as one-fourth of the American public seek to employ maximum retaliation through nuclear weapons. As time passes and experience develops, Americans become more measured in their support for military invasion, though support does not collapse, as might be expected of a feckless public feared by traditionalists. In none of this do we find clear evidence of an irresponsible or emotionally volatile public.

Yet another opportunity for the public to display irresponsible overreaction to a traumatic event is in the domestic response to the terror attacks. Again, as we report in chapter 4, the evidence suggests a more measured response. While the perceived threat of terrorism did rise, it was well above midscale several years before the 9/11 strikes. The public assessment of government's capacity to fight terrorism, previously seen as a mixed bag, rose modestly after the strikes then settled again to a level moderately above midscale. Measures to gather information about terror groups (domestic spying), seize weapons from suspected terror groups, and expel foreigners deemed threatening—all of which were quite popular before 2001—temporarily gained support after 9/11. At the same time, infringements on free speech or domestic travel were opposed by majorities even after the 9/11 attacks, and support for national identification cards shifted both moderately and temporarily. In aggregate, this does not paint a picture of a public eager to sell its freedoms for protection against terrorists, nor does it imply unwillingness to pay some price for greater security.

Other data we describe in earlier chapters similarly point to remarkably nuanced and measured responses to changes over time. Our point is that, taken as a whole, the pattern of changing public beliefs over time supports neither a view that the public is a volatile emotive herd, nor one that the public is insensitive or unresponsive to changing contexts and events.

The Structure of Public Beliefs

The third strand of our assessment of public beliefs concerns the degree and nature of structure that is evident in public opinion. The structure of public opinion—or, more properly, its absence—has long been the focus of concerns about the role of the public in policymaking. While we recount the debate concerning the structure of public beliefs in detail in chapters 1 and 5, the central traditionalist point is made by Converse (1964) in asserting that the great majority of citizens lack the capacity to organize beliefs in accord with overarching normative principles such as ideology.[8] Absent this organizing capacity, members of the public are unable to relate specific policy preferences to more general beliefs, or to logically reconcile beliefs in distinct policy domains. Were it to be verified, the absence of structured beliefs could be taken to indicate the absence of a necessary condition for a rational public.

Quite contrary to the traditionalist concern, we find coherent and stable structure in public beliefs about security issues. As we detail in chapter 6, relatively complex core beliefs such as political culture and ideology are systematically and sensibly linked to policy beliefs and preferences. Ideology, as the core belief most extensively measured in our series of surveys, is shown to be quite stable both in aggregate over the entire decade and at the individual level in our 2001–2002 panel study. Political ideology, in turn, is both strongly and reliably linked to partisan positions over time.

To be meaningful, of course, core beliefs must constrain more specific policy beliefs in systematic ways. This is indeed the case, as political ideology and partisanship are predictive of general policy dispositions and more specific policy preferences. Political conservatives or Republicans are more likely to believe that the benefits of the nuclear arsenal (both at home and abroad) are larger, and that the risks of maintaining the US arsenal at home are smaller, than are liberals or Democrats. On more specific policy issues, ranging from the perceived importance of retaining nuclear weapons, to issues of testing and ballistic missile defenses, to nuclear spending, consistent and statistically significant relationships hold over time. Similar patterns of relationships hold between ideology, partisanship, and beliefs about policies concerning terrorism.

We also find that domain beliefs (those reflecting fundamental orientations and strategies that apply across a given policy domain) constrain more specific policy preferences. Beliefs about general risks and benefits of nuclear weapons, or normative dispositions to be hawks or doves on nuclear issues, predict substantial fractions of the variation in specific policy preferences. And this is what we would expect if people make policy choices that are consistent with their more general policy beliefs and values.

When we couple core and domain beliefs with policy preferences, our analyses show patterns of expressed public opinions that are consistent with hierarchically structured systems of beliefs. Core beliefs constrain more inter-mediate domain beliefs, which in turn constrain specific policy preferences. While we do not suppose our measures tapped the full fabric of public beliefs about security, our measures provide clear evidence that ordinary American citizens can and do employ complex structured belief systems in making sense of public policy choices. These systems of beliefs, in which general policy dispositions and specific preferences are grounded in enduring attributes of the individual (such as gender, age, education, and ethnicity) and quite stable core beliefs, act to stabilize expressed policy preferences temporally. This, we believe, is why we find durable security policy beliefs over time (both in ag-gregate and at the individual level) despite a sometimes radically changing international and domestic security environment.

But we also find that the structure of beliefs, as measured by the strength of the associations among components of belief systems, evolves in important ways over time. The role of core beliefs such as political ideology and partisan-ship grows in importance over time as a predictor of security policy prefer-ences. At the same time, the domain-level belief concerning threats posed by other nations' nuclear arsenals begins as an influential predictor of security policy beliefs, but that influence wanes and disappears over the decade of our measurements. We consider these kinds of changes to be essential by-products of the ongoing security policy debate. Our analyses suggest that, very early in the post–Cold War period, the role of political ideology and partisanship in shaping security policy positions of the mass public was evolving. Over time, repeated iterations of policy debates in political campaigns, arguments over budgets, and struggles to shape policy priorities—all prominently portrayed in the news media—provide the kinds of cues and context that link policy positions to ideological and partisan placement.[9] At the same time, repeated exposure to ongoing security policy debates changes the ways in which im-portant substantive policy beliefs are related. Initially in our time series, the perception of greater threats from other countries' nuclear arsenals is system-atically linked to more support for retaining the US nuclear stockpile and in-creased spending on the infrastructure needed to develop new nuclear weap-ons in the future. But the changing context as reflected in the policy debate made these relationships ambiguous, reducing their force in the structure of public beliefs. As previously described, nuclear abolitionists argue that the US nuclear stockpile itself increases the risk of nuclear conflict by encourag-ing other nations to retain or enhance their nuclear capabilities, spawning more weapons, and increasing the chance of a new arms race. At the same time, nuclear realists contend that the added nuclear risks from proliferation only increase the value of the US stockpile. In addition, the collapse of the Soviet Union coupled with the rise of the threat of nuclear terrorism decreases the public's sense of the *relative* importance of deterrence (and hence the US nuclear weapons stockpile). These kinds of arguments weaken the links between external nuclear threats and the perceived need for US nuclear capabilities. And, we believe, the evolving policy debate is reflected in the observed changes in the structure of public beliefs about nuclear security policy.

Public Wisdom and Public Policy

The pattern of public beliefs we describe is, of course, a far cry from either an emotionally volatile mass lacking structure or an inert and disengaged one that might be inferred from a critical reading of the traditionalist literature. Public beliefs are subject to a significant degree of hierarchical structure and at the same time are dynamic in ways that appear to reflect the workings of the political process and evolving policy contexts. The role of such composite core values as ideology in shaping security preferences appears to be growing, and substantive connections among beliefs appear to be subject to change over time. Despite far-reaching and traumatic changes in the policy domain, public beliefs appear to be reasonably stable, both in aggregate and at the individual level. Based on these findings, what can we conclude about the policy wisdom of the public?

We first note that the belief structures, as we map them in figures 6.7 through 6.10, are moderately predictive, with explanatory powers ranging from 16 percent to 38 percent of explained variation in the policy preferences that are modeled. The remaining variation (84 percent to 62 percent of the total) is likely some combination of unexplained structure and truly stochastic (random) variation in public beliefs.[10] At the same time, even completely structured beliefs in which *all* variance is explained by hierarchical constraints need not, in themselves, be evidence of wisdom. Converse's (1964) concerns about the absence of the constraining effects of political ideology were more in the nature of a necessary condition for reasoned participation in policy debates, not a sufficient one. Rigid adherence to an ideological position would scarcely qualify as the kind of wisdom Lippmann (1955) or Yankelovich (1991) were concerned about. One would hope that structured beliefs leave room for learning, which may require the attenuation of some elements of structure as others are emerging and strengthening. The role of emotions, as might be induced by trauma and crisis, may be to facilitate such transitions (Marcus and MacKuen 1993; Marcus 2002).

Rather than finding wisdom in public beliefs, it is more accurate to say that we fail to rule it out. We can say with some confidence that the patterns of beliefs of mass publics share many essential characteristics with those of elite groups, who presumably would not be deemed incompetent to participate in politics. We are not suggesting that mass views are as tightly connected and hierarchically constrained as the views of some elites.[11] However, much like members of the political and scientific elite (Barke and Jenkins-Smith 1993; Barke, Jenkins-Smith and Slovic 1997; Rothman and Lichter 1987), mass publics appear to rely partially on such abstract concepts as political ideology to formulate preferences (Herron and Jenkins-Smith 2002; Herron, Jenkins-Smith, Mitchell, and Whitten 2003). Structures of public beliefs evolve over time, similar to the ways in which it appears that structures of beliefs among elites evolve over time.[12] Utilizing these structures, mass publics are capable of placing policy debates within a larger context provided by ideology, partisanship, and other frames of reference such as political culture. In short, members of the public have the capacity to link values and beliefs in sensible ways to policy preferences, even in the unusually complex domain of national security policy. Put in terms of the scholarly debate about the capacities of mass publics to engage meaningfully and constructively in policy processes, the findings of our decade-long series of surveys are consistent with the revisionist perspective.

It is important to note that our evidence of structured and coherent public views does not suggest how publics should participate in security policy processes. There are practical issues of how to access policy processes and how to incorporate public opinion that are not addressed by our research. We agree with Lupia and McCubbins (1998) that citizens are best understood as cognitive misers who must choose which information to assimilate and which to ignore, and they must do that not just about selected issues of nuclear security and terrorism but about the full spectrum of domestic, foreign, and security policy issues. Ordinary citizens depend on the critical roles played by policy experts and advocates, but if the views of the general public are not discredited and ignored, they can provide important guidelines about the boundaries within which acceptable and sustainable public policies can be shaped. We do not agree that the only roles for mass publics are to elect public officials or (conversely) to "throw the bastards out," nor do we advocate policymaking by opinion poll and referendum. But if policymakers reject traditionalist assumptions about the lack of coherence of mass opinions, the American public can play an important role in helping shape the contours of policies, even when the issues are complex and technical. Policymakers ignore such public guidance at their own—and the country's—peril.

APPENDIX 1   Research Methodology

Sampling

For each of our telephone surveys of the US general public, we purchased national sample frames of randomly selected and randomly ordered households having one or more telephones from Survey Sampling, Incorporated, of Fairfield, Connecticut. The sample frames were drawn from a random digit database, stratified by county, in which each telephone exchange and working block had a probability of selection equal to its share of listed telephone households. This was accomplished as follows. All blocks within a county were organized in ascending order by area code, exchange, and block number. After a proportional quota had been allocated to all counties in the frame, a sampling interval was calculated by summing the number of listed residential numbers in each eligible block within the county and dividing that sum by the number of sampling points assigned to the county. From a random start between zero and the sampling interval, blocks were systematically selected in proportion to their density of listed households. After a block was selected, a two-digit random number in the range 00–99 was appended to the exchange and block to form a ten-digit telephone number. Known business numbers were eliminated.

The sample frames were loaded into a computer-assisted telephone interviewing system at the Survey Research Center of the University of New Mexico's Institute for Public Policy (IPP) that selected and dialed the individual numbers. Each household in each sample had an equal chance of being called. Probability sampling was extended within each household by interviewing only the member of the household over the age of eighteen with the most recent birthday. Up to ten attempts were made to contact the individual selected for the sample. No substitutions were made.

Table A1.1 compares key demographic characteristics of survey participants in 2003 to national and regional population parameters.

Table A1.1. Demographic representativeness of respondents, 2003

Demographic category	US national population (%)	Respondents 2003 (%)	Demographic category	US national population (%)	Respondents 2003 (%)
Gender[a]			*Household income*		
Men	48.1	45.2	$0–49,999	57.3	50.6
Women	51.9	54.8	$50,000–99,999	29.3	36.6
Age			$100,000 and above	13.4	12.8
18–24	13.2	8.7	*Region*[d]		
25–54	57.0	57.2	Northeast[e]	19.1	19.5
>54	28.8	34.1	Midwest[f]	23.3	26.0
Education[b]			South[g]	35.7	33.0
High school grad or higher	83.1	95.1	West[h]	21.9	21.5
College grad or higher	24.3	41.6			
Race/ethnicity[c]					
White, non-Hispanic	72.7	84.7			
Black	11.5	5.4			
Hispanic (any race)	11.0	4.5			
American Indian/ Alaskan Native	0.7	2.8			
Asian/Pacific Islander	4.0	1.3			
Other	NA	1.3			

Sources: U.S. Census Bureau 2003a, 2003b, 2003c; for household income, U.S. Bureau of Labor Statistics and U.S. Census Bureau 2001; for region, U.S. Census Bureau, 2003d.

[a]The proportion of men and women 18 years old and above is used for comparison, because by design we excluded individuals below the age of 18 from participating in our survey.

[b]The proportion of the population 18 years of age and above having graduated high school or having a bachelor's degree or higher is used for comparison, because by design we excluded individuals below the age of 18 from participating in our survey.

[c]National population data include all ages.

[d]Alaska, Hawaii, Micronesia, Guam, Marshall Islands, Northern Mariana Islands, Palau, Puerto Rico, Midway Islands, and the Virgin Islands were not included in the sample frame. Regional population data include all ages.

[e] The Northeast region included Connecticut, Maine, Massachusetts, New Hampshire, New Jersey, New York, Pennsylvania, Rhode Island, and Vermont.

[f]The Midwest region included Illinois, Indiana, Iowa, Kansas, Michigan, Minnesota, Missouri, Nebraska, North Dakota, Ohio, South Dakota, and Wisconsin.

[g]The South region included Alabama, Arkansas, Delaware, Florida, Georgia, Kentucky, Louisiana, Maryland, Mississippi, North Carolina, Oklahoma, South Carolina, Tennessee, Texas, Virginia, and West Virginia.

[h]The West region included Arizona, California, Colorado, Idaho, Montana, Nevada, New Mexico, Oregon, Utah, Washington, and Wyoming.

Data Collection

In Table A1.2, we identify samples, report collection methods and dates, *n*-sizes, and type four (highest) cooperation rates calculated in accordance with guidelines from the American Association for Public Opinion Research (2004).

Before data collection for each survey began, an extensive review of the survey

Table A1.2. Survey descriptions

Year	Collection method	Collection dates	n-size	Cooperation rates
1993	phone	July–August	1,301	67.0
1995	phone	September–November	2,490	55.7
1997	phone	September–November	1,639	54.8
1999	phone	September–October	1,483	52.0
2001	phone	September–November	1,226	53.7
(2002 panel)	phone	September–November	474	76.8
2003	phone	September–November	1,520	51.5

instrument was conducted by the UNM Institute for Public Policy's senior interviewing staff, survey research center supervisors, and the research design team. During this step the survey was checked for content that might be culturally insensitive or threatening to different socioeconomic or demographic groups. This process reduced the likelihood that the instrument would inadvertently induce respondents from different groups or classes to drop out before completing the survey. Also during this step, the skip patterns used were checked to ensure that the specified research parameters were met. Then a verbal protocol test was conducted with senior interviewers to identify any remaining problematic question wording or computer programming errors.

When the survey instrument was in final form, training was conducted with each of the interviewers and supervisors to ensure they were proficient in the standardized procedures and terminology. This process entailed oral reading of the survey instrument in group training sessions to make sure that proper and consistent emphasis was given to the various words and phrases specified in the survey, and to assure that respondents were interviewed using consistent phrasing, emphasis, and protocols during the data collection process. Data collection did not begin until each interviewer demonstrated thorough competence with the survey instructions and reading aloud the questions.

The interviews were conducted in the IPP Survey Research Center by experienced interviewers using a computer-assisted telephone interviewing system that recorded data in a centralized collection file. Rigorous supervision and quality control measures were applied throughout the data collection process. No interviews were conducted without the presence of a supervisor. A silent monitor was used by supervisors to evaluate individual interviewers and to ensure high quality and continuity in application of the survey protocols throughout the data collection phase. The quality of the data collected was continually monitored to assure that intended collection standards were maintained. These procedures included daily downloading and analysis of responses, and diagnostics such as the degree of "reluctance" of survey participants, the proportions of collections by region, and standardized recording of verbatim responses where appropriate.

The sample size and random selection procedures provide plus or minus 3.0 percent sampling errors for all surveys.

APPENDIX 2

Questions, Distributions, and Means

Q1_edu What is your highest level of education?

% Public	2003	2001	1999	1997	1995	1993
<High school graduate	5	5	5	7	6	6
High school graduate	24	26	25	27	28	24
Some college/vocational school	30	30	32	32	30	32
College graduate	22	22	22	18	20	20
Some graduate work	5	4	3	4	4	5
Master's degree	12	10	8	8	8	9
J.D. or higher law degree	NA	NA	1	1	NA	NA
Other doctorate	3	2	2	1	3	3
Other degree	0	1	1	1	NA	1

Q2_age How old are you?

	Mean
2003	47.6
2001	45.0
1999	44.0
1997	44.3
1995	42.2
1993	42.3

Q3_gend As part of the survey, I am required to ask: are you male or female?

	% Female	% Male
2003	54.8	45.2
2001	55.2	44.8
1999	55.6	44.4
1997	54.6	45.4
1995	54.5	45.5
1993	50.8	49.2

Now I want to ask you some questions about how you think the world may have changed since the end of the Cold War. We are interested in your perceptions. There are no right or wrong answers.

Q4_natsec Considering the international environment as a whole, and using a scale from one to seven where one means the world is much less secure, and seven means the world is much more secure, how do you think international security has changed since the end of the Cold War?

Much less secure ← → Much more secure

% Public	1	2	3	4	5	6	7	Mean
2003	9	9	23	18	26	9	6	3.93
2001	9	8	20	20	26	9	7	4.02
1999	7	7	19	21	29	9	7	4.14
1997	8	6	15	19	34	10	9	4.30

1997–2003: $p < .0001$; 2001–2003: $p = .1226$

Q5_USec Focusing more specifically on the US, and using the same scale from one to seven where one means much less secure, and seven means much more secure, how has US security changed since the end of the Cold War?

Much less secure ← → Much more secure

% Public	1	2	3	4	5	6	7	Mean
2003	10	10	19	17	23	12	8	4.04
2001	10	10	20	19	21	11	9	3.97
1999	7	9	16	18	26	14	10	4.30
1997	8	8	14	19	26	15	11	4.36

1997–2003: $p < .0001$; 2001–2003: $p = .2675$

Q6_USwar Turning now to nuclear considerations, on a scale from one to seven where one means the chances have decreased greatly, and seven means the chances have increased greatly, how has the breakup of the Soviet Union affected the chances that the US will be involved in a war with any country in which nuclear weapons are used?

Decreased greatly ← → Increased greatly

% Public	1	2	3	4	5	6	7	Mean
2003	9	12	16	18	21	13	11	4.13
2001	7	13	17	14	20	13	15	4.28
1999	7	8	17	16	24	14	13	4.35
1997	10	13	19	16	18	13	12	4.04
1995	14	11	16	15	19	9	16	4.07
1993	11	16	18	15	19	10	11	3.85

1993–2003: $p < .0001$; 2001–2003: $p = .0386$

Q7_nucwar Using a scale from one to seven where one means the chances have decreased greatly, and seven means the chances have increased greatly, how do you think the breakup of the Soviet Union has affected the possibility that nuclear weapons will be used by any country against any other country?

Decreased greatly ← *No change* → Increased greatly

% Public	1	2	3	4	5	6	7	Mean
2003	7	8	13	17	24	17	14	4.50
2001	5	9	13	17	23	15	17	4.61
1999	6	6	13	18	22	19	17	4.66
1997	7	9	15	17	21	16	14	4.41
1995	8	7	12	14	22	13	23	4.67
1993	6	8	14	18	22	14	18	4.54

1993–2003: $p = .5951$; 2001–2003: $p = .1106$

The next several questions ask for your perceptions about risks to American society associated with managing US nuclear weapons. Using a scale from zero to ten where zero means no risk, and ten means extreme risk, how would you rate the risk of each of the following items:

Q8_manu Manufacturing nuclear weapons in the US

No risk ← → Extreme risk

% Public	0	1	2	3	4	5	6	7	8	9	10	Mean
2003	6	6	8	11	8	22	9	11	8	4	8	5.06
2001	5	5	11	10	9	21	9	9	9	3	9	5.07
1999	3	3	8	9	10	22	9	12	10	3	10	5.42
1997	5	5	9	10	10	19	9	11	8	2	10	5.10
1995	4	2	4	5	5	13	6	11	13	6	31	5.74
1993	3	3	6	6	6	14	8	11	13	8	22	6.54

1993–2003: $p < .0001$; 2001–2003: $p = .9542$

Q9_trans Transporting nuclear weapons in the US

No risk ← → Extreme risk

% Public	0	1	2	3	4	5	6	7	8	9	10	Mean
2003	4	5	8	9	7	18	11	13	11	4	11	5.49
2001	4	5	8	9	10	17	9	13	11	4	10	5.44
1999	3	4	8	10	7	18	11	14	9	4	12	5.68
1997	4	5	8	11	9	17	9	12	11	4	11	5.42
1995	3	2	3	4	4	12	5	10	13	9	34	5.96
1993	2	2	5	5	6	13	8	13	15	7	25	6.84

1993–2003: $p < .0001$; 2001–2003: $p = .6655$

Q10_store Storing existing nuclear weapons in the US

% Public	No risk ⟵ 0	1	2	3	4	5	6	7	8	9	⟶ Extreme risk 10	Mean
2003	4	5	9	9	7	16	10	14	10	5	12	5.60
2001	4	6	9	9	9	16	10	12	10	5	11	5.46
1999	2	4	6	8	8	17	10	14	11	5	15	5.94
1997	4	4	8	9	8	15	9	13	11	5	14	5.71
1995	3	2	4	5	4	13	6	11	12	8	30	6.07
1993	2	2	5	7	7	13	9	11	13	7	23	6.57

1993–2003: $p < .0001$; 2001–2003: $p = .2137$

Q11_dsmbl Disassembling nuclear weapons in the US

% Public	No risk ⟵ 0	1	2	3	4	5	6	7	8	9	⟶ Extreme risk 10	Mean
2003	5	6	10	12	10	18	9	10	7	4	8	4.94
2001	5	7	9	11	9	19	10	10	8	3	9	4.95
1999	3	5	8	11	11	18	10	12	7	5	10	5.34
1997	5	6	10	10	11	19	9	10	8	3	10	5.06
1995	4	3	5	7	6	14	7	9	12	6	26	5.51
1993	4	3	7	8	8	17	7	10	14	6	17	6.02

1993–2003: $p < .0001$; 2001–2003: $p = .9582$

Q12_rwaste Storing radioactive materials in the US from disassembled weapons

% Public	No risk ⟵ 0	1	2	3	4	5	6	7	8	9	⟶ Extreme risk 10	Mean
2003	3	4	6	8	8	17	10	13	11	6	14	5.92
2001	3	4	7	8	8	14	11	12	11	7	14	5.86
1999	2	3	4	7	8	15	11	13	11	8	19	6.39
1997	3	3	5	7	8	14	9	15	11	6	17	6.12
1995	3	2	3	5	4	10	5	10	15	9	36	6.25
1993	2	1	2	3	4	9	7	10	18	11	34	7.64

1993–2003: $p < .0001$; 2001–2003: $p = .6034$

Q13_unauth Some people worry that a nuclear weapon might someday be used by US forces without the president's authorization. On a scale from zero to ten, where zero means not at all likely, and ten means highly likely, how would you rate the likelihood of a US nuclear weapon being used within the next 25 years without presidential authorization?

Not at all likely ← → Highly likely

% Public	0	1	2	3	4	5	6	7	8	9	10	Mean
2003	19	16	15	11	5	10	3	6	6	2	7	3.50
2001	22	17	16	10	5	9	4	5	5	2	5	3.08
1999	15	12	12	11	6	11	5	7	9	4	9	4.23
1997	17	13	14	10	5	12	4	7	7	3	9	3.91
1995	19	11	9	7	4	14	5	7	7	2	14	4.34
1993	15	13	11	12	6	14	4	6	8	2	10	4.06

1993–2003: $p < .0001$; 2001–2003: $p = .0005$

Q14_expl Some people are concerned about the possibility of an accidental explosion of a nuclear weapon. On the same scale where zero means not at all likely, and ten means highly likely, how would you rate the likelihood of an accident involving a US nuclear weapon causing an unintended nuclear explosion?

Not at all likely ← → Highly likely

% Public	0	1	2	3	4	5	6	7	8	9	10	Mean
2003	9	13	14	12	8	14	6	8	5	3	7	4.09
2001	10	15	15	14	9	14	6	5	6	2	5	3.78
1999	7	8	11	12	8	16	7	10	9	3	8	4.70
1997	7	11	13	10	8	14	8	9	8	3	9	4.57
1995	8	9	8	10	7	19	6	9	9	2	13	4.98
1993	5	10	12	11	8	18	8	9	7	3	10	4.79

1993–2003: $p < .0001$; 2001–2003: $p = .0051$

Q15_nsprd On a scale from zero to ten where zero means the likelihood for the future spread of nuclear weapons is greatly reduced, and ten means it is greatly increased, how do you think the breakup of the Soviet Union has affected the likelihood that nuclear weapons will spread to other countries?

Greatly reduced ← → Greatly increased

% Public	0	1	2	3	4	5	6	7	8	9	10	Mean
2003	2	1	3	7	8	17	11	15	16	6	13	6.34
2001	2	2	6	7	9	19	10	14	14	6	12	6.10
1999	1	1	3	6	6	17	11	16	15	8	16	6.62
1997	3	2	4	8	8	19	10	14	13	5	13	6.04
1995	2	4	4	8	9	18	9	16	10	4	16	6.02
1993	7	6	0	10	0	13	20	0	17	0	26	6.49

1993–03: $p = .1560$; 2001–2003: $p = .0167$

Q16_USrisk Now I would like to know how you think the spread of nuclear weapons to other countries influences the security of the US. On a scale from zero to ten where zero means the spread of nuclear weapons poses no risk to the US, and ten means the spread of nuclear weapons poses extreme risk, how would you rate the risk to the US if more countries have nuclear weapons?

| | No risk | | | | | | | | | | Extreme risk | |
% Public	0	1	2	3	4	5	6	7	8	9	10	Mean
2003	1	1	1	2	3	8	7	16	21	13	27	7.67
2001	1	0	1	3	4	9	8	14	20	10	28	7.59
1999	1	1	1	3	3	8	9	15	22	12	26	7.65
1997	1	1	1	3	5	10	8	15	18	11	27	7.45
1995	1	1	1	2	3	10	7	16	16	8	36	7.81
1993	1	0	2	3	3	9	9	16	18	8	32	7.65

1993–2003: $p = .7413$; 2001–2003: $p = .3179$

Q17_ternow Now I would like to know about your perceptions of today's threat of nuclear terrorism. On a scale from zero to ten where zero means there is no threat of nuclear weapons being used by terrorists, and ten means there is extreme threat, how would you rate today's threat of nuclear terrorism occurring anywhere in the world?

| | No threat | | | | | | | | | | Extreme threat | |
% Public	0	1	2	3	4	5	6	7	8	9	10	Mean
2003	1	1	3	4	5	11	9	16	19	11	20	7.10
2001	1	1	3	6	6	11	10	13	16	10	23	7.01
1999	1	1	2	4	6	11	10	14	18	11	22	7.14
1997	2	1	3	5	6	12	10	13	17	10	22	7.03
1995	1	1	2	4	5	13	10	14	15	7	27	7.16
1993	1	2	3	5	6	13	10	14	18	6	22	6.89

1993–2003: $p = .0237$; 2001–2003: $p = .3362$

Q18_10yrs On the same scale from zero to ten where zero means no threat, and ten means extreme threat, how would you rate the threat of nuclear weapons being used by terrorists anywhere in the world during the next ten years?

| | No threat | | | | | | | | | | Extreme threat | |
% Public	0	1	2	3	4	5	6	7	8	9	10	Mean
2003	1	1	3	5	4	11	9	16	19	11	20	7.11
2001	1	1	4	4	5	12	9	13	17	10	23	7.06
1999	1	1	3	5	4	11	10	17	18	9	21	7.09
1997	2	1	4	4	7	13	10	15	16	8	21	6.83
1995	1	1	3	4	5	12	9	15	14	7	28	7.23
1993	0	1	3	5	5	15	9	16	17	6	23	7.00

1993–2003: $p =. 2432$; 2001–2003: $p = .6372$

Next we turn to broad issues of US leadership. The next four questions use a scale from zero to ten where zero means not at all important, and ten means extremely important.

Q19_influ First, how important are US nuclear weapons for US influence over international events?

	Not at all important										Extremely important	
% Public	0	1	2	3	4	5	6	7	8	9	10	Mean
2003	2	1	3	5	6	16	10	13	15	8	21	6.74
2001	3	1	4	4	6	15	8	12	15	8	24	6.84
1999	2	1	3	5	6	18	10	13	15	8	19	6.70
1997	4	1	5	5	8	15	11	14	14	6	17	6.32
1995	4	2	4	6	6	17	10	13	15	4	20	6.39
1993	4	3	5	7	7	18	10	15	12	5	16	6.10

1993–2003: $p < .0001$; 2001–2003: $p = .3538$

Q20_stat How important are US nuclear weapons for maintaining US status as a world leader?

	Not at all important										Extremely important	
% Public	0	1	2	3	4	5	6	7	8	9	10	Mean
2003	2	2	3	5	6	10	8	12	17	9	27	7.12
2001	3	1	3	4	5	11	8	12	15	9	29	7.16
1999	3	1	2	3	6	13	8	13	15	10	26	7.06
1997	4	2	4	5	7	12	9	13	15	7	22	6.59
1995	4	3	4	5	5	15	8	14	14	6	24	6.67
1993	3	4	5	6	7	15	8	16	11	6	19	6.25

1993–2003: $p < .0001$; 2001–2003: $p = .6907$

Q21_spwr How important is it for the US to remain a military superpower?

	Not at all important										Extremely important	
% Public	0	1	2	3	4	5	6	7	8	9	10	Mean
2003	2	1	1	2	2	7	4	7	12	12	50	8.32
2001	1	0	1	1	1	3	4	6	12	11	59	8.76
1999	1	1	1	1	2	6	4	8	13	12	51	8.46
1997	1	1	2	2	3	6	6	9	14	11	46	8.18
1995	2	2	1	3	2	9	6	12	13	7	44	8.00
1993	1	2	2	3	3	8	7	15	10	8	39	7.61

1993–2003: $p < .0001$; 2001–2003: $p < .0001$

Q22_amway How important have nuclear weapons been to preserving America's way of life?

	Not at all important ←									→ Extremely important		
% Public	0	1	2	3	4	5	6	7	8	9	10	Mean
2003	5	4	5	6	6	15	7	10	14	7	20	6.22
2001	4	2	4	5	5	13	10	11	17	6	21	6.57
1999	4	2	4	6	5	15	9	12	14	7	20	6.47
1997	6	2	5	6	7	14	9	13	15	6	18	6.28
1995	5	3	4	6	7	15	9	12	14	5	20	6.30
1993	4	4	5	7	7	15	9	13	15	6	15	6.07

1993–2003: $p < .0001$; 2001–2003: $p = .0034$

The next three questions ask about your perceptions of nuclear deterrence, which means preventing someone from using nuclear weapons against us, because they expect that we would retaliate by using nuclear weapons against them.

Q23_pdet Using the same scale from zero to ten where zero is not at all important, and ten is extremely important, how important was nuclear deterrence in preventing nuclear conflict during the Cold War?

	Not at all important ←									→ Extremely important		
% Public	0	1	2	3	4	5	6	7	8	9	10	Mean
2003	1	0	1	3	2	9	6	10	19	12	38	8.02
2001	1	0	1	2	3	9	7	10	19	11	35	7.88
1999	2	1	1	2	3	11	7	11	18	12	31	7.66
1997	2	1	1	2	4	10	9	11	19	10	31	7.63
1995	1	1	1	2	3	10	7	13	16	9	36	7.79

1995–2003: $p = .0023$; 2001–2003: $p = .1122$

Q24_ndet Again, using the same scale from zero to ten, how important are US nuclear weapons for preventing other countries from using nuclear weapons against us today?

	Not at all important ←									→ Extremely important		
% Public	0	1	2	3	4	5	6	7	8	9	10	Mean
2003	2	1	3	3	3	10	8	11	18	9	31	7.47
2001	2	1	2	2	5	8	8	12	16	11	33	7.62
1999	1	1	2	3	4	10	7	12	19	11	31	7.66
1997	2	1	2	3	4	11	9	11	18	11	29	7.41
1995	2	1	2	3	3	10	8	13	16	8	34	7.60

1995–2003: $p = .1458$; 2001–2003: $p = .1518$

Q25_fdet For this question, zero means not at all effective, and ten means extremely effective. If more countries acquire nuclear weapons in the future, how effective will nuclear deterrence be in preventing nuclear wars from occurring anywhere in the world?

Not at all effective ⟵——————————————————————⟶ Extremely effective

% Public	0	1	2	3	4	5	6	7	8	9	10	Mean
2003	6	3	7	8	8	15	6	11	13	5	17	5.85
2001	6	2	6	8	7	16	9	10	11	6	18	5.99
1999	6	3	5	8	8	16	8	12	13	6	16	5.92
1997	7	2	5	8	7	15	7	11	14	5	18	6.00
1995	7	4	4	7	6	16	8	13	12	4	20	5.99

1995–2003: $p = .1741$; 2001–2003: $p = .2320$

Q26_detcb Now we want you to think about preventing the use of chemical and biological weapons against the US today. Using a scale from zero to ten where zero means not at all important, and ten means extremely important, how important are US nuclear weapons for preventing other countries from using chemical or biological weapons against us today?

Not at all important ⟵——————————————————————⟶ Extremely important

% Public	0	1	2	3	4	5	6	7	8	9	10	Mean
2003	7	4	6	7	6	12	8	10	14	6	21	6.08
2001	8	4	7	8	5	11	6	11	12	6	22	6.03
1999	5	2	5	6	5	11	9	11	15	9	22	6.57

1999–2003: $p < .0001$; 2001–2003: $p = .7156$

Q27_reduce Under the terms of arms reductions agreements, the US and Russia are reducing their stockpiles of nuclear weapons. Recent published reports estimate that the US and Russia each have between 6,000 and 7,000 strategic warheads deployed today. For this question, assume that 7,000 is the maximum number and zero is the minimum. If mutual reductions in the number of US and Russian nuclear weapons can be verified, to approximately what level would you be willing to reduce the number of US nuclear weapons?

% Public	7,000–6,501	6,500–6,001	6,000–5,501	5,500–5,001	5,000–4,501	4,500–4,001	4,000–3,501	3,500–3,001
2003	13	0	2	0	11	0	6	5
2001	14	1	4	0	13	0	6	5
1999	11	1	4	1	11	1	7	6
1997	11	1	2	0	11	1	6	7

% Public	3,000–2,501	2,500–2,001	2,000–1,501	1,500–1,001	1,000–501	500–1	0	Median
2003	7	0	4	0	9	25	16	1,000–501
2001	6	1	5	1	8	15	19	3,000–2,501
1999	5	1	7	0	9	16	20	2,000–1,501
1997	7	2	7	1	8	17	21	2,000–1,501

If China does not enter into arms control agreements to reduce the number of its nuclear weapons, I would like to know how that would influence your views about US reductions. Please respond to the following two statements about China, using a scale from one to seven where one means strongly disagree, and seven means strongly agree.

Q28_PRC1 The number of China's nuclear weapons should not influence the number of US nuclear weapons.

% Public	Strongly disagree 1	2	3	4	5	6	Strongly agree 7	Mean
2003	32	9	8	7	8	8	27	3.83
2001	37	9	6	5	10	8	25	3.64
1999	40	9	7	5	9	8	23	3.47
1997	38	8	6	6	10	7	24	3.59

1997–2003: $p = .0125$; 2001–2003: $p = .0641$

Q29_PRC2 The US should not reduce below the number of nuclear weapons that China maintains.

% Public	Strongly disagree 1	2	3	4	5	6	Strongly agree 7	Mean
2003	14	6	6	6	9	10	50	5.20
2001	12	4	5	5	10	9	55	5.45
1999	14	4	6	5	8	9	54	5.32
1997	15	5	5	7	10	8	50	5.16

1997–2003: $p = .6158$; 2001–2003: $p = .0072$

Q30_udrgrd Some experts argue that underground nuclear test explosions are important to ensure the safety and reliability of US nuclear weapons. Other experts argue that nuclear safety and reliability can be assured through other means such as computer simulations. Using a scale from zero to ten where zero is not at all important, and ten is extremely important, how do you rate the importance of underground nuclear testing for assuring the safety and reliability of US nuclear weapons?

% Public	Not at all important 0	1	2	3	4	5	6	7	8	9	Extremely important 10	Mean
2003	12	11	9	8	7	14	6	8	8	3	15	4.82
2001	11	7	9	6	8	13	7	9	8	3	17	5.24
1993*	17	8	0	11	0	14	15	0	7	0	28	5.63

(*1–7 scale converted to 0–10 scale)
1993–2003: $p < .0001$; 2001–2003: $p = .0025$

The next three questions address arms control policies. Each uses a scale from one to seven where one means strongly oppose, and seven means strongly support.

Q31_CTBT First, how do you feel about the US participating in a treaty that bans all nuclear test explosions?

% Public	Strongly oppose						Strongly support	
	1	2	3	4	5	6	7	Mean
2003	12	5	8	7	11	12	44	5.14
2001	12	6	9	8	12	12	41	4.99
1999	13	3	5	6	11	13	49	5.34
1997	12	4	5	7	10	11	52	5.39
1995*	6	5	3	15	13	11	46	5.43

(*0–10 scale converted to 1–7 scale)
1995–2003: $p < .0001$; 2001–2003: $p = .0891$

Q32_FMC On the same scale from one to seven, how do you feel about the US participating in a treaty that bans production of nuclear materials that could be used to make nuclear weapons?

% Public	Strongly oppose						Strongly support	
	1	2	3	4	5	6	7	Mean
2003	11	5	7	8	13	11	44	5.17
2001	13	6	7	11	15	12	36	4.90
1999	11	5	6	8	12	13	46	5.28
1997	12	4	7	8	11	11	46	5.18
1995*	6	6	4	16	16	10	43	5.30

(*0–10 scale converted to 1–7 scale)
1995–2003: $p = .0555$; 2001–2003: $p = .0019$

Q33_darm Again, using the same scale from one to seven, how do you feel about the US agreeing to a provision that requires us to eventually eliminate all of our nuclear weapons?

% Public	Strongly oppose						Strongly support	
	1	2	3	4	5	6	7	Mean
2003	27	8	7	8	11	8	31	4.16
2001	29	10	10	8	10	6	26	3.86
1999	25	8	7	8	10	9	32	4.27
1997	23	8	9	7	10	8	35	4.40
1995*	12	12	7	18	12	7	32	4.57

(*0–10 scale converted to 1–7 scale)
1995–2003: $p < .0001$; 2001–2003: $p = .0023$

Using a scale from one to seven where one means you strongly disagree, and seven means you strongly agree, please respond to the following two statements.

Q34_nonucs It is feasible to eliminate all nuclear weapons worldwide within the next 25 years.

Strongly disagree ←————————→ Strongly agree

% Public	1	2	3	4	5	6	7	Mean
2003	35	10	9	7	9	7	24	3.62
2001	37	10	9	7	10	6	22	3.48
1999	33	10	9	8	12	5	23	3.64
1997	31	11	9	6	11	6	26	3.76
1995	26	9	10	9	13	8	24	3.95
1993	29	14	8	6	11	7	25	3.78

1993–2003: $p = .0952$; 2001–2003: $p = .1649$

Q35_future Even if all the nuclear weapons could somehow be eliminated worldwide, it would be extremely difficult to keep other countries from building them again.

Strongly disagree ←————————→ Strongly agree

% Public	1	2	3	4	5	6	7	Mean
2003	8	3	3	4	8	13	61	5.84
2001	7	3	3	4	10	13	60	5.86
1999	7	2	3	3	8	15	61	5.95
1997	8	4	2	4	11	14	58	5.79
1995	5	2	3	6	14	17	52	5.83
1993	5	3	3	4	12	16	56	5.89

1993–2003: $p = .4543$; 2001–2003: $p = .8103$

Q36_retain On a scale from zero to ten where zero is not at all important, and ten is extremely important, how important is it for the US to retain nuclear weapons today?

Not at all important ←————————————→ Extremely important

% Public	0	1	2	3	4	5	6	7	8	9	10	Mean
2003	3	2	2	3	3	11	9	15	14	7	32	7.30
2001	1	1	1	2	3	10	7	17	12	6	39	7.75
1999	2	2	1	3	3	9	9	14	15	7	34	7.50
1997	3	1	2	3	4	14	7	18	13	5	30	7.19
1995*	7	0	6	10	0	11	0	18	12	0	36	6.78
1993*	6	6	0	11	0	14	20	0	13	0	30	6.59

(*1–7 scale converted to 0–10 scale)
1993–2003: $p < .0001$; 2001–2003: $p < .0001$

Q37_tanks Using a scale from one to seven where one means you strongly disagree, and seven means you strongly agree, please respond to the following statement. "Having a nuclear arsenal means the US can spend less for national defense than would be necessary without nuclear weapons."

% Public	Strongly disagree 1	2	3	4	5	6	Strongly agree 7	Mean
2003	23	13	10	9	16	9	20	3.87
2001	25	14	10	9	17	10	15	3.69
1999	21	10	10	11	17	11	19	4.02
1997	20	9	10	11	18	10	22	4.15
1995	22	9	11	14	17	10	18	3.94
1993	24	15	15	12	17	9	9	3.43

1993–2003: $p < .0001$; 2001–2003: $p = .0591$

The next two questions deal with the economic value of defense industry jobs and defense-related technologies. Both use a scale from one to seven where one means little economic value, and seven means great economic value.

Q38_jobs First, how do you rate the economic value of defense industry jobs in America?

% Public	Little economic value 1	2	3	4	5	6	Great economic value 7	Mean
2003	4	3	6	13	25	21	28	5.26
2001	3	2	5	10	26	22	33	5.50
1999	4	3	7	13	28	21	25	5.22
1997	4	3	8	14	28	18	25	5.13
1995	7	4	9	16	25	15	23	4.88
1993	7	9	13	15	23	15	18	4.55

1993–2003: $p < .0001$; 2001–2003: $p = .0003$

Q39_tectran Next, how do you rate the economic value of technological advances in defense industries for other areas of the US economy?

% Public	Little economic value 1	2	3	4	5	6	Great economic value 7	Mean
2003	3	2	5	8	22	23	38	5.67
2001	2	2	2	8	20	25	41	5.82
1999	2	2	4	9	22	25	37	5.69
1997	2	2	4	9	24	23	35	5.60
1995	4	3	8	13	24	19	30	5.29

1995–2003: $p < .0001$; 2001–2003: $p = .0100$

Next we want your views about spending priorities. Please indicate how you think government spending on nuclear weapons issues should change in each of the following areas. Use a scale from one to seven where one means spending should substantially decrease, and seven means spending should substantially increase.

Q40_devtest First, how should government spending change for developing and testing new nuclear weapons?

Substantially decrease ←——→ *Substantially increase*

% Public	1	2	3	4	5	6	7	Mean
2003	19	13	21	19	16	6	7	3.42
2001	13	13	19	19	19	6	11	3.79
1999	18	14	19	19	18	5	7	3.45
1997	25	16	20	15	13	3	7	3.13
1995	44	14	14	10	9	2	7	2.61
1993	40	16	12	9	11	3	8	2.77

1993–2003: $p < .0001$; 2001–2003: $p < .0001$

Q41_mtain For maintaining existing nuclear weapons in reliable condition

Substantially decrease ←——→ *Substantially increase*

% Public	1	2	3	4	5	6	7	Mean
2003	7	5	12	18	22	15	22	4.76
2001	4	3	8	13	22	18	32	5.26
1999	6	4	10	15	21	16	29	5.03
1997	10	6	12	15	20	15	22	4.62
1995	17	6	12	14	17	11	24	4.35
1993	12	6	13	15	19	10	25	4.53

1993–2003: $p = .0024$; 2001–2003: $p < .0001$

Q42_safwpn For research to increase the safety of existing nuclear weapons

Substantially decrease ←——→ *Substantially increase*

% Public	1	2	3	4	5	6	7	Mean
2003	5	3	7	11	19	18	38	5.42
2001	3	3	3	8	16	19	49	5.83
1999	4	2	4	7	15	16	52	5.84
1997	5	2	5	9	14	17	47	5.65
1995	11	4	7	7	14	12	45	5.24
1993	8	3	8	10	17	14	40	5.24

1993–2003: $p = .0113$; 2001–2003: $p < .0001$

Q43_tng For training to assure competence of those who manage US nuclear weapons

Substantially decrease ⟵⟶ Substantially increase

% Public	1	2	3	4	5	6	7	Mean
2003	3	1	5	7	13	17	54	5.92
2001	2	1	2	5	10	14	66	6.27
1999	3	1	2	5	12	13	64	6.18
1997	3	1	2	7	11	14	60	6.04
1995	8	2	3	6	10	10	61	5.82
1993	6	2	4	8	14	13	52	5.69

1993–2003: $p = .0005$; 2001–2003: $p < .0001$

Q44_sustain For maintaining the ability to develop and improve US nuclear weapons in the future

Substantially decrease ⟵⟶ Substantially increase

% Public	1	2	3	4	5	6	7	Mean
2003	13	8	11	14	19	15	21	4.47
2001	7	7	8	10	21	14	32	5.02
1999	10	7	9	13	20	13	28	4.78
1997	13	9	12	13	19	10	24	4.45
1995	23	8	11	12	16	8	22	4.00
1993	23	12	16	12	14	8	16	3.68

1993–2003: $p < .0001$; 2001–2003: $p < .0001$

Q45_prolif For preventing the spread of nuclear weapons

Substantially decrease ⟵⟶ Substantially increase

% Public	1	2	3	4	5	6	7	Mean
2003	6	2	2	6	10	17	57	5.91
2001	4	2	2	5	11	12	63	6.07
1999	6	2	3	5	9	12	62	5.94
1997	9	2	3	6	10	13	57	5.72
1995	18	3	3	5	9	10	52	5.21
1993	14	4	5	6	12	12	46	5.19

1993–2003: $p < .0001$; 2001–2003: $p = .0197$

Q46_terror For preventing nuclear terrorism

Substantially decrease ⟵⟶ Substantially increase

% Public	1	2	3	4	5	6	7	Mean
2003	4	2	2	4	7	11	70	6.23
2001	3	1	1	1	5	9	80	6.51
1999	4	1	1	3	5	9	76	6.34
1997	7	1	1	3	6	9	73	6.18
1995	13	2	1	2	5	7	69	5.84
1993	7	2	4	5	8	12	61	5.83

1993–2003: $p < .0001$; 2001–2003: $p < .0001$

On a scale from zero to ten where zero means no trust, and ten means complete trust, how much do you trust the following organizations to safely manage nuclear resources such as nuclear weapons or radioactive materials?

(NOTE: Questions 47–50 were asked in random order)

Q47_DoD The Department of Defense

% Public	No trust 0	1	2	3	4	5	6	7	8	9	Complete trust 10	Mean
2003	5	4	5	5	7	15	11	18	13	6	10	5.92
2001	2	2	3	4	4	12	11	20	17	9	16	6.75
1999	5	4	6	6	7	17	12	18	12	5	8	5.67
1997	6	4	5	8	6	18	12	18	10	5	7	5.51
1995	5	6	6	10	8	21	11	14	9	2	7	5.15

1995–2003: $p < .0001$; 2001–2003: $p < .0001$

Q48_util Public utility companies

% Public	No trust 0	1	2	3	4	5	6	7	8	9	Complete trust 10	Mean
2003	9	9	10	13	12	19	9	10	5	1	3	4.18
2001	9	7	10	10	11	19	9	12	6	3	4	4.49
1999	10	8	10	13	11	21	9	9	5	2	3	4.17
1997	10	8	9	13	11	20	10	10	5	1	4	4.20
1995	8	11	8	14	13	18	8	10	6	1	4	4.20

1995–2003: $p = .8382$; 2001–2003: $p = .0047$

Q49_DOE The Department of Energy

% Public	No trust 0	1	2	3	4	5	6	7	8	9	Complete trust 10	Mean
2003	5	4	6	9	10	21	15	13	8	3	6	5.19
2001	4	4	4	7	8	19	13	16	12	5	8	5.77
1999	6	5	5	9	11	21	13	13	10	3	5	5.13
1997	6	4	6	9	9	22	12	15	8	3	5	5.12
1995	5	6	7	11	11	22	11	12	8	2	5	4.87

1995–2003: $p = .0044$; 2001–2003: $p < .0001$

Q50_labs National laboratories

% Public	No trust 0	1	2	3	4	5	6	7	8	9	Complete trust 10	Mean
2003	4	4	4	10	11	24	13	13	10	3	5	5.26
2001	4	3	4	8	8	20	14	17	12	5	6	5.67
1999	6	5	4	9	10	24	12	14	10	2	4	5.09
1997	6	4	5	9	10	24	14	13	9	3	4	5.07
1995	5	5	5	10	11	23	13	14	8	2	5	5.08

1995–2003: $p = .0923$; 2001–2003: $p < .0001$

Now we want your overall assessment of current and future threats to the US from two sources.

Q51_Rusnow First, on a scale from zero to ten where zero means no threat, and ten means extreme threat, how would you rate the current threat to the US posed by Russia's nuclear weapons?

No threat ←————————————————————————→ Extreme threat

% Public	0	1	2	3	4	5	6	7	8	9	10	Mean
2003	6	6	14	15	11	18	8	8	5	2	6	4.35
2001	6	7	13	16	13	18	8	7	5	1	7	4.39
1999	4	4	8	11	13	22	9	11	8	2	8	5.14
1997	5	4	11	14	12	19	9	9	8	2	7	4.77

1997–2003: $p < .0001$; 2001–2003: $p = .7472$

Q52_PRCnow Next, using the same scale from zero to ten where zero means no threat, and ten means extreme threat, how would you rate the current threat to the US from China's nuclear weapons?

No threat ←————————————————————————→ Extreme threat

% Public	0	1	2	3	4	5	6	7	8	9	10	Mean
2003	3	3	7	8	9	16	12	16	10	5	11	5.76
2001	2	4	8	8	11	20	12	12	11	4	8	5.47
1999	2	2	4	6	8	15	13	16	15	7	13	6.27
1997	3	2	5	8	8	19	13	16	11	5	10	5.84

1997–2003: $p = .4177$; 2001–2003: $p = .0069$

Q53_Rus10 Turning now to your outlook for the future, and using the same scale from zero to ten, how would you rate the threat to the US in the next ten years from Russia's nuclear weapons?

No threat ←————————————————————————→ Extreme threat

% Public	0	1	2	3	4	5	6	7	8	9	10	Mean
2003	7	7	13	17	11	17	8	7	7	1	5	4.26
2001	5	9	13	16	12	18	7	6	6	2	6	4.32
1999	4	3	10	12	12	19	10	10	8	3	8	5.08
1997	6	5	11	15	11	21	8	8	6	3	7	4.65

1997–2003: $p = .0002$; 2001–2003: $p = .5681$

Q54_PRC10 On the same scale from zero to ten, how would you rate the threat to the US in the next ten years from China's nuclear weapons?

No threat ←————————————————————————→ Extreme threat

% Public	0	1	2	3	4	5	6	7	8	9	10	Mean
2003	3	3	7	9	8	14	12	14	12	7	11	5.84
2001	2	4	7	9	12	18	10	12	10	4	10	5.56
1999	2	2	4	5	7	15	12	16	13	8	16	6.45
1997	3	3	5	8	8	17	13	14	12	6	11	5.84

1997–2003: $p = .9782$; 2001–2003: $p = .0130$

Q55_bmd Now I want to shift the discussion to defense against missile attacks. There is an ongoing debate about defending the US from attacks by long-range nuclear-armed ballistic missiles. To the best of your knowledge, does the US currently have a defensive system for shooting down long-range ballistic missiles that have been launched against the US homeland?

% Public	No	Yes	Don't know
2003	31	61	8
2001	31	60	9
1999	26	63	10

Actually, we do NOT currently have any defenses that can shoot down long-range ballistic missiles. People opposed to national missile defenses say that they are not needed, because the threat of US nuclear retaliation will deter all missile launches against us except for those that are accidental. They argue that missile defenses cost too much, will not work, and will lead to another arms race.

People in favor of national missile defenses say that our government has a responsibility to protect us, and that it is both feasible and affordable to construct a limited missile defense system. They argue that such a system would defend against a few missiles launched accidentally or from an attack by a rogue state like North Korea.

[NOTE: The order of the pro and con arguments in the above lead-in was rotated so that approximately one-half of respondents heard the "con" argument first, and approximately one-half heard the "pro" argument first.]

Please respond to the following statements about missile defenses on a scale from one to seven where one means strongly disagree, and seven means strongly agree.

[NOTE: Questions 56–58 were asked in random order.]

Q56_govbmd The US government has a responsibility to build a national ballistic missile defense system to protect us from attacks by nuclear missiles.

	Strongly disagree			←	→	Strongly agree		
% Public	1	2	3	4	5	6	7	Mean
2003	12	6	8	7	17	13	37	4.97
2001	9	5	8	8	17	14	39	5.17
1999	8	4	6	10	17	16	39	5.27

1999–2003: $p = .0003$; 2001–2003: $p = .0202$

Q57_$bmd Money to build a national ballistic missile defense system for the US would be better spent on other programs.

% Public	Strongly disagree ←				→ Strongly agree			Mean
	1	2	3	4	5	6	7	Mean
2003	19	11	11	10	13	10	26	4.19
2001	21	10	12	11	14	11	20	4.01
1999	19	10	12	14	16	9	20	4.06

1999–2003: p = .1680; 2001–2003: p = .0628

Q58_racebmd A US national ballistic missile defense system would lead to a new arms race with Russia and China.

% Public	Strongly disagree ←				→ Strongly agree			Mean
	1	2	3	4	5	6	7	Mean
2003	17	14	13	12	16	9	19	3.99
2001	13	12	13	14	17	13	18	4.20
1999	17	13	11	14	19	11	15	3.98

1999–2003: p = .9612; 2001–2003: p = .0159

Q59_buildbmd On a scale from one to seven where one means the US definitely should not build a national ballistic missile defense system, and seven means the US definitely should build such a system, what is your preference about building a system to defend the US against attacks by long-range nuclear-armed ballistic missiles?

% Public	Definitely should not ←				→ Definitely should			Mean
	1	2	3	4	5	6	7	Mean
2003	13	5	7	8	16	16	36	5.00
2001	9	5	6	10	15	15	39	5.19
1999	8	5	6	12	19	16	34	5.15

1999–2003: p = .0638; 2001–2003: p = .0309

As shown in Afghanistan and Iraq, precision-guided munitions, often called smart bombs, can be delivered very accurately by airplanes and cruise missiles. Some people argue that smart bombs that do NOT have nuclear warheads can take the place of nuclear weapons for preventing attacks against the US. Others disagree, arguing that nothing except our own nuclear weapons can reliably prevent others from using nuclear weapons against us.

Q60_replace On a scale from zero to ten where zero means not at all and ten means completely, to what degree, if any, do you think smart bombs can replace US nuclear weapons for purposes of deterrence?

% Public	Not at all ←									→ Completely		Mean
	0	1	2	3	4	5	6	7	8	9	10	Mean
2003	8	8	9	10	9	19	9	12	8	3	6	4.69
1999	17	8	8	8	10	17	9	8	9	2	5	4.18

1999–2003: p < .0001

Currently there is a debate in the US about developing new lower-energy nuclear weapons that can penetrate deep into the ground before exploding. Although these small-yield nuclear weapons would have much less destructive power than current large-yield nuclear weapons, the devices would be ten times or more as powerful as the largest non-nuclear weapons used in the war against Iraq. The primary purpose for these small-yield nuclear weapons is to destroy deeply buried weapons of mass destruction and command bunkers that cannot be destroyed with non-nuclear weapons.

Supporters of small-yield nuclear weapons argue that the US needs these weapons for two reasons. First, they believe such weapons will allow the US to destroy existing deeply buried targets while producing less radioactive fallout. Second, they believe these new weapons will strengthen deterrence, because such weapons will make it more difficult for other countries to protect weapons of mass destruction and their command bunkers located underground, which would limit their ability to retaliate against the US.

Opponents of small-yield nuclear weapons argue that the US should not develop these new weapons for two reasons. First, they believe such weapons will weaken deterrence, because developing these new nuclear weapons would encourage other countries to build new nuclear weapons. Second, if the US were to use such weapons to destroy deeply buried targets, other countries could then justify their use of nuclear weapons, which would increase the chances for widespread nuclear war.

[NOTE: The order of the pro and con arguments in the above lead-in was rotated so that approximately one-half of respondents heard the "con" argument first, and approximately one-half heard the "pro" argument first.]

With this in mind, please respond to the following statements using a scale from one to seven where one means strongly disagree, and seven means strongly agree.

Q61_sdeter If the US had small-yield nuclear weapons, other countries and terrorists would be less likely to use their weapons of mass destruction against us.

Strongly disagree ← → Strongly agree

% Public	1	2	3	4	5	6	7	Mean
2003	23	12	11	10	14	10	21	3.91

Q62_swmd If the US had small-yield nuclear weapons, other countries and terrorists would be less likely to successfully protect their weapons of mass destruction by burying them deep underground.

Strongly disagree ← → Strongly agree

% Public	1	2	3	4	5	6	7	Mean
2003	13	7	9	10	17	15	28	4.71

Q63_snuke On a scale from one to seven where one means the US definitely should not develop new small-yield nuclear weapons, and seven means the US definitely should develop such weapons, what is your view?

Definitely should not ←————————→ Definitely should

% Public	1	2	3	4	5	6	7	Mean
2003	23	8	7	9	16	13	24	4.24

Q64_stest Now consider that the US has not conducted a nuclear test explosion since 1992, but a limited number of underground nuclear tests might be required if we develop a new nuclear warhead. Using a scale from one to seven where one means the US definitely should not develop new small-yield nuclear weapons, if doing so requires nuclear testing, and seven means the US definitely should develop such weapons, even if it does require some testing, what is your view?

Definitely should not ←————————→ Definitely should

% Public	1	2	3	4	5	6	7	Mean
2003	28	12	9	11	14	10	17	3.68

Q65_terror Now I am going to ask several questions about terrorism. Considering both foreign and domestic sources of terrorism, and both the likelihood of terrorism and its potential consequences, how would you rate today's threat of all kinds of terrorism in the US on a scale from zero to ten where zero means no threat, and ten means extreme threat?

No threat ←————————————————————→ Extreme threat

% Public	0	1	2	3	4	5	6	7	8	9	10	Mean
2003	1	1	3	4	4	10	10	15	22	8	21	7.20
2001	1	0	1	2	1	4	4	11	14	10	51	8.57
1997	1	2	4	8	7	17	12	15	13	5	16	6.34

1997–2003: $p < .0001$; 2001–2003: $p < .0001$

The terrorist bombing in Oklahoma City on April 19, 1995, and the terrorist attacks in New York and Washington DC on September 11, 2001, have raised questions about what can be done to stop terrorism. Using a scale from one to seven where one means you strongly disagree, and seven means you strongly agree, please respond to the following statements:

Q66_stopter There is nothing the government can do to stop determined terrorists.

Strongly disagree ←————————→ Strongly agree

% Public	1	2	3	4	5	6	7	Mean
2003	26	14	11	7	13	13	16	3.70
2001	41	12	7	5	9	9	16	3.22
1995	31	11	10	6	13	8	20	3.65

1995–2003: $p = .6296$; 2001–2003: $p < .0001$

Q67_nointrde The government could stop terrorists, but only with unacceptable intrusions on people's rights and privacy.

Strongly disagree ⟵—————————⟶ Strongly agree

% Public	1	2	3	4	5	6	7	Mean
2003	21	12	14	7	14	12	21	4.02
2001	20	11	12	9	15	11	21	4.07
1995	16	10	8	9	17	12	28	4.48

1995–2003: $p < .0001$; 2001–2003: $p = .5798$

Q68_yesintrde The government must try to stop terrorists, even if it intrudes on some people's rights and privacy.

Strongly disagree ⟵—————————⟶ Strongly agree

% Public	1	2	3	4	5	6	7	Mean
2003	16	8	9	10	14	12	30	4.55
2001	8	4	6	7	13	16	47	5.49
1995	10	5	8	8	17	15	38	5.12

1995–2003: $p < .0001$; 2001–2003: $p < .0001$

Using a scale where one means strongly oppose, and seven means strongly support, how would you feel about giving the federal government the following powers to prevent terrorism?

[NOTE: Questions 69–76 were asked in random order.]

Q69_expel The power to quickly expel from the US any citizen of another country who is suspected of planning a terrorist act, even if the person has not been convicted of any crime.

Strongly oppose ⟵—————————⟶ Strongly support

% Public	1	2	3	4	5	6	7	Mean
2003	16	7	7	7	13	12	38	4.84
2001	8	5	7	8	13	13	46	5.36
1995	9	5	6	9	14	16	41	5.26

1995–2003: $p < .0001$; 2001–2003: $p < .0001$

Q70_spy The power to infiltrate and spy on organizations in this country that the government suspects of planning terrorist acts, even if the groups have not been convicted of any crime.

Strongly oppose ⟵—————————⟶ Strongly support

% Public	1	2	3	4	5	6	7	Mean
2003	10	7	9	10	15	13	36	4.97
2001	6	4	6	7	16	16	45	5.52
1995	11	7	9	9	21	12	29	4.77

1995–2003: $p = .0388$; 2001–2003: $p < .0001$

Q71_seize The power to search for and seize weapons from groups that are suspected of planning terrorist acts, even if the groups have not been convicted of any crime.

Strongly oppose ← — — — — — → Strongly support

% Public	1	2	3	4	5	6	7	Mean
2003	10	6	7	9	14	14	40	5.12
2001	6	4	6	8	16	15	45	5.50
1995	12	8	6	10	17	13	34	4.88

1995–2003: $p = .0129$; 2001–2003: $p < .0001$

Q72_ID The power to require national identification cards for all US citizens.

Strongly oppose ← — — — — — → Strongly support

% Public	1	2	3	4	5	6	7	Mean
2003	24	7	5	7	11	11	34	4.46
2001	14	7	6	7	13	11	43	5.04
1995	27	6	7	8	13	7	32	4.23

1995–2003: $p = .0427$; 2001–2003: $p < .0001$

Q73_radio The power to ban people from speaking on radio or television if they advocate anti-government violence.

Strongly oppose ← — — — — — → Strongly support

% Public	1	2	3	4	5	6	7	Mean
2003	32	13	8	6	10	7	23	3.64
2001	30	10	8	8	11	8	25	3.86
1995	28	11	10	7	9	10	25	3.85

1995–2003: $p = .0579$; 2001–2003: $p = .0377$

Q74_Cnet The power to ban information about bomb-making from computer networks.

Strongly oppose ← — — — — — → Strongly support

% Public	1	2	3	4	5	6	7	Mean
2003	11	6	5	6	10	11	51	5.33
2001	9	5	5	4	7	9	61	5.66
1995	10	4	5	6	9	12	54	5.54

1995–2003: $p = .0359$; 2001–2003: $p = .0004$

Q75_within The power to restrict travel within the US.

Strongly oppose ← — — — — — → Strongly support

% Public	1	2	3	4	5	6	7	Mean
2003	38	12	9	7	10	6	18	3.27
2001	32	12	8	10	12	8	18	3.56

2001–2003: $p = .0034$

Q76_tofrom The power to restrict travel to and from the US.

% Public	1	2	3	4	5	6	7	Mean
2003	15	8	8	11	15	11	32	4.65
2001	13	7	7	11	17	13	32	4.77

Strongly oppose ←——————→ *Strongly support*

2001–2003: *p* = .1922

Q77_into Using the same scale from one to seven, how would you feel about the US government restricting immigration into the US to prevent terrorism?

% Public	1	2	3	4	5	6	7	Mean
2003	12	6	8	8	13	13	40	5.03
2001	8	5	7	8	14	12	45	5.33

Strongly oppose ←——————→ *Strongly support*

2001–2003: *p* = .0013

Responding to the terrorist attacks on New York and Washington DC poses difficult choices involving a range of options. If our government determines to a high degree of certainty that another country actively participated in these acts of terrorism by providing personnel or training for the terrorists, would you support the following responses by the US?

Q78_dip Apply strong diplomatic and political pressures against that country.

% Public	No	Yes
2003	5	95
2001	3	97

Q79_sanc Apply strong economic and trade sanctions against that country.

% Public	No	Yes
2003	8	92
2001	5	95

Q80_bombs Conduct air strikes against that country using conventionally armed weapons such as bombs and cruise missiles.

% Public	No	Yes
2003	49	51
2001	21	79

Q81_invade Use US military forces to invade that country.

% Public	No	Yes
2003	48	52
2001	19	81

Q82_nukes Attack that country using US nuclear weapons.

% Public	No	Yes
2003	86	14
2001	77	23

Q83_certain Now I would like to know how certain you think the government should be in the future that a country supported terrorist acts against the US before we take military action. Using a scale from zero to ten where zero means not at all certain and ten means completely certain, how certain should the government be before it retaliates using military force?

Not at all certain ⟵⟶ Completely certain

% Public	0	1	2	3	4	5	6	7	8	9	10	Mean
2003	1	1	0	1	0	4	5	9	16	16	47	8.60
2001	1	1	1	0	0	4	2	8	19	19	46	8.71

2001–2003: $p = .1395$

The next series of questions deals with critical infrastructures in the US such as telecommunications, electrical power systems, gas and oil supplies and services, banking and finance, transportation systems, water supply systems, emergency services, and continuity of government.

First I want to know your perceptions about potential threats to these kinds of infrastructures as a group. On a scale from zero to ten where zero means no threat, and ten means extreme threat, please rate each of the following as potential threats to critical US infrastructures.

Q84_CIfor Significant damage to critical US infrastructures resulting from terrorism sponsored by foreign groups or individuals.

No threat ⟵⟶ Extreme threat

% Public	0	1	2	3	4	5	6	7	8	9	10	Mean
2001	0	1	2	2	3	12	11	19	16	6	28	7.40
1997	2	3	4	8	8	15	12	16	15	4	11	6.07

1997–2001: $p < .0001$

Q85_CIUS Significant damage to critical US infrastructures resulting from terrorism sponsored by US groups or individuals.

No threat ⟵⟶ Extreme threat

% Public	0	1	2	3	4	5	6	7	8	9	10	Mean
2001	2	3	5	10	11	20	13	12	10	2	13	5.71
1997	2	4	8	14	14	20	11	12	7	2	6	4.96

1997–2001: $p < .0001$

Turning now to individual types of US infrastructures, some people have suggested that terrorists might pose physical threats to property and people and electronic threats to computer networks and other technologies. On a scale where zero means no threat, and ten means extreme threat, please rate the threat that you think terrorists pose to each of the following categories of essential services in the US. Please consider both the likelihood of such terrorist acts occurring and their potential consequences.

Q86_tele Telecommunications such as telephones, television, radio, and the internet.

	No threat									Extreme threat		
% Public	0	1	2	3	4	5	6	7	8	9	10	Mean
2001	1	3	5	6	7	15	11	13	14	7	17	6.42
1997	2	4	5	7	8	14	12	13	14	7	14	6.12

1997–2001: $p = .0072$

Q87_elec Electrical power systems, including generating, transmitting, and distributing electrical power.

	No threat									Extreme threat		
% Public	0	1	2	3	4	5	6	7	8	9	10	Mean
2001	1	2	4	7	7	14	12	15	14	7	18	6.56
1997	3	3	5	9	9	16	12	15	11	5	11	5.83

1997–2001: $p < .0001$

Q88_oil Gas and oil supplies and services, including producing, refining, transporting, and distributing petroleum products and natural gas.

	No threat									Extreme threat		
% Public	0	1	2	3	4	5	6	7	8	9	10	Mean
2001	1	1	3	4	6	12	10	17	16	9	21	7.01
1997	2	2	4	8	8	14	13	15	14	6	12	6.14

1997–2001: $p < .0001$

Q89_bank Banking and finance, including checking services, credit cards, and stock markets.

	No threat									Extreme threat		
% Public	0	1	2	3	4	5	6	7	8	9	10	Mean
2001	1	3	6	7	8	14	12	15	12	6	18	6.39
1997	3	4	8	10	9	15	11	13	11	5	11	5.61

1997–2001: $p < .0001$

Q90_tran Transportation systems, including capabilities for all forms of travel and freight shipments.

	No threat									Extreme threat		
% Public	0	1	2	3	4	5	6	7	8	9	10	Mean
2001	0	1	4	3	5	14	11	17	15	8	21	6.96
1997	2	4	7	8	9	16	14	13	10	5	12	5.73

1997–2001: $p < .0001$

Q91_H2O Water supply systems, including watersheds, aquifers, water treatment, and water distribution for all purposes.

| | No threat | | | | | | | | | | Extreme threat | |
% Public	0	1	2	3	4	5	6	7	8	9	10	Mean
2001	1	2	4	4	5	12	11	16	13	8	22	6.86
1997	3	3	6	10	10	15	10	13	12	6	12	5.83

1997–2001: $p < .0001$

Q92_emer Emergency services, such as medical, police, fire, and rescue.

| | No threat | | | | | | | | | | Extreme threat | |
% Public	0	1	2	3	4	5	6	7	8	9	10	Mean
2001	3	5	8	10	9	17	11	10	10	4	13	5.60
1997	5	7	11	14	12	16	9	8	7	3	9	4.80

1997–2001: $p < .0001$

Q93_govt Continuity of government, meaning preserving institutions and functions of government at all levels.

| | No threat | | | | | | | | | | Extreme threat | |
% Public	0	1	2	3	4	5	6	7	8	9	10	Mean
2001	2	5	8	9	9	15	10	12	10	5	14	5.72
1997	4	6	9	10	11	17	10	12	8	2	9	5.06

1997–2001: $p < .0001$

Q94_aptsec Since the terrorist attacks on the US in September 2001, the government has taken several actions intended to improve airport security. On a scale from zero to ten where zero means not at all effective, and ten means completely effective, how do you rate efforts to improve US airport security thus far?

| | Not at all effective | | | | | | | | | | Completely effective | |
% Public	0	1	2	3	4	5	6	7	8	9	10	Mean
2003	4	3	6	8	10	22	13	16	10	2	5	5.40

Q95_WOT On the same scale from zero to ten where zero means not at all effective, and ten means completely effective, how effective do you believe US efforts in the war on terrorism have been thus far?

| | Not at all effective | | | | | | | | | | Completely effective | |
% Public	0	1	2	3	4	5	6	7	8	9	10	Mean
2003	3	3	5	8	9	18	14	18	12	3	6	5.60

For the next two questions, suppose that winning the war on terrorism is defined by a reduction in the threat of terrorism by half of that which existed immediately after the September 2001 terrorist attacks.

Q96_win First, on a scale from zero to ten, where zero means not at all confident, and ten means completely confident, how confident are you that the US will eventually win the war on terrorism?

Not at all confident ←————————————————→ Completely confident

% Public	0	1	2	3	4	5	6	7	8	9	10	Mean
2003	7	5	7	7	8	17	10	11	11	5	12	5.49

Q97_long Next, assuming that the US can win the war on terrorism, how many years do you think it will take to win?

% Public	Already won 0	1	2	3	4	5	6–10	11–20	21–30	>30	Can never be won	Mean
2003	0	0	1	2	2	11	33	25	10	15	12	19.9

Q98_outlook Using a scale from zero to ten where zero means not at all likely, and ten means extremely likely, how likely do you think it is that we will be able to prevent all large-scale terrorist attacks against the US in the next five years?

Not at all likely ←————————————————→ Extremely likely

% Public	0	1	2	3	4	5	6	7	8	9	10	Mean
2003	10	8	10	12	9	19	9	9	7	2	5	4.39

On a scale from zero to ten where zero means the terrorists who attacked the US in September 2001 were not at all successful, and ten means they were completely successful, how successful do you believe the terrorists were at bringing about each of the following?

[NOTE: Questions 99–101 were asked in random order.]

Q99_suspic Causing Americans to be more suspicious of other people.

Not at all successful ←————————————————→ Completely successful

% Public	0	1	2	3	4	5	6	7	8	9	10	Mean
2003	1	1	2	2	2	9	9	16	17	10	32	7.68

Q100_rights Causing Americans to give up important rights and freedoms.

Not at all successful ←————————————————→ Completely successful

% Public	0	1	2	3	4	5	6	7	8	9	10	Mean
2003	6	6	9	9	8	13	8	11	12	4	15	5.48

Q101_fear Causing Americans to become more fearful in their everyday lives.

Not at all successful ←————————————————→ Completely successful

% Public	0	1	2	3	4	5	6	7	8	9	10	Mean
2003	2	3	5	6	5	14	8	13	15	6	22	6.53

Q102_life On a scale from zero to ten where zero means not at all changed, and ten means completely changed, to what degree, if any, has your way of life changed as a result of the terrorist attacks in September 2001?

	Not at all changed									Completely changed		
% Public	0	1	2	3	4	5	6	7	8	9	10	Mean
2003	17	13	14	10	8	12	7	7	6	1	5	3.65

On a scale from one to seven where one means greatly decreased, four means no change, and seven means greatly increased, how has the threat of terrorism affected your willingness to participate in the following activities?

[NOTE: Questions 103–105 were asked in random order.]

Q103_flyUS Flying on commercial airliners in the US.

	Greatly decreased	No change				Greatly increased		
% Public	1	2	3	4	5	6	7	Mean
2003	13	3	5	59	6	3	11	3.95

Q104_abroad Traveling outside the US.

	Greatly decreased	No change				Greatly increased		
% Public	1	2	3	4	5	6	7	Mean
2003	14	5	6	47	7	5	17	4.09

Q105_crowds Attending public events or visiting public places where there are large crowds of people, such as sporting events, shopping centers, parades, and political rallies.

	Greatly decreased	No change				Greatly increased		
% Public	1	2	3	4	5	6	7	Mean
2003	15	4	5	60	6	4	7	3.77

Now I want you to compare very different kinds of risks. When assessing these risks, please consider both the likelihood of an event occurring and its potential consequences. Using a scale from zero to ten where zero means no risk, and ten means extreme risk, how do you rate each of the following?

Q106_nwar The risks to you and your family of war involving the US in which nuclear weapons are used.

	No risk									Extreme risk		
% Public	0	1	2	3	4	5	6	7	8	9	10	Mean
2003	5	10	13	14	9	17	9	8	5	2	8	4.47

Q107_cbwar The risks to you and your family of war involving the US in which chemical or biological weapons are used.

	No risk										Extreme risk	
% Public	0	1	2	3	4	5	6	7	8	9	10	Mean
2003	3	5	7	9	9	19	11	13	9	3	11	5.51

Q108_cvwar The risks to you and your family of war involving the US in which conventional weapons such as bombs and missiles are used, but nuclear, chemical, or biological weapons are not used.

	No risk										Extreme risk	
% Public	0	1	2	3	4	5	6	7	8	9	10	Mean
2003	5	8	12	11	10	17	9	8	9	3	10	4.88

Q109_twar The risks to you and your family of attacks in the US by terrorists.

	No risk										Extreme risk	
% Public	0	1	2	3	4	5	6	7	8	9	10	Mean
2003	3	5	8	10	8	14	10	15	10	4	13	5.64

Q110_vcrime The risks to you and your family of violent crime.

	No risk										Extreme risk	
% Public	0	1	2	3	4	5	6	7	8	9	10	Mean
2003	3	8	12	13	13	17	9	9	7	2	7	4.69

Q111_nvcrime The risks to you and your family of nonviolent crime such as burglary or credit card fraud.

	No risk										Extreme risk	
% Public	0	1	2	3	4	5	6	7	8	9	10	Mean
2003	2	4	6	9	8	17	12	15	12	5	10	5.77

For the next series, I will read several pairs of opposing statements, and I want you to tell me which statement you agree with the most. It's OK if you do not completely agree with either statement. I just need to know which statement you agree with the most.

[NOTE: Items 112–120 were included only in our 1999 and 2001 surveys. Their order was randomized, and the order of individual statements within each pair of contrasting statements was rotated.]

Q112_nwfw Which of these statements that contrast views about the desirability of a world without nuclear weapons do you agree with the most?

	% Public 1999	% Public 2001
A. If all nuclear weapons were eliminated, the world would be safer, because wars would be less likely to destroy civilization.	69	63
B. If all nuclear weapons were eliminated, the world would be more dangerous, because large conflicts like World Wars I and II would be more likely.	31	37

Q113_viewdet Which of these statements that contrast views about nuclear deterrence do you agree with the most?

	% Public 1999	% Public 2001
A. Nuclear deterrence is dangerous, unstable, and does not prevent war.	40	40
B. Nuclear deterrence is safe, stable, and prevents large conflicts like World Wars I and II.	60	60

Q114_rskben Which of these statements that contrast views about risks and benefits of the US nuclear arsenal do you agree with the most?

	% Public 1999	% Public 2001
A. The US nuclear arsenal deters attacks and ensures our security, and these benefits far outweigh any risks from US nuclear weapons.	73	79
B. The US nuclear arsenal threatens civilization and cannot be safely managed, and these risks far outweigh any benefits from US nuclear weapons.	27	21

Q115_values Which of these statements that contrast views about US nuclear weapons and personal values do you agree with the most?

	% Public 1999	% Public 2001
A. US nuclear weapons threaten institutions that support freedom, self-determination, and human rights.	28	19
B. US nuclear weapons protect institutions that support freedom, self-determination, and human rights.	72	81

Q116_wldsec Which of these statements that contrast views about world security today do you agree with the most?

	% Public 1999	% Public 2001
A. Today the world is a less dangerous place for the US than it was during the Cold War.	36	24
B. Today the world is a more dangerous place for the US than it was during the Cold War.	64	76

Q117_elim Which of these statements that contrast views about eliminating nuclear weapons worldwide do you agree with the most?

	% Public 1999	% Public 2001
A. Eliminating all nuclear weapons worldwide can be achieved if the US sets the example and uses its influence to persuade other countries.	16	13
B. Eliminating all nuclear weapons worldwide cannot be achieved, because knowledge about them is too widespread, and the US cannot prevent others from acquiring them.	84	87

Q118_fpol Which of these statements that contrast views about US foreign policy do you agree with the most?

	% Public 1999	% Public 2001
A. Unless it is directly attacked, the US should use military force only when it is authorized by the United Nations.	53	46
B. The US should use military force when the US thinks it's necessary, even if the United Nations does not authorize it.	47	54

Q119_uses Which of these statements that contrast views about the uses of nuclear weapons do you agree with the most?

	% Public 1999	% Public 2001
A. US nuclear weapons have no use except for deterring others from using their nuclear weapons against us.	42	40
B. US nuclear weapons are useful both for deterring others from using their nuclear weapons against us and for winning wars if necessary.	58	60

Q120_milpwr Which of these statements that contrast views about US military power do you agree with the most?

	% Public 1999	% Public 2001
A. US military power is less important today than it was during the Cold War.	28	19
B. US military power is more important today than it was during the Cold War.	72	81

Now we want to understand more about how you feel about American society. On a scale from one to seven, where one means you strongly disagree, and seven means you strongly agree, please respond to each of the following statements.

[NOTE: Questions 121–140 were asked only in the years shown. Though grouped here by the political culture category they are intended to measure, actual order in each survey was randomized.]

Measures of Hierarchy

Q121_ahead The best way to get ahead in life is to work hard and do what you are told to do.

Strongly disagree ⟵⟶ Strongly agree

% Public	1	2	3	4	5	6	7	Mean
1995	10	6	10	13	18	13	30	4.81
1993	7	7	11	14	20	16	25	4.81

Q122_auth Our society is in trouble, because we don't obey those in authority.

Strongly disagree ⟵⟶ Strongly agree

% Public	1	2	3	4	5	6	7	Mean
1995	15	9	10	11	19	11	26	4.45

Q123_auth One of the problems with people today is that they have lost their respect for authority.

Strongly disagree ⟵⟶ Strongly agree

% Public	1	2	3	4	5	6	7	Mean
1993	5	5	7	9	20	20	35	5.32

Q124_rules Society would be much better off if we imposed strict and swift punishment on those who break the rules.

Strongly disagree ⟵⟶ Strongly agree

% Public	1	2	3	4	5	6	7	Mean
1995	5	3	6	7	13	15	50	5.66
1993	6	4	5	10	17	18	40	5.44

Measures of Individualism

Q125_fail Even if some people are at a disadvantage, it is best for society to let people succeed or fail on their own.

Strongly disagree ⟵⟶ Strongly agree

% Public	1	2	3	4	5	6	7	Mean
1995	9	6	10	14	18	12	31	4.86
1993	8	7	10	13	18	17	26	4.83

Q126_disadv Even the disadvantaged should have to make their own way in the world.

Strongly disagree ⟵⟶ Strongly agree

% Public	1	2	3	4	5	6	7	Mean
1995	14	8	16	15	18	10	19	4.22

Q127_rich People who get rich in business have a right to keep and enjoy their wealth.

Strongly disagree ←――――――――――→ Strongly agree

% Public	1	2	3	4	5	6	7	Mean
1995	7	3	5	10	17	18	39	5.40
1993	5	3	7	11	22	19	33	5.31

Q128_indiv We are all better off when we compete as individuals.

Strongly disagree ←――――――――――→ Strongly agree

% Public	1	2	3	4	5	6	7	Mean
1995	10	7	9	11	15	13	35	4.95

Q129_intrfer Society should never interfere in how people choose to live their lives.

Strongly disagree ←――――――――――→ Strongly agree

% Public	1	2	3	4	5	6	7	Mean
1993	11	11	12	16	17	12	21	4.38

Measures of Egalitarianism

Q130_fair What our society needs is a fairness revolution to make the distribution of goods more equal.

Strongly disagree ←――――――――――→ Strongly agree

% Public	1	2	3	4	5	6	7	Mean
1995	24	11	11	10	15	8	21	3.91
1993	22	12	13	13	16	9	16	3.78

Q131_pwr Society works best if power is shared equally.

Strongly disagree ←――――――――――→ Strongly agree

% Public	1	2	3	4	5	6	7	Mean
1995	13	7	10	12	17	11	30	4.65

Q132_fairness It is our responsibility to reduce the differences in income between the rich and the poor.

Strongly disagree ←――――――――――→ Strongly agree

% Public	1	2	3	4	5	6	7	Mean
1995	24	11	11	12	15	8	19	3.84

Q133_taxes I support a tax shift so that the burden falls more heavily on corporations and people with large incomes.

Strongly disagree ←――――――――――→ Strongly agree

% Public	1	2	3	4	5	6	7	Mean
1993	12	6	7	10	21	16	29	4.84

Q134_corps Most of the harm done in society comes from big corporations and the government.

| | Strongly disagree ← | | | | | → Strongly agree | | |
% Public	1	2	3	4	5	6	7	Mean
1993	10	12	14	16	18	13	17	4.26

Measures of Fatalism

Q135_random Most of the important things that take place in life happen by random chance.

| | Strongly disagree ← | | | | | → Strongly agree | | |
% Public	1	2	3	4	5	6	7	Mean
1995	31	19	12	10	12	5	11	3.11

Q136_chance For the most part, succeeding in life is a matter of chance.

| | Strongly disagree ← | | | | | → Strongly agree | | |
% Public	1	2	3	4	5	6	7	Mean
1995	34	18	13	9	10	5	11	3.02

Q137_luck For the most part, getting ahead in life is a matter of being lucky.

| | Strongly disagree ← | | | | | → Strongly agree | | |
% Public	1	2	3	4	5	6	7	Mean
1993	31	20	15	12	11	5	6	2.90

Q138_fate No matter how hard we try, the course of our lives is largely determined by forces beyond our control.

| | Strongly disagree ← | | | | | → Strongly agree | | |
% Public	1	2	3	4	5	6	7	Mean
1995	25	15	12	9	13	7	19	3.65

Q139_plans It would be foolish to make serious plans in such an uncertain world.

| | Strongly disagree ← | | | | | → Strongly agree | | |
% Public	1	2	3	4	5	6	7	Mean
1993	40	19	9	9	10	4	9	2.79

Q140_same In politics, no matter how hard we try, things go on pretty much the same.

| | Strongly disagree ← | | | | | → Strongly agree | | |
% Public	1	2	3	4	5	6	7	Mean
1993	4	5	6	9	20	20	36	5.39

Finally, I need some basic background information about you.

Q141_reside Including yourself, how many people currently live at your residence?

% Public	Means
2003	2.60
2001	2.76
1999	2.77
1997	2.70
1995	2.80
1993	2.79

Q142_ovr18 How many of those are 18 years of age or older?

% Public	Means
2003	2.24
2001	2.23
1999	2.24
1997	2.23
1995	2.22

Q143_party With which political party do you most identify?

% Public	Democratic (1)	Republican (2)	Independent (3)	Other (4)
2003	41	45	10	5
2001	44	45	7	4
1999	47	41	6	6
1997	43	44	10	3
1995	37	37	23	3
1993	43	39	16	2

Q144_iden Do you completely, somewhat, or slightly identify with that political party?

% Public	Slightly (1)	Somewhat (2)	Completely (3)	Mean
2003	11	56	33	2.22
2001	8	53	39	2.31
1999	19	60	22	2.03
1997	18	61	21	2.03
1995	21	58	21	1.99
1993	18	55	26	2.08

Q145_ideol On a scale of political ideology, individuals can be arranged from strongly liberal to strongly conservative. Which of the following categories best describes your views?

% Public	Strongly liberal (1)	Liberal (2)	Slightly liberal (3)	Middle of the road (4)	Slightly Conservative (5)	Conservative (6)	Strongly Conservative (7)	Mean
2003	6	12	10	27	18	19	9	4.34
2001	4	12	11	27	18	19	9	4.35
1999	4	13	8	29	17	20	8	4.37
1997	4	10	11	28	17	24	7	4.43
1995	2	10	11	28	21	20	7	4.46
1993	4	12	12	28	17	19	9	4.34

1993–2003: $p = .9685$; 2001–2003: $p = .8495$

Q146_race Which of the following best describes your race or ethnic background?

% Public	American Indian	Asian	Black	Hispanic	White, non-Hispanic	Other
2003	3	1	5	4	85	1
2001	3	3	6	5	81	3
1999	2	2	7	5	79	4
1997	2	1	6	4	81	5
1995	2	2	7	4	79	6
1993	2	2	6	4	84	2

Q147_inc Please indicate which of the following income categories approximates the total estimated annual income for your household for the year 2002.

% Public	<$10K (1)	$10–20K (2)	$20–30K (3)	$30–40K (4)	$40–50K (5)	$50–60K (6)
2003	5	9	11	11	15	10

% Public	$60–70K (7)	$70–80K (8)	$80–90K (9)	$90–100K (10)	>$100K (11)	Median
2003	9	8	5	4	13	5

Median Ranges

Public 2003	Public 2001	Public 1999	Public 1997	Public 1995	Public 1993
$40K–50K	$50K–60K	$40K–50K	$40K–50K	$30K–40K	$35K–40K

NOTES

Chapter 1: Objectives, Concepts, and Theories

1. The Treaty on the Non-proliferation of Nuclear Weapons (NPT) opened for signature in 1968, entered into force March 5, 1970, for an initial period of twenty-five years, and was extended indefinitely in 1995. It recognizes five nuclear weapon states: China, France, the United Kingdom, the United States, and the Union of Soviet Socialist Republics (succeeded by Russia). Israel is not a signatory to the treaty and does not officially acknowledge possessing nuclear weapons but is widely recognized as having an operational nuclear arsenal. In 1974 India conducted its first nuclear weapon test, and in 1998 both India and Pakistan conducted multiple underground nuclear test explosions, followed by the development of respective operational nuclear weapons capabilities. Neither India nor Pakistan are signatories to the NPT.

2. Though not examined in this book, we also conducted surveys of elite groups during the same ten-year period to include members of the technical staffs of four US national laboratories (Jenkins-Smith, Barke, and Herron 1994), members of the prestigious American Men and Women of Science (Herron and Jenkins-Smith 1998), state legislators from all fifty states (Herron and Jenkins-Smith 1998), and members of the American Association for the Advancement of Science in the US and fifteen member states of the European Union (Herron, Jenkins-Smith, Mitchell, and Whitten 2003). Also, we conducted and qualitatively analyzed in-depth interviews with fifty prominent US security policy experts (Herron, Jenkins-Smith, Hughes, Gormley, and Mahnken 2000). Though the focus of this book is on mass opinions, our studies of elite groups are designed to afford comparisons of mass and elite belief structures and to contrast the views of less informed and less technically sophisticated publics with those of elite groups possessing more information about nuclear security and, presumably, higher average cognitive skills.

3. For a concise review of the evolution of the concept of public opinion from its roots in ancient political theory to contemporary interpretations, see Peters 1995.

4. For further elaboration of Converse's views on public opinion, see Campbell et al. 1960, 1966; Converse 1970, 1975, 1987; and Converse and Markus 1979.

5. For a description of the evolution of survey research in the US, see Jean Converse 1987.

6. For a different and less sanguine view of the importance of political knowledge for public participation in policy processes, see Delli Carpini and Keeter 1996.

7. Noting that society's own mandates can exert social tyranny of the majority that is more formidable than many kinds of political oppression, John Stuart Mill cautions in *On Liberty* ([1859] 1992) that there must be a limit to the legitimate interference of collective opinion with individual independence.

Chapter 2: Trends in Nuclear Security Assessments

1. Our biennial surveys were conducted in the fall period of each survey year, and in 2001 our survey began by coincidence on September 12, the day following the terrorist attacks in New York and Washington DC, providing a rare snapshot during a national emergency. Dates and methods of data collection, sample sizes, and cooperation rates for each survey are in appendix 1, table A1.2.

2. Ungrouped distributions of responses to all survey questions are in appendix 2. Throughout, we report the results of analyses of variance (ANOVAs) in terms of p-value, which is a measure of the probability that differences in means would have occurred by chance. Statistical significance is attributed to those differences that would have occurred by chance fewer than five times in 100 (equivalent to a 95 percent confidence level). In figure 2.1, the difference in means between respondents in 1997 and 2003 would have occurred by chance fewer than once in 10,000 occurrences ($p < .0001$), and therefore is considered statistically significant. In the same figure, the difference in means between public responses in 2001 and 2003 would have occurred by chance 1,226 times in 10,000 occurrences ($p = .1226$), and therefore is not considered statistically significant at the 95 percent confidence level. However, statistical significance does not always equate to policy relevance. The relevance of statistically significant differences in means must be judged in the context of the variables being measured and the groups being compared.

3. The elusive "peace dividend" can be interpreted many different ways. In general, it refers to the concept of redirecting portions of defense expenditures to non-defense uses. The U.S. Department of State estimates that worldwide military spending declined 4.6 percent in real terms in the first decade of the post–Cold War era (1989–1999). During the same period, US military expenditures (expressed in constant 1999 dollars) declined from approximately 5.5 percent of US gross national product to 3.0 percent (U.S. Department of State 2002). The purposes for which "peace dividends" have been used are much less clear.

4. However, differences in 2003 paired comparisons of current and future mean nuclear threats from neither Russia ($p = .0561$) nor China ($p = .0747$) are large enough to be statistically significant at the 95 percent confidence level.

5. The scales for Q6 and Q7 are converted from 1–7 to 0–10, then responses from each of the six questions are averaged, ignoring missing values, to form the external nuclear risk index.

6. Note that in figure 2.8 and in subsequent trend graphs, we truncate the vertical scale to better illustrate the data. We identify the scale midpoint to help orientation.

7. Responses to each of the seven questions are averaged, ignoring missing values, to form the domestic nuclear risk index.

8. These three questions about nuclear deterrence were not asked in 1993.

9. Responses to each of the questions are averaged, ignoring missing values, to form the external nuclear benefit index.

10. See Schwartz 1998 for one approach to estimating nuclear weapons–related expenditures.

11. This question was not asked of the public in 1993.

12. For ease of comparison with other nuclear benefit and risk indices, we convert responses from each of the three questions from a 1–7 scale to a 0–10 scale and average them, ignoring missing values, to form the domestic nuclear benefit index.

Chapter 3: Trends in Policy and Spending Preferences

1. Wordings of and distributions of responses to all survey questions are found in appendix 2.

2. Note that throughout this chapter vertical scales in figures vary to better illustrate changes and do not always show full response ranges.

3. The US public appears to clearly differentiate between the "desirability" and "feasibility" dimensions of the nuclear abolition issue. Though the desirability question is not asked in these surveys, we reported in 2002 that about two out of three US respondents and three out of four British respondents in nationwide surveys agreed that eliminating nuclear weapons is *desirable*, but only about one in three US participants and four in ten British participants consider nuclear abolition *feasible* (Jenkins-Smith and Herron 2002a).

4. Article VI of the NPT reads as follows: "Each of the Parties to the Treaty undertakes to pursue negotiations in good faith on effective measures relating to cessation of the nuclear arms race at an early date and to nuclear disarmament, and on a treaty on general and complete disarmament under strict and effective international control."

5. Only about 10 percent of the weapons used in Operation Desert Storm were so-called smart bombs; estimates are that in Afghanistan about 60 percent of the bombs dropped were precision guided. While in the 1991 Gulf War and the 1999 Kosovo conflict less than half of precision munitions hit their targets, the US air campaign in Afghanistan achieved a 75 to 85 percent success rate (Burgess 2002). The increasing effectiveness of precision munitions has sparked debate about their potential effectiveness for deterrence. For arguments calling for precision munitions to replace nuclear weapons, see Nitze 1994, 1999; Nitze and McCall 1997; and Krepinevich and Kosiak 1998. For a critique of those arguments, see Gormley and Mahnken 2000. For a discussion of the strategic implications and limitations of precision weapons, see Pape 1997/98; Reese 2003; and Younger 2000.

6. In 1999, the lead-in began as follows: "As shown in the Persian Gulf War and more recently in Yugoslavia, precision-guided. . . ."

7. The Treaty on Strategic Offensive Reductions, signed by President George W. Bush and President Vladimir Putin in Moscow on May 24, 2002, requires the United States and the Russian Federation to reduce and limit aggregate strategic nuclear warheads to 1,700–2,200 for each party by December 31, 2012. The treaty was ratified by the US Senate on March 6, 2003. It was ratified by Russia's lower house of parliament on May 14, 2003, and by the upper house of parliament on May 29, 2003.

8. The increase in the percentage of correct answers, while modest, was statistically significant (chi-square $p = .032$).

9. The order of the pro and con arguments was rotated so that approximately half of respondents heard the "con" argument first, and the other half heard the "pro" argument first.

10. The order in which the statements were asked was randomized to reduce unintended order effects.

11. For open source estimates of historical investment levels in US nuclear weapons capabilities, see Schwartz 1998.

12. The explosive yield of such weapons could vary widely and could greatly exceed the example cited in the lead-in to this series of questions. Most members of the general public are not conversant in the terms of varying nuclear yields. Media discussions often describe nuclear yields relative to the nuclear device used in 1945 against Hiroshima, Japan. We avoided that application because of pejorative connotations associated with the detonation of a nuclear weapon over a densely populated metropolitan area. The applications being considered here are deep underground explosions that would produce very different effects. The explosive size of such warheads and the specific effects they may produce under differing conditions cannot be specified in detail.

13. The order in which the questions were asked was randomized to reduce unintended order effects.

14. The component questions for each of our four risk and benefit indices are discussed in chapter 2. Question wordings, distributions of responses, and mean values for each component question are in appendix 2.

Chapter 4: Terrorism

1. Distributions of responses and wordings of all survey questions are in appendix 2. As in the preceding chapters, note that vertical scales vary and are truncated to better illustrate change. We specify scale midpoints to help orientation.

2. Responses to questions 17, 18, and 65 are averaged, ignoring missing values, to form the terrorism threat index.

3. The eight questions about individual infrastructures were asked in random order to reduce unintended order effects.

4. After the scales for questions 66 and 67 are reversed, we average them with responses to question 68 (ignoring missing values) to form the preventing terrorism index.

5. These nine questions were asked in random sequence to avoid unintended order effects.

6. Because questions 75–77 were not asked in 1995, we compute the domestic intrusion index only for the years 2001 and 2003.

7. Questions were randomly ordered to reduce response bias.

Chapter 5: Opinion Stability at the Individual Level

1. Madison, no. 50, p. 317: "But it is the reason, alone, of the public, that ought to control and regulate the government. The passions ought to be controlled and regulated by the government." Madison, no. 50, p. 319: "When men exercise their reason coolly and freely on a variety of distinct questions, they inevitably fall into different opinions on some of them. When they are governed by a common passion, their opinions, if they are so to be called, will be the same." Madison no. 63, p. 384: "[T]here are particular moments in public affairs when the people, stimulated by some irregular passion, or some illicit advantage, or misled by the artful representations of interested men, may call for measures which they themselves will afterwards be the most ready to lament and condemn." See also Hamilton, no. 15, p. 110; Hamilton, no. 71, p. 432; and Madison no. 52, pp. 324–25.

2. For additional analysis of public "mood theory" and foreign policy see Caspary 1970; Cohen 1957; Furniss and Snyder 1955; Holsti 1996; Needler 1966; and Rosenau 1961.

3. Reports consist of instances in which the words "terrorist" or "terrorism" appear in the headline or lead paragraph in articles published between January 1, 1991, and September 30, 2002, in the following eight periodicals: *Chicago Sun-Times, Houston Chronicle, Miami Herald, New York Times, Philadelphia Enquirer, San Francisco Chronicle, USA Today,* and the *Wall Street Journal.*

4. Demographic characteristics of each of the five increments did not differ significantly from those of the entire sample.

5. Component questions and descriptions of how we calculated the terrorism threat index, preventing terrorism index, domestic intrusion index, and terrorism response index are provided in chapter 4. Question wordings, distributions of responses, and mean values for all component questions are in appendix 2.

6. In part, the high variance in view among the minority respondents over time reflects a small sample of minority respondents in the 2001–2002 panel survey.

7. For further discussion and illustration of panel stability see Jenkins-Smith and Herron 2005.

8. We also modeled age using nonlinear (polynomial) relationships. Because these models produce few statistically significant results and very small explanatory values, they add little to the linear model and are omitted from our discussion.

9. For a list of component questions and explanations of how external and domestic nuclear risk and benefit indices are calculated, see chapter 2. Question wordings, distributions, and mean values for all component questions are in appendix 2.

10. Coefficients for models estimating nonlinear relationships (e.g., polynomial models) were not significant, indicating that the overall relationship between age and perceptions of deterrence is essentially linear.

11. The one exception among the indices in six surveys occurs in 2003 when women rate mean external nuclear benefits at 7.01, and men rate them at 7.22, a difference of 0.21 that does reach statistical significance ($p = .0421$).

12. This is consistent with expectations about public anxiety promoting less reliance on predispositions (Marcus 2002).

13. So-called dummy variables are dichotomous measures in which a value of one indicates the presence of an attribute (male gender; college degree; racial/ethnic minority status), and a value of zero indicates its absence (not male; no college degree; not a member of a racial/ethnic minority).

Chapter 6: Mass Belief Structures

1. This level of beliefs among elites is referred to as "deep core" by Sabatier and Jenkins-Smith (1999, 133) and as "standard heuristics" by Peffley and Hurwitz (1992, 433).

2. This level of beliefs among elite groups is termed "policy core" by Sabatier and Jenkins-Smith (1999, 133).

3. Our primary concern in this book is with such policy preferences. More general characterizations of belief systems incorporate specific beliefs about states of the world, causal mechanisms, and other elements. See, for example, the discussion of the "secondary aspects" of belief systems in Sabatier and Jenkins-Smith (1999, 133).

4. According to Sabatier and Jenkins-Smith (1999, 130–31): "The most important beliefs are those in the policy core—that is, those that relate to the subsystem as a whole—because these are more salient to the individual than deep core beliefs and serve as more efficient guides to behavior than specific policy preferences in the secondary aspects."

5. For further discussions about methodological issues associated with ideological self-measurement, see Brown 1970; Feldman 1988; Herron and Jenkins-Smith 2002; Huber 1989; Kerlinger 1967; Laponce 1970, 1981; Levitin and Miller 1979; Luttbeg and Gant 1993; Marcus, Tabb, and Sullivan 1974; and Peffley and Hurwitz 1985.

6. These sensible relationships between self-assessed ideology and self-assessed partisanship do not address causality. We are not suggesting that ideology drives partisanship or the reverse. In fact, some evidence suggests that changes in macroideology and macropartisanship may not always be related systematically (Box-Steffensmeier, Knight, and Sigelman 1998).

7. See chapter 2 for descriptions of how the risk and benefit indices are constructed. Question wordings, distributions of responses, and mean values for all component questions are in appendix 2.

8. Put differently, both Republicans and Democrats see substantial risks (on average), even though their policy remedies may differ substantially.

9. Question wordings, distributions of responses, and mean values for all survey questions are in appendix 2.

10. The change in the strength of association is captured by calculating a regression in which the policy preferences are regressed on partisanship (a six-point scale running from strong Republican to strong Democrat) and an interactive term that multiplies the

partisanship variable by a counter representing the wave of the survey. If the estimated coefficient for the latter is positive and significant, it indicates that the strength of the association is positive and getting stronger.

11. For that, a prior hypothesis would be required or fresh data with which to test the newly generated hypothesis.

12. The origin of this variant of "cultural theory" is found in the work of Mary Douglas. In *Natural Symbols* (1970), she introduces the grid/group typology that is the basis of cultural theory. The typology was applied to risk analysis by Mary Douglas and Aaron Wildavsky in 1982. For other important contributions to the study of culture and risk see: Schwartz and Thompson 1990; Thompson, Ellis, and Wildavsky 1990; and Thompson and Wildavsky 1982. For a quantitative test of cultural theory hypotheses see Jenkins-Smith and Smith 1994. For the evolution of cultural theory as it is applied to risk analysis, see Rayner 1992.

13. The measures are modifications of similar metrics originated by Wildavsky and Dake (1990). Their original formulations were iteratively revised based on opinion survey research conducted during the 1990s (Jenkins-Smith and Smith 1994; Jenkins-Smith et al. 1994). We list them in appendix 2.

14. See chapter 2 for a list of component questions for each of our risk and benefit indices. Exceptions in 1993 are as follows. The external nuclear benefit index for 1993 does not include the three questions about the value of nuclear deterrence (Q23–25) that were added in 1995 and incorporated in the external benefit indices for 1995–2003. The domestic nuclear benefit index for 1993 does not include the question about the value of technological advances in defense industries for other areas of the US economy (Q39) that was added in 1995 and incorporated in the domestic nuclear benefit indices for 1995–2003. Question wordings, distributions of responses, and mean values for all component questions are in appendix 2.

15. To reduce systematic order effects, we randomized the pairs of contrasting statements in two ways: the order of the component statements in each pair was rotated, and the sequence of the nine pairs of statements was randomized.

16. Because percentages indicate the proportion of respondents who identify *most* with each statement, they should not be interpreted to imply that those proportions agree completely with either statement.

17. Our survey in 2001 began on September 12, immediately following the terrorist attacks of 9/11 in New York City, Washington DC, and Pennsylvania. Some of the changes in 2001 compared to responses in 1999 may be partially a function of the proximity of our survey to the terrorist attacks.

18. Based on chi-square tests, differences in means would have occurred by chance fewer than five times out of a hundred.

19. The nuclear security domain belief index is created by summing scored responses. Cases having one or more missing values for any of the nine component pairs of beliefs are omitted from the index.

20. So-called "dummy" variables are dichotomous measures in which a value of one indicates the presence of an attribute (male gender; college degree; racial/ethnic minor-

ity status), and a value of zero indicates its absence (not male; no college degree; not a member of a racial/ethnic minority).

21. Though we do not comparatively address elite views in this book, for discussions of elite perspectives on nuclear security, see Jenkins-Smith, Barke, and Herron 1994; Herron and Jenkins-Smith 1998; Herron, Jenkins-Smith, and Hughes 2000; Herron and Jenkins-Smith 2002; and Herron, Jenkins-Smith, Mitchell, and Whitten 2003.

Chapter 7: Making Sense of Public Beliefs

1. Theorists differ markedly in what they expect of a public in a successful democracy, ranging from relatively demanding requirements of democratic citizenship in Delli Carpini and Keeter (1996) to the more relaxed requirements for reasoned public choice in Lupia and McCubbins (1998). More generally, see Mueller's (1999) survey of the requirements for functioning democracy.

2. It is quite easy to ask factual knowledge questions that illustrate how little some Americans know about technical details associated with complex policy areas such as nuclear security and terrorism. Answers to knowledge questions in some polls, particularly about science or geography, are sometimes reported as evidence that the public largely is ignorant. To some experts, a lack of factual knowledge about technical aspects of security issues and foreign policies disqualifies most citizens from having an important role in their debate. These kinds of assumptions are at the heart of traditional theory about public capacities.

3. Similar confusion was evident in our focus group discussions. The group participants' beliefs were based on recollections of the widely televised use of Patriot missiles to defend (poorly, as it turned out) against Iraqi Scud missiles in the first Gulf War.

4. On September 11, 1996, the United Nations approved the CTBT. To date, the treaty has been signed by 175 states and ratified by 120 states. On October 13, 1999, the US Senate declined to ratify the CTBT. As of this writing, the US government continues to voluntarily abide by the provisions of the treaty.

5. Among other distinguished international personalities, Canberra Commission members included two prominent former leaders charged with responsibilities for US nuclear forces and resources: Robert McNamara, US Secretary of Defense 1961–1968; and General Lee Butler, USAF (Retired), Commander in Chief of the US Strategic Air Command 1991–1992, and subsequently the US Strategic Command 1992–1994.

6. For a small sample of expert analyses during the period of our surveys, see: Bailey 1994; Blackwill and Carnesale 1993; Bundy, Crowe, and Drell 1993; Cimbala 1993, 1998; Clausen 1993; Daalder 1995; Flournoy 1993; Garrity and Maaranen 1992; Gray 1999; Harknett and Wirtz 1998; Iklé 1996; Mazarr 1992; Morgan 2003; National Academy of Sciences 1997; Payne 1996, 2001; Reiss and Litwak 1994; Roberts 1995; Rotblatt, Steinberger, and Udgaonkar 1993; Schneider and Dowdy 1998; Utgoff 2000; van Creveld 1993.

7. One highly popular song by country singer Toby Keith announced that, in response to the unnamed enemy behind the 9/11 attacks, "we'll put a boot in your ass, it's the American Way."

8. Zaller (1992) added the view that most members of the public are susceptible to quite different apparent belief structures depending on which of many competing "considerations" are activated.

9. In electoral systems (like that in the United States) with single-member districts with plurality elections, the iterative process of policy debate is theorized by Anthony Downs (1957) to result in two-dimensional distributions of policy positions. All else being equal, we would expect the "fit" of the dimension of the policy dispute to partisan positions to become more tightly aligned as the number of opportunities for policy dispute and debate increases. Of course, if the policy context changes fundamentally, the public's ability to make the linkage between partisan positions and policy preferences may be attenuated pending clarification in subsequent iterations of partisan dispute.

10. Of course measurement error and model specification limitations also influence the explained and residual variation, but these issues are unlikely to change our central findings.

11. Though not reported here, our research into the security views of elite groups (Herron and Jenkins-Smith 2002) finds more highly structured patterns of beliefs than are evident among mass publics. Our findings are not that mass and elite views are *equally* structured, but that clear, replicable patterns of beliefs are evident among mass publics, and that those structures parallel the general patterns of beliefs we find among elite groups.

12. Compare the results of Rothman and Lichter (1987) with those of Plutzer, Maney, and O'Connor (1998). Models of nuclear risk perceptions of samples of scientists, taken in similar ways a decade apart, show markedly different correlations between perceived risk and political ideology.

REFERENCES

Achen, Christopher H. 1975. "Mass Political Attitudes and the Survey Response." *American Political Science Review* 69 (4): 1218–31.

Almond, Gabriel A. 1950. *The American People and Foreign Policy.* New York: Harcourt Brace.

———. 1956. "Public Opinion and National Security Policy." *Public Opinion Quarterly* 20 (2): 371–78.

American Association for Public Opinion Research. 2004. *Standard Definitions: Final Dispositions of Case Codes and Outcome Rates for Surveys.* Ann Arbor, MI: AAPOR.

Asher, Herbert B. 1980. *Presidential Elections and American Politics.* Homewood, IL: Dorsey Press.

Bailey, Kathleen C., ed. 1994. *Weapons of Mass Destruction: Costs Versus Benefits.* New Delhi: Manohar Publishers.

Bailey, Thomas A. 1948. *The Man in the Street: The Impact of American Public Opinion on Foreign Policy.* New York: Macmillan.

Barke, Richard P., and Hank C. Jenkins-Smith. 1993. "Politics and Scientific Expertise: Scientists, Risk Perceptions, and Nuclear Waste Policy." *Risk Analysis* 13 (4): 425–39.

Barke, Richard P., Hank C. Jenkins-Smith, and Paul Slovic. 1997. "Risk Perceptions of Men and Women Scientists." *Social Science Quarterly* 78 (1): 167–76.

Bentham, Jeremy. [1838–1843] 1962. *The Works of Jeremy Bentham.* Ed. J. Browning. 11 vols. New York: Russell and Russell.

Berelson, Bernard R., Paul F. Lazarsfeld, and William N. McPhee. 1954. *Voting: A Study of Opinion Formation in a Presidential Campaign.* Chicago: University of Chicago Press.

Blackwill, Robert D., and Albert Carnesale, eds. 1993. *New Nuclear Nations: Consequences for U.S. Policy.* New York: Council on Foreign Relations Press.

Bless, Herbert. 2000. "The Interplay of Affect and Cognition: The Mediating Role of General Knowledge Structures." In *Feeling and Thinking: the Role of Affect in Social Cognition,* ed. Joseph P. Forgas. New York: Cambridge University Press.

Box-Steffensmeier, Janet M., Kathleen Knight, and Lee Sigelman. 1998. "The Interplay of Macropartisanship and Macroideology: A Time Series Analysis." *Journal of Politics* 69 (4): 1031–49.

Brown, Steven R. 1970. "Consistency and Persistence of Ideology: Some Experimental Results." *Public Opinion Quarterly* 34 (1): 60–68.

Bundy, McGeorge, William J. Crowe Jr., and Sidney D. Drell. 1993. *Reducing Nuclear Danger: The Road Away from the Brink.* New York: Council on Foreign Relations Press.

Burgess, Mark. 2002. "Smart Bombs." Washington, DC: Center for Defense Information. <http://www.cdi.org/terrorism/smartbombs.cfm>

Campbell, Angus, Philip E. Converse, Warren E. Miller, and Donald E. Stokes. 1960. *The American Voter.* New York: Wiley.

———. 1966. *Elections and the Political Order.* New York: John Wiley and Sons.

Caspary, William R. 1970. "The 'Mood Theory': A Study of Public Opinion and Foreign Policy." *American Political Science Review* 64 (2): 536–47.

Chittick, William O., Keith R. Billingsley, and Rick Travis. 1995. "A Three-Dimensional Model of American Foreign Policy Beliefs." *International Studies Quarterly* 39:313–31.

Christenson, Reo M., Alan S. Engel, Dan N. Jacobs, Mostafa Rejai, and Herbert Waltzer. 1975. *Ideologies and Modern Politics.* New York: Dodd, Mead.

Cimbala, Stephen J. 1993. "Nuclear Weapons in the New World Order." *Journal of Strategic Studies* 16 (2): 173–99.

———. 1998. *The Past and Future of Nuclear Deterrence.* Westport, CT: Praeger Publishers.

Clausen, Peter A. 1993. *Nonproliferation and the National Interest.* New York: HarperCollins.

Cohen, Bernard C. 1957. *The Political Process and Foreign Policy.* Princeton, NJ: Princeton University Press.

Congleton, Roger. 1991. "Ideological Conviction and Persuasion in the Rent-Seeking Society." *Journal of Public Economics* 44 (1): 65–86.

Conover, Pamela Johnston, and Stanley Feldman. 1981. "The Origins and Meaning of Liberal/Conservative Self-Identifications." *American Journal of Political Science* 25 (4): 617–45.

Converse, Jean. 1987. *Survey Research in the United States: Roots and Emergence 1890–1960.* Berkeley: University of California Press.

Converse, Philip E. 1964. "The Nature of Belief Systems in Mass Publics." In *Ideology and Discontent,* ed. David E. Apter. New York: Free Press.

———. 1970. "Attitudes and Non-Attitudes: Continuation of a Dialogue." In *The Quantitative Analysis of Social Problems,* ed. Edward R. Tufte. Reading, MA: Addison-Wesley.

———. 1975. "Public Opinion and Voting Behavior." In *Handbook of Political Science,* volume 4, ed. Fred Greenstein and Nelson Polsby. Reading, MA: Addison-Wesley.

———. 1987. "Changing Conceptions of Public Opinion in the Political Process." *Public Opinion Quarterly* 51 (Part 2: Supplement): S12–S24.

Converse, Philip E., and Gregory B. Markus. 1979. "Plus ça change . . . : The New CPS Election Study Panel." *American Political Science Review* 73 (1): 32–49.

Daalder, Ivo H. 1995. "What Vision for the Nuclear Future?" *Washington Quarterly* 18 (2): 127–42.

Delli Carpini, Michael X., and Scott Keeter. 1996. *What Americans Know about Politics and Why It Matters.* New Haven, CT: Yale University Press.

Domhaff, William. 1983. *Who Rules America Now?* Englewood Cliffs, NJ: Prentice-Hall.

Douglas, Mary. 1970. *Natural Symbols: Explorations in Cosmology.* London: Barrie and Rockliff.

———. 1982. *In the Active Voice.* London: Routledge.

Douglas, Mary, and Aaron Wildavsky. 1982. *Risk and Culture: An Essay on the Selection of Technical and Environmental Dangers.* Berkeley: University of California Press.

Downs, Anthony. 1957. *An Economic Theory of Democracy.* New York: Harper and Row.

Ellis, Richard J., and Dennis J. Coyle. 1994. "Introduction." In *Politics, Policy and Culture,* ed. Richard J. Ellis and Dennis J. Coyle. Boulder, CO: Westview Press.

Enelow, James, and Melvin Hinich. 1984. *The Spatial Theory of Voting.* New York: Cambridge University Press.

Erikson, Robert S., Michael B. MacKuen, and James A Stimson. 2002. *The Macro Polity.* New York: Cambridge University Press.

Feldman, Stanley. 1988. "Structure and Consistency in Public Opinion: The Role of Core Beliefs and Values." *American Journal of Political Science* 32 (2): 416–40.

Fishkin, James. 1991. *Democracy and Deliberation.* New Haven, CT: Yale University Press.

Fiske, Susan T., and Shelly E. Taylor. 1992. *Social Cognition.* New York: McGraw-Hill.

Flournoy, Michèle A., ed. 1993. *Nuclear Weapons After the Cold War: Guidelines for U.S. Policy.* New York: HarperCollins.

Furniss, Edgar S., Jr., and Richard C. Snyder. 1955. *An Introduction to American Foreign Policy.* New York: Rinehart.

Garrity, Patrick J., and Steven A. Maaranen, eds. 1992. *Nuclear Weapons in the Changing World: Perspectives from Europe, Asia, and North America.* New York: Plenum Press.

Gormley, Dennis M., and Thomas G. Mahnken. 2000. "Facing Nuclear and Conventional Reality." *Orbis* 44 (1): 109–25.

Gray, Colin S. 1999. *The Second Nuclear Age.* Boulder, CO: Lynne Rienner Publishers.

Gutmann. Amy. 1987. *Democratic Education.* Princeton, NJ: Princeton University Press.

Habermas, Jürgen. 1979. *Communication and the Evolution of Society.* Trans. Thomas McCarthy. Boston: Beacon Press.

———. 1984. *The Theory of Communicative Action.* Boston: Beacon Press.

Hamilton, Alexander, James Madison, and John Jay. [1788] 1961. *The Federalist Papers.* New York: The New American Library.

Harknett, Richard J., and James J. Wirtz, eds. 1998. *The Absolute Weapon Revisited: Nuclear Arms and the Emerging International Order.* Ann Arbor, MI: University of Michigan Press.

Herron, Kerry G., and Hank C. Jenkins-Smith. 1998. *Public Perspectives on Nuclear Security: U.S. National Security Surveys, 1993–1997*. Sandia Report: SAND98-1707. Albuquerque, NM: Sandia National Laboratories.

———. 2002. "U.S. Perceptions of Nuclear Security in the Wake of the Cold War: Comparing Public and Elite Belief Systems." *International Studies Quarterly* 46 (4): 450–79.

Herron, Kerry G., Hank C. Jenkins-Smith, and Scott D. Hughes. 2000. *Mass and Elite Views on Nuclear Security: U.S. National Security Surveys, 1993–1999. Volume I: General Public*. Sandia Report: SAND2000-1267. Albuquerque, NM: Sandia National Laboratories.

Herron, Kerry G., Hank C. Jenkins-Smith, Scott D. Hughes, Dennis M. Gormley, and Thomas G. Mahnken. 2000. *U.S. National Security Surveys, 1993–1999. Volume II: Policy Elites*. Sandia Report: SAND2000-2081. Albuquerque, NM: Sandia National Laboratories.

Herron, Kerry G., Hank C. Jenkins-Smith, Neil J. Mitchell, and Guy Whitten. 2003. *Scientists' Perspectives on Nuclear Energy and Nuclear Security in the U.S. and Europe: U.S. National Security Surveys, 1993–2002*. Sandia Report: SAND2003-3098P. Albuquerque, NM: Sandia National Laboratories.

Higgs, Robert, and Charlotte Twight. 1987. "National Emergency and the Erosion of Private Property Rights." *Cato Journal* 6 (3): 747–73.

Hinckley, Ronald H. 1991. *People, Polls, and Policymakers: American Public Opinion and National Security*. New York: Lexington Books.

Hinich, Melvin J., and Michael C. Munger. 1996. *Ideology and the Theory of Political Choice*. Ann Arbor, MI: University of Michigan Press.

Holm, John D., and John P. Robinson. 1978. "Ideological Identification and the American Voter." *Public Opinion Quarterly* 42 (2): 235–46.

Holsti, Ole R. 1992. "Public Opinion and Foreign Policy: Challenges to the Almond-Lippmann Consensus." *International Studies Quarterly* 36:439–66.

———. 1996. *Public Opinion and American Foreign Policy*. Ann Arbor, MI: University of Michigan.

Huber, John D. 1989. "Values and Partisanship in Left-Right Orientations: Measuring Ideology." *European Journal of Political Research* 17 (5): 599–621.

Hurwitz, Jon, and Mark Peffley. 1987. "How Are Foreign Policy Attitudes Structured? A Hierarchical Model." *American Political Science Review* 81 (4): 1099–120.

———. 1990. "Public Images of the Soviet Union: the Impact on Foreign Policy Attitudes." *Journal of Politics* 52 (1): 2–28.

Hurwitz, Jon, Mark Peffley, and Mitchell A. Seligson. 1993. "Foreign Policy Belief Systems in Comparative Perspective: The United States and Costa Rica." *International Studies Quarterly* 37 (3): 245–70.

Iklé, Fred Charles. 1996. "The Second Coming of the Nuclear Age." *Foreign Affairs* 75 (January/February): 119–28.

Jackson, Thomas H., and George E. Marcus. 1975. "Political Competence and Ideological Constraint." *Social Science Research* 4:93–111.

Jenkins-Smith, Hank C., Richard P. Barke, and Kerry G. Herron. 1994. *Public Perspectives of Nuclear Weapons in the Post-Cold War Environment.* Sandia Report: SAND94-1265. Albuquerque, NM: Sandia National Laboratories.

Jenkins-Smith, Hank C., John Gastil, Judith Palier, Carol Silva, and Laura Stevens. 1994. "A Cognitive Filtering Model of the Perceived Risk of Environmental Hazards." In *Waste Management: From Risk to Remediation,* volume 1, ed. Rohinton K. Bhada, Abbas Ghassemi, Timothy J. Ward, M. Jamshidi, and M. Shahinpoor. Albuquerque, NM: ECM Press.

Jenkins-Smith, Hank C., and Kerry G. Herron. 2002a. *Comparing Public Views on Security: U.S. National Security Surveys, 1993–2002. Volume I: U.S./British Public Views on Nuclear Weapons and Nuclear Energy.* Sandia Report: SAND2002-1187P. Albuquerque, NM: Sandia National Laboratories.

———. 2002b. *Comparing Public Views on Security: U.S. National Security Surveys, 1993–2002. Volume II: Trends in U.S. Perspectives on Nuclear Security, Terrorism, and Energy.* Sandia Report: SAND2002-2401P. Albuquerque, NM: Sandia National Laboratories.

———. 2005. "United States Public Response to Terrorism: Fault Lines or Bedrock?" *Review of Policy Research* 22 (5): 599–623.

Jenkins-Smith, Hank C., Neil J. Mitchell, and Kerry G. Herron. 2004. "Foreign and Domestic Policy Belief Structures in the U.S. and Britain." *Journal of Conflict Resolution* 48 (3): 287–309.

Jenkins-Smith, Hank C., and Walter K. Smith. 1994. "Ideology, Culture, and Risk Perception." In *Politics, Policy and Culture,* ed. Dennis J. Coyle and Richard J. Ellis. Boulder, CO: Westview Press.

Jentleson, Bruce W. 1992. "The Pretty Prudent Public: Post Post-Vietnam American Opinion on the Use of Military Force." *International Studies Quarterly* 36 (1): 49–73.

Jentleson, Bruce W., and Rebecca L. Britton. 1998. "Still Pretty Prudent: Post-Cold War American Public Opinion on the Use of Military Force." *Journal of Conflict Resolution* 42 (4): 395–417.

Jovrasky, David. 1970. *The Lysenko Affair.* Cambridge, MA: Harvard University Press.

Kennan, George F. 1951. *American Diplomacy, 1900–1950.* New York: Mentor Books.

Kerlinger, Fred N. 1967. "Social Attitudes and Their Criterial Referents: A Structural Theory." *Psychological Review* 74 (2): 110–22.

Knopf, Jeffrey W. 1998. "How Rational Is 'The Rational Public'?" *Journal of Conflict Resolution* 42 (5): 544–71.

Krepinevich, Andrew F., and Steven M. Kosiak. 1998. "Smarter Bombs, Fewer Nukes." *Bulletin of the Atomic Scientists* 54 (6): 26–32.

Krouse, Richard, and George E. Marcus. 1984. "Electoral Studies and Democratic Theory Reconsidered." *Political Behavior* 6 (1): 23–39.

Laponce, Jean. A. 1970. "Note on the Use of the Left–Right Dimension." *Comparative Political Studies* 2 (4): 481–502.

———. 1981. *Left and Right: The Topography of Political Perceptions.* Toronto: University of Toronto Press.

Levitin, Teresa E., and Warren E. Miller. 1979. "Ideological Interpretations of Presidential Elections." *American Political Science Review* 73 (3): 751–71.

Lippmann, Walter. 1922. *Public Opinion.* New York: Macmillan.

———. 1925. *The Phantom Public.* New York: Harcourt Brace.

———. 1955. *Essays in Public Philosophy.* Boston: Little, Brown.

Lodge, George C. 1976. *The New American Ideology.* New York: Knopf.

Lodge, Milton, Marco R. Steenbergen, and Shawn Brau. 1995. "The Responsive Voter: Campaign Information and the Dynamics of Candidate Evaluation." *American Political Science Review* 89 (2): 309–26.

Lupia, Arthur, and Mathew D. McCubbins. 1998. *The Democratic Dilemma: Can Citizens Learn What They Need to Know?* Cambridge: Cambridge University Press.

Luttbeg, Norman R., and Michael M. Gant. 1993. "The Failure of Liberal/Conservative Ideology as a Cognitive Structure." *Public Opinion Quarterly* 49 (1): 80–93.

Macridis, Roy C. 1980. *Contemporary Political Ideologies: Movements and Regimes.* Cambridge, MA: Winthrop.

Marcus, George E. 2002. *The Sentimental Citizen: Emotion in Democratic Politics.* University Park, PA: Pennsylvania State University Press.

Marcus, George E., and Russell L. Hanson, eds. 1993. *Reconsidering the Democratic Public.* University Park, PA: Pennsylvania State University Press.

Marcus, George E., and Michael MacKuen. 1993. "Anxiety, Enthusiasm, and the Vote: The Emotional Underpinnings of Learning and Involvement during Presidential Campaigns." *American Political Science Review* 87 (3): 688–701.

Marcus, George, David Tabb, and John L. Sullivan. 1974. "The Application of Individual Differences Scaling to the Measurement of Political Ideology." *American Journal of Political Science* 18 (2): 405–20.

Markel, Lester. 1949. "Opinion—A Neglected Instrument." In *Public Opinion and Foreign Policy,* ed. Lester Markel. New York: Harper and Brothers.

Mayer, William G. 1993. *The Changing American Mind: How and Why American Public Opinion Changed between 1960 and 1988.* Ann Arbor, MI: University of Michigan Press.

Mazarr, Michael J. 1992. "Nuclear Weapons After the Cold War." *Washington Quarterly* 15 (Summer): 185–201.

Mill, John Stuart. [1859] 1992. "On Liberty." In *Classics of Moral and Political Theory,* ed. Michael L. Morgan. Indianapolis, IN: Hackett Publishing.

———. [1863] 1992. "Utilitarianism." In *Classics of Moral and Political Theory,* ed. Michael L. Morgan. Indianapolis, IN: Hackett Publishing.

Minar, David W. 1960. "Public Opinion in the Perspective of Political Theory." *Western Political Quarterly* 13 (1): 31–44.

Monroe, Alan D. 1998. "Public Opinion and Public Policy, 1980–1993." *Public Opinion Quarterly* 62 (1): 6–28.

Morgan, Patrick M. 2003. *Deterrence Now.* New York: Cambridge University Press.

Morgenthau, Hans. 1948. *Politics Among Nations: The Struggle for Power and Peace.* New York: Knopf.

Mueller, John E. 1973. *War, Presidents, and Public Opinion.* New York: John Wiley.

———. 1999. *Capitalism, Democracy and Ralph's Pretty Good Grocery.* Princeton, NJ: Princeton University Press.

Nagourney, Adam, and Janet Elder. 2004. "Americans Show Clear Concerns on Bush Agenda," *New York Times,* November 23:A1.

National Academy of Sciences. 1997. *The Future of U.S. Nuclear Weapons Policy.* Washington, DC: National Academy Press.

National Commission on Terrorist Attacks Upon the United States. 2004. *The 9/11 Commission Report: Final Report of the National Commission on Terrorist Attacks Upon the United States.* New York: W. W. Norton.

Needler, Martin C. 1966. *Understanding Foreign Policy.* New York: Holt: Rinehart, and Winston.

Nie, Norman H., Jane Junn, and Kenneth Stehlik-Barry. 1996. *Education and Democratic Citizenship in America.* Chicago: University of Chicago Press.

Nitze, Paul H. 1994. "Is It Time to Junk Our Nukes?" *Washington Post,* January 16:C1.

———. 1999. "A Threat Mostly to Ourselves." *New York Times,* October 28:A31.

Nitze, Paul H., and J. H. McCall. 1997. "Contemporary Strategic Deterrence and Precision-Guided Munitions." In *Post–Cold War Conflict Deterrence.* Naval Studies Board, National Research Council. Washington, DC: National Academy Press.

Noelle-Neumann, Elisabeth. 1984. *The Spiral of Silence: Public Opinion—Our Social Skin.* Chicago: University of Chicago Press.

North, Douglas. 1981. *Structure and Change in Economic History.* New York: Norton.

———. 1990. *Institutions, Institutional Change, and Economic Performance.* New York: Cambridge University Press.

———. 1994. "Economic Performance Through Time." *American Economic Review* 84 (3): 803–32.

Oldendick, Robert W., and Barbara Ann Bardes. 1982. "Mass and Elite Foreign Policy Opinions." *Public Opinion Quarterly* 46 (3): 368–82.

Page, Benjamin I., and Jason Barabas. 2000. "Foreign Policy Gaps between Citizens and Leaders." *International Studies Quarterly* 44:339–64.

Page, Benjamin I., and Robert Y. Shapiro. 1983. "Effects of Public Opinion on Policy." *American Political Science Review* 77 (1): 175–90.

———. 1992. *The Rational Public: Fifty Years of Trends in Americans' Policy Preferences.* Chicago: University of Chicago Press.

Pape, Robert A. 1997/98. "The Limits of Precision-Guided Air Power." *Security Studies* 7 (2): 93–114.

Payne, Keith B. 1996. *Deterrence in the Second Nuclear Age.* Lexington, KY: University Press of Kentucky.

———. 2001. *The Fallacies of Cold War Deterrence and a New Direction.* Lexington, KY: University Press of Kentucky.

Peffley, Mark A., and Jon Hurwitz. 1985. "A Hierarchical Model of Attitude Constraint." *American Journal of Political Science* 29 (4): 871–90.

———. 1992. "International Events and Foreign Policy Beliefs: Public Responses to Changing Soviet-U.S. Relations." *American Journal of Political Science* 36 (2): 431–61.

Peters, John Durham. 1995. "Historical Tensions in the Concept of Public Opinion." In *Public Opinion and the Communication of Consent,* ed. Theodore L. Glasser and Charles T. Salmon. New York: The Guilford Press.

Plutzer, Eric, Ardith Maney, and Robert E. O'Conner. 1998. "Ideology and Elites' Perceptions of the Safety of New Technologies." *American Journal of Political Science* 42 (1): 190–209.

Price, Vincent. 1992. *Public Opinion.* Newbury Park, CA: SAGE Publications.

Rayner, Steve. 1992. "Cultural Theory and Risk Analysis." In *Social Theories of Risk,* ed. Sheldon Krimsky and Dominic Golding. Westport, CT: Praeger Publishers.

Reese, Timothy R. 2003. "Precision Firepower: Smart Bombs, Dumb Strategy." *Military Review* July–August (4): 46–54.

Reichley, James. 1981. *Conservatives in an Age of Change: The Nixon and Ford Administrations.* Washington, DC: Brookings Institution.

Reiss, Mitchell, and Robert S. Litwak, eds. 1994. *Nuclear Proliferation after the Cold War.* Washington, DC: Woodrow Wilson Center, Johns Hopkins University Press.

Roberts, Brad, ed. 1995. *Weapons Proliferation in the 1990s.* Cambridge, MA: MIT Press.

Rosenau, James N. 1961. *Public Opinion and Foreign Policy.* New York: Random House.

Rotblat, Joseph, Jack Steinberger, and Bhalchandra Udgaonkar, eds. 1993. *A Nuclear-Weapon-Free World: Desirable? Feasible?* Boulder, CO: Westview Press.

Rothman, Stanley, and Robert S. Lichter. 1987. "Elite Ideology and Risk Perception in Nuclear Energy Policy." *American Political Science Review* 81 (2): 383–404.

Russett, Bruce. 1990. *Controlling the Sword: The Democratic Governance of National Security.* Cambridge, MA: Harvard University Press.

Sabatier, Paul A., and Hank C. Jenkins-Smith. 1993. *Policy Change and Learning: An Advocacy Coalition Approach.* Boulder, CO: Westview Press.

———. 1999. "The Advocacy Coalition Framework: An Assessment." In *Theories of the Policy Process,* ed. Paul A. Sabatier and Hank C. Jenkins-Smith. Boulder, CO: Westview Press.

Sartori, Giovanni. 1969. "Politics, Ideology, and Belief Systems." *American Political Science Review* 63 (2): 398–420.

Schneider, Barry R., and William L. Dowdy. 1998. *Pulling Back from the Nuclear Brink: Reducing and Countering Nuclear Threats.* Portland, OR: Frank Cass Publishers.

Schwartz, Michael, and Michael Thompson. 1990. *Divided We Stand: Redefining Politics, Technology and Social Choice.* Philadelphia, PA: University of Pennsylvania Press.

Schwartz, Stephen, ed. 1998. *Atomic Audit: The Costs and Consequences of U.S. Nuclear Weapons Since 1940.* Washington, DC: Brookings Institution Press.

Schwarz, Norbert, and Herbert Bless. 1991. "Happy and Mindless, But Sad and Smart? The Impact of Affective States on Analytic Reasoning." In *Emotion and Social Judgments,* ed. Joseph P. Forgas. Elmsford, NY: Pergamon Press.

Shapiro, Robert Y., and Benjamin I. Page. 1988. "Foreign Policy and the Rational Public." *Journal of Conflict Resolution* 32 (2): 211–47.

———. 1994. "Foreign Policy and Public Opinion." In *The New Politics of American Foreign Policy,* ed. David A. Deese. New York: St. Martin's Press.

Sheehan, Colleen A. 2004. "Madison v. Hamilton: The Battle Over Republicanism and the Role of Public Opinion." *American Political Science Review* 98 (3): 405–24.

Sniderman, Paul M., Richard A Brody, and Philip E. Tetlock. 1991. *Reasoning and Choice: Explorations in Political Psychology.* New York: Cambridge University Press.

Sniderman, Paul M., and Philip E. Tetlock. 1986. "Interrelationship of Political Ideology and Public Opinion." In *Political Psychology,* ed. Margaret E. Hermann. San Francisco: Jossey-Bass.

Sniderman, Paul, Philip Tetlock, and Laurel Elms. 1999. "Public Opinion and Democratic Politics: The Problem of Non-Attitudes and the Social Construction of Political Judgment." In *Citizens and Politics: Perspectives from Political Psychology,* ed. James Kuklinski. New York: Cambridge University Press.

Stimson, James A. 1991. *Public Opinion in America: Moods, Cycles, and Swings.* Boulder, CO: Westview Press.

———. 2001. "The Macro Foundations of Mood." In *Citizens and Politics: A Political Psychology Perspective,* ed. James Kuklinski. New York: Cambridge University Press.

Surowiecki, James. 2004. *The Wisdom of Crowds: Why the Many Are Smarter than the Few and How Collective Wisdom Shapes Business, Economies, Societies, and Nations.* New York: Doubleday.

Thompson, Dennis. 1970. *The Democratic Citizen: Social Science and Democratic Theory in the Twentieth Century.* New York: Cambridge University Press.

Thompson, Michael, Richard Ellis, and Aaron Wildavsky. 1990. *Cultural Theory.* Boulder, CO: Westview Press.

Thompson, Michael, and Aaron Wildavsky. 1982. "A Proposal to Create a Cultural Theory of Risk." In *The Risk Analysis Controversy: An Institutional Perspective,* ed. Howard C. Kunreuther and E. V. Ley. New York: Springer-Verlag.

Tocqueville, Alexis de. [1835, 1840] 1945. *Democracy in America.* 2 volumes. New York: Knopf.

U.S. Bureau of Labor Statistics and U.S. Census Bureau. 2001. Income Distribution to $250,000 or More for Households: 2000 (Table HINC-07). Washington, DC. <http://ferret.bls.census.gov/macro/032001/hhinc/new07_000.html>

U.S. Census Bureau. 2003a. Annual Projections of the Resident Population by Age, Sex, Race, and Hispanic Origin: Lowest, Middle, Highest, and Zero International Migration Series, 1999 to 2100 (NP-D1-A). Washington, DC. <http://www.census.gov/population/www/projections/natdet.html>

———. 2003b. Educational Attainment of the Population 15 Years and Over, by Age, Sex, Race, and Hispanic Origin: March 2002. Washington, DC. <http://www.census.gov/population/socdemo/education/ppl-169.html>

———. 2003c. Projections of the Total Resident Population by 5-Year Age Groups, Race, and Hispanic Origin with Special Age Categories: Middle Series, 2001 to 2005 (NP-T$-B). Washington, DC. <http://www.census.gov/population/projections/nation/summary/np-t4-b.pdf>

———. 2003d. Projections of the Total Population of States: 1995 to 2025 (PPL-47). Washington, DC. <http://www.census.gov/population/projections/state/stpjpoptxt>

U.S. Department of State, Bureau of Verification and Compliance. 2002. "World Military Expenditures and Arms Transfers 1999–2000." Washington, DC. <http://www.state.gov/t/vc/rls/rpt/wmeat/1999_2000>

Utgoff, Victor A., ed. 2000. *The Coming Crisis: Nuclear Proliferation, U.S. Interests, and World Order.* Cambridge, MA: MIT Press.

van Creveld, Martin. 1993. *Nuclear Proliferation and the Future of Conflict.* New York: Free Press.

Warren, Mark E. 1996. "Deliberative Democracy and Authority." *American Political Science Review* 90 (1): 46–90.

Weisberg, Herbert F., and Jerrold G. Rusk. 1970. "Dimensions of Candidate Evaluation." *American Political Science Review* 64 (4): 1167–85.

Weissberg, Robert. 2001. "Why Policymakers Should Ignore Public Opinion Polls." *Policy Analysis* 402 (May 29): 1–16.

Wildavsky, Aaron, and Karl Dake. 1990. "Theories of Risk Perception: Who Fears What and Why?" *Daedalus* 119 (4): 41–60.

Wittkopf, Eugene R. 1981. "The Structure of Foreign Policy Attitudes; An Alternative View." *Social Science Quarterly* 62 (1): 108–23.

———. 1983. "The Two Faces of Internationalism: Public Attitudes Toward American Foreign Policy in the 1970s and Beyond." *Social Science Quarterly* 64:288–304.

———. 1986. "On the Foreign Policy Beliefs of the American People: A Critique and Some Evidence." *International Studies Quarterly* 30 (4): 425–45.

———. 1987. "Elites and Masses: Another Look at Attitudes toward America's World Role." *International Studies Quarterly* 31:131–59.

———. 1990. *Faces of Internationalism: Public Opinion and American Foreign Policy.* Durham, NC: Duke University Press.

———. 1994. "Faces of Internationalism in a Transitional Environment." *Journal of Conflict Resolution* 38 (3): 376–401.

Yankelovich, Daniel. 1991. *Coming to Public Judgment: Making Democracy Work in a Complex World.* Syracuse, NY: Syracuse University Press.

Younger, Stephen M. 2000. "Nuclear Weapons in the Twenty-First Century." Los Alamos Report: LAUR-00-2850. Los Alamos, NM: Los Alamos National Laboratory.

Zaller, John R. 1992. *The Nature and Origins of Mass Opinion.* Cambridge: Cambridge University Press.

INDEX

Note: Page numbers in *italic* type indicate tables or figures.

Achen, Christopher H., 13, 96
Afghanistan war (2001), 44
age: nuclear deterrence and, 110–12, *111–12*; nuclear security beliefs and, 151; policy preferences and, 109–10, *110*; security beliefs and, 108–9, *109*; terrorism beliefs and, 153
air travel, 91, *91*
airport security, 85, *86*
Almond, Gabriel A., 95
antiterrorism measures: freedom of expression restrictions, 77–78, *78*; immigration policies, 79–81, *81*; infiltration and spying, 76–77, *77*; national identification cards, 78–79, *79*; after 9/11, 174; rights/privacy versus, 74–76, 81–82, *82*, 89, *90*, 91, 104–6, *106*, 165–66; search and seizure, 76–77, *77*; travel restrictions, 79, *80*; trends in, 165–66
anxiety, 97–98
arms control, 48–49
arms race, *52*
arms reductions, 38, 45–48, 223n3
assembly, attitudes toward, 91, *92*

Barabas, Jason, 15
Bardes, Barbara Ann, 15

Belarus, 169
beliefs and belief structures: coherence of, 156–59; core, 124–39; domain, 124, 139–47; of elites, 123, 178, 229n11; about nuclear security, elite versus mass, 168–71; about nuclear security, modeling, 148–52; policy role of, 10–11, 14, 123, 178; predictive value of, 177; about terrorism, modeling, 152–56. *See also* structure of public beliefs
Bentham, Jeremy, 8
biological weapons, nuclear deterrence against, *43*
Bless, Herbert, 98
Britton, Rebecca L., 17

Canberra Commission on the Elimination of Nuclear Weapons, 169
Caspary, William R., 13, 96
Catholic Church, 170
causality: national security beliefs and, 148–52; terrorism beliefs and, 152–56
censorship, 77–78, *78*
chemical weapons, nuclear deterrence against, *43*
China: national missile defense leading to arms race with, *52*; nuclear arsenal,

241